The Future
of Children
PRINCETON - BROOKINGS

VOLUME 17   NUMBER 2   FALL 2007

The Next Generation of Antipoverty Policies

Introducing the Issue

Ron Haskins and Isabel Sawhill

Hurricane Katrina forced Americans to confront inner-city poverty and misery, not least by bringing indelible images of poverty onto the nation's TV screens. The predictable reaction of the news media was that Katrina revealed poverty as a major problem in the United States, a problem that neither the government nor the average American was doing much to fight.[1]

Although the nation is no longer making major advances against poverty as it did during the 1960s and early 1970s, it has still made some gains in recent years, especially among particular demographic groups. And there is every reason to believe that further progress is possible. The purpose of this volume of *The Future of Children* is to present and explain several specific public policies that would, if well implemented, achieve further reductions in poverty. Before reviewing these policies, we briefly survey historical trends in poverty in the United States and examine several of the forces that shaped them.

Poverty and Its Causes

A surprising fact about poverty in the United States is that it declined steeply throughout the 1960s and then increased in an uneven pattern thereafter, never again equaling its low point during the early 1970s. Children's poverty has followed this pattern, with increases in many years after the early 1970s. By contrast, the poverty rate among the elderly continued to fall throughout the period, from nearly 25 percent in 1970 to 10 percent by 2005. The decline in poverty among the elderly has a straightforward explanation—Social Security.[2] Congress increased Social Security benefits several times during the 1970s and indexed benefits to inflation, boosting millions of low-income elderly Americans above the poverty line. The case of the elderly shows that if government gives people enough money, their poverty rate will drop. But Americans generally do not support taxing one group of Americans, only to give the money away to another group, especially if the receiving group is able-bodied but not working.

Poverty and the Economy

As background for proposing new ways to attack poverty, we briefly explore three forces that are widely thought to shape poverty rates: the economy, changes in family composition, and changes in government spending. Perhaps surprisingly, the overall performance

www.futureofchildren.org

Ron Haskins and Isabel Sawhill are senior editors of *The Future of Children,* co-directors of the Center on Children and Families, and senior fellows in the Economic Studies program at the Brookings Institution, where Sawhill holds the Cabot Family Chair. Haskins is also a senior consultant at the Annie E. Casey Foundation.

of the American economy does not explain the nation's inability to make substantial gains against poverty since the 1970s. Although the 1960s saw the highest economic growth rate of the last half of the twentieth century, the following three decades all enjoyed growth of more than 20 percent in per capita gross domestic product (GDP). Yet between the early 1970s and the mid-1990s, poverty increased. Why, with the economy growing, was the nation not able to continue the progress it made against poverty during the 1960s? To paraphrase President Kennedy's famous aphorism, why didn't a rising tide lift more boats?

One reason was wage stagnation at the bottom of the income distribution, which led to growing wage inequality. Between 1979 and 1996, inflation-adjusted wages at the tenth percentile of the distribution fell in most years, ending up about 12 percent below where they started. Wages recovered during the vibrant economy of the second half of the 1990s as poverty fell once again, but even so wound up in 2003 almost exactly where they were in 1979.[3] If the impressive reductions in poverty during the 1960s and the second half of the 1990s were caused in part by increasing wages, wages in turn were responding to tight labor markets, as signaled by low unemployment rates. During the 1960s unemployment averaged 4.8 percent and fell as low as 3.5 percent. By contrast, during the 1970s and 1980s, when wages were falling and poverty rising, unemployment averaged 6.2 percent and 7.3 percent, respectively. Only when tight labor markets returned, after the mid-1990s, and unemployment fell to an average of 4.8 percent between 1995 and 2000, did wages once again rise and poverty fall. Economic growth itself will not necessarily lower poverty rates. A better formula for fighting poverty effectively is tight labor markets accompanied by rising wages.

Poverty and Family Dissolution

Changes in family composition have been a major force driving Americans into poverty. The story of family composition and poverty is straightforward. In most years, poverty in female-headed families is four or five times greater than poverty in married-couple families. High divorce rates, falling marriage rates, and rising nonmarital birthrates over the past three decades have more than doubled the share of children living with single mothers. Even if everything else had stayed the same, having a higher share of people in female-headed families would have increased the poverty rate because of the high poverty rate of this family form. One group of prominent scholars estimated that changes in family structure alone would have raised the poverty rate from 13.3 percent in 1967 to 17 percent by 2003.[4] Offsetting forces slowed the rise of poverty, but there is no doubt that one major factor underlying the nation's difficulty in cutting poverty rates is the dramatic increase in female-headed families. If a greater share of American children were living with their married parents, poverty would decline. In fact, according to a recent Brookings analysis, if the marriage rate were the same today as it was in 1970, holding all other population characteristics constant, the child poverty rate would fall more than 25 percent.[5]

Poverty and Government Spending

Government spending also affects poverty rates. After all, with the exception of the large insurance programs like Social Security, Medicare, and unemployment compensation, most of the nation's social programs have their roots in the War on Poverty declared by Lyndon Johnson in 1965. Since the mid-1960s, when relatively few government programs were directed at the poor, programs intended to reduce poverty or soften its effect have proliferated. Total federal and state spending on these programs has increased almost every year, on average at rates much greater than inflation and even greater than GDP growth. According to the Congressional Research Service, means-tested spending increased in inflation-adjusted dollars in all but four of the thirty-six years between 1968 and 2004. Over nearly three decades, real spending grew from about $89 billion to nearly $585 billion, driven in large part by exploding health care costs. If spending had grown at the rate of inflation and in proportion to the rise in GDP, in 2004 spending would have been about $220 billion, less than 40 percent of the actual rate. Yet poverty was higher in 2004 than it was in 1968.[6] In part this is because the way the federal government computes poverty rates ignores many means-tested benefits,[7] in part because health care costs have risen so rapidly, and in part because substantial sums are spent on families without bringing them quite to the poverty line, while additional billions are spent on people above the poverty line.

We conclude that although the American economy has enjoyed a healthy growth rate over the past four decades, stagnant wages among the least skilled have made it hard for people holding low-wage jobs to escape poverty. This problem has been exacerbated by changes in family composition. And government spending, which has grown rapidly, has reduced poverty less than had been hoped and in some cases may even have been counterproductive, by reducing incentives to work and supporting young women who have births outside marriage.

Policy Initiatives Can Reduce Poverty: A Success Story

The stubbornness of poverty over the past several decades makes it clear that cutting poverty is a difficult business. But there is some good news on which to build a strategy for reducing poverty. Between 1991 and 2000, poverty among children in female-headed families plummeted from a little more than 47 percent to 33 percent, by far its lowest rate ever. This abrupt decline—30 percent in less than a decade—comes close to rivaling the 45 percent fall in the overall poverty rate during the 1960s. Even after

By any measure, the 1990s decline in poverty among female-headed households is impressive and demonstrates that progress against poverty is possible.

four straight years of increases, caused in part by the recession of 2001, which saw poverty in female-headed families rise from 33 percent to nearly 36 percent, the poverty rate for these families was still nearly 25 percent below its 1991 peak.

By any measure, the 1990s decline in poverty among female-headed households is impressive and demonstrates that progress against poverty is possible. The poverty rate for these families before any government benefits in 1999 was 11 percentage points lower than the 1990 rate (50 percent as against 39 percent), reflecting the dramatic increase in employment and earnings achieved by single mothers during the intervening years. One explanation for this increase in work was the 1996 welfare reform legislation that imposed a five-year time limit on mothers receiving welfare and required them to search for work or have their cash benefit reduced or terminated. These reforms were followed by a huge increase in the number of poor mothers leaving welfare and increasing both their employment and their earnings, which in turn substantially lowered their poverty rate.

Adding government transfer payments, including Social Security, food stamps, housing, and the earned income tax credit (EITC), to these women's market income produces a decline of 12 percentage points in a comprehensive measure of poverty—from 37 percent to 25 percent. By this broader definition, if the poverty rate in 1999 (25 percent) had been the same as in 1990 (37 percent), a total of nearly 4.5 million additional people, many of them children, would have been poor.

In sum, this combination of policy based on sticks (such as the work requirements, time limits, and sanctions of welfare reform) and carrots (such as child care and the earned income tax credit) is an effective strategy for fighting poverty. Moreover, it is consistent with the domestic philosophies of the nation's two major political parties. Republicans emphasize that progress will not be possible unless individuals behave more responsibly—and more in accord with traditional American values—than they have in the past. Democrats emphasize that serious personal effort and responsible behavior alone will not be enough to allow millions of poorly educated adults and their families to escape poverty. Both individuals and government, in other words, have major roles to play in reducing poverty, and both parties can—and indeed have—supported work requirements and work support programs. Keeping this winning combination of approaches in mind, let us review some specific proposals for government action that will lead to further reductions in poverty.

Extending Sticks and Carrots to Young Men

A major limitation of the current stick-and-carrot approach to fighting poverty and reducing inequality is that it is confined almost exclusively to single mothers. At the same time as poor women were entering the labor force by the millions during the 1990s, the work rate among less-educated men fell. That decline is particularly remarkable because during the second half of the 1990s the unemployment rate fell to 4 percent and wage rates at the bottom of the wage distribution rose for the first time in two decades. The stick-and-carrot approach of encouraging or requiring work and reinforcing it with work support benefits has not been tried with men, in part because most are not eligible for public benefits. Thus, we asked two of our authors, Gordon Berlin, president of MDRC, and Lawrence Mead of New York University, to focus their antipoverty analysis and recommendations on young men.

Providing Work Incentives for Fathers

As noted, falling wages and the striking increase in children living with a lone parent, usually the mother, are the two principal explanations for the lack of progress against poverty since 1973. The problems of falling wages and single parenthood are intertwined. As the wages of men with a high school education or less began to tumble, their employment rates also fell. The result was that the share of men who could support a family above the poverty line began to decline, reducing the willingness of low-income women to marry the fathers of their children. Low-income men and women consistently tell interviewers that they weigh these issues when making decisions about marriage.

Berlin's proposal would partially overcome the low wages and income of poorly educated males by using the earned income tax credit to supplement the earnings of all low-wage workers aged twenty-one or older who work full time—regardless of whether they have children or whether they are married. Berlin argues that by conditioning the benefit on full-time work, by targeting individuals regardless of their family status, and by treating EITC payments as individual income rather than as joint income for income tax purposes, this earnings-based supplement would restore equity to the American social compact without distorting incentives to work, marry, and bear children. In addition, the policy would create social policy parity between poor men and women, help noncustodial fathers in low-wage jobs meet their child support obligations, and raise the opportunity cost of criminal activity. The largest benefits by far would accrue to two-parent households in which both adults work full time. The policy would come with a price tag of nearly $30 billion a year when fully implemented.

Helping Fathers with Special Problems

Although increasing wage subsidies could increase work rates among poor males, Mead argues that low wages are not the primary reason for their lack of employment. Many poor men appear to resist taking or keeping low-paid jobs because of an oppositional culture in which the search for respect takes precedence over maximizing income. Thus, although work subsidies like Berlin's EITC proposal would likely make some difference, Mead believes that restoring work discipline among many of these men requires special measures. He recommends that government link new benefits with work requirements, as it has for welfare mothers. Two groups of disadvantaged men present an opportunity to test Mead's approach of combining the government's authority to require work with its ability to provide rewards for work. Specifi-

cally, disadvantaged men who owe child support and ex-offenders who have been released from prison on parole would be assigned to a mandatory work program if they did not work regularly. There, in return for supervised employment, they might receive the enhanced work subsidies recommended by Gordon Berlin. Large child support arrears might also be reduced. Such a work program might cost from $2.4 billion to $4.8 billion annually. A similar child support model was tested during the 1990s with partial success, and evaluations of prison reentry programs along these lines are currently under way.[8] If these studies show positive results, Mead favors federal funding of additional demonstrations to help settle on the best model for mandatory work programs.

Improving Supports for Working Families

Like the stick-and-carrot approach for mothers, these approaches with fathers try to capitalize on policies that both push and pull men into the workforce. But many observers believe that the current work supports for low-income workers, whether male or female, are inadequate. The new combination of work requirements, sanctions, and work supports has been moderately effective, but it should be regarded as an evolving system that needs constant attention and improvement to bring still more adults into the workforce and to provide them with supports that will allow them to better their material lives and those of their children. Two of the most important problems in the current system are the shortage of funding for child care and the number of poor working adults who are not covered by health insurance. The work support system would be greatly improved if the nation could guarantee child care and health coverage to all parents who are willing to work. Thus we asked Mark Greenberg, a noted child care expert at the Center for American Progress, to propose a plan to expand child care, and we asked Alan Weil, executive director of the National Academy for State Health Policy, to propose a plan to cover all poor working families with health insurance.

Providing Good Child Care

Greenberg's proposal is based on the view that a national child care strategy should pursue four goals. First, every parent who needs child care to get or keep employment should be able to afford care without having to leave the children in unhealthy or dangerous environments; second, all families should have the opportunity to place their children in settings that foster education and healthy development; third, parental choice should be respected; and fourth, a set of good child care choices should be available. To attain these goals, the nation should revamp both federal child care subsidy programs and federal tax policy related to child care. Today subsidies are principally provided through a block grant structure in which states must restrict eligibility, access, or the extent of assistance to husband limited federal and state funds. Tax policy principally involves a modest non-refundable credit that provides little or no assistance to poor and low-income families.

To improve this flawed system, Greenberg would replace the block grant with a federal guarantee of child care assistance for all working families with income under 200 percent of poverty. This federal assistance program would be administered by the states under a federal-state matching formula, with the federal government paying most of the cost. States would be responsible for developing and implementing plans to improve the quality of child care, coordinate child care with other early education programs, and ensure that child care payment rates are

sufficient to allow families to purchase care that fosters healthy child development. In addition, Greenberg would restructure the federal dependent care tax credit as a refundable tax credit, with the credit set at 50 percent of covered child care costs for the lowest-income families and gradually phasing down to 20 percent as family income increases.

Taken together, the subsidy and tax changes would lead to a better-coordinated system of child care subsidies in which working families below 200 percent of poverty would be assured of substantial financial help, while tax-based help would ensure continued, albeit significantly reduced, assistance for families with higher incomes. Greenberg estimates that the additional cost of these two reforms would be on the order of $13.5 billion a year, of which the federal share would be about $8.5 billion if that share remained the same as under current law.

Providing Health Insurance

Another work support that is needed by low-income working families is health insurance. Medicaid was created in 1965 to provide health insurance to poor and disabled individuals and families. The original program, however, created a major work disincentive because virtually the only way to get Medicaid coverage was to be on welfare. If a mother on welfare went to work, in most cases both the mother and her children lost their Medicaid coverage. Beginning in the mid-1980s, Congress gradually began to loosen the link between welfare and Medicaid for children. Then, in 1997 Congress enacted the State Children's Health Insurance Program (SCHIP), which provides coverage to children in families with income well above the poverty level. Now, regardless of welfare status, nearly all children in families with incomes under 200 percent of poverty are covered by either Medicaid or SCHIP. Despite being a great improvement over the old system, the new one nonetheless suffers from a serious flaw: poor parents are often not covered. Parents who leave welfare normally get a year of coverage, but after that they are uncovered unless their employer provides a subsidized plan—which is rarely the case in the low-wage market in which most of these parents participate. Similarly, parents who avoid welfare but take one of the millions of jobs that do not provide employee benefits usually have no coverage at all. This lack of coverage for adults constitutes a disincentive to work and may indirectly affect the health of children, because adults without health insurance are less likely to take their children for preventive care.[9]

Alan Weil proposes creating a federal earned income health credit (EIHC) combined with redefining the federal floor of coverage through Medicaid and SCHIP. His proposal is designed to address the two key requirements for an effective policy of covering all members of poor and low-income families: overcoming the affordability barrier that so many families face and making sure enough options are available that individuals and families can obtain coverage using a combination of their own, their employer's, and public resources.

The EIHC, which borrows heavily in its design from the EITC, would be a refundable tax credit claimed each year on the federal tax return but available during the year in advance of filing. The credit would be based on taxpayer earnings and family structure, with the amount phasing in as earnings increase, reaching a plateau, and then phasing out farther up the income scale. The credit would be larger for families with dependents, reflecting

the higher cost of health insurance for a family than for an individual. The EIHC would be available only to adults who demonstrate that they had health insurance coverage during the year and, in the case of adults with children, only if their eligible dependent children were enrolled in either a private or the appropriate public program. For recipients whose children are enrolled in a public program, the value of the EIHC would be reduced.

Now, regardless of welfare status, nearly all children in families with incomes under 200 percent of poverty are covered by either Medicaid or SCHIP.

Weil's proposal includes provisions for handling individuals who receive coverage from their employer and those who do not. The EIHC is designed to function seamlessly with the employee payroll withholding system. The proposal smooths transitions from public to private coverage, and it anticipates a substantial role for states. Weil estimates that his policy would cost about $45 billion a year ($35 billion in federal dollars and $10 billion in state dollars).

Creating Longer-Term Strategies

A distinguishing characteristic of the carrot-and-stick policies discussed so far is that they lead to almost immediate payoffs. The goal is to provide requirements or inducements for poor and low-income adults to enter the labor force and to provide government work supports that would reward work and improve the family's economic well-being as soon as they begin working. But these policies do not do much to reduce poverty in the long term by promoting children's development. Especially in a nation that prides itself on the claims that all children have a chance to do better than their parents and that education is the primary route to such self-improvement, policies to reduce poverty and inequality in the long run are essential. The United States remains a society with much economic mobility—although not as much as the public seems to assume. In fact, as suggested in a recent volume of *The Future of Children*, education in America now seems to reinforce rather than compensate for the differences between economic and social groups.[10] The work strategy outlined above could affect children's development by increasing family resources that could be used to purchase services—such as high-quality child care—that would benefit children. But careful analyses of welfare-to-work experiments that achieved high work rates have shown only modest effects on children.[11] To boost the development of poor children, policymakers will need to go beyond work-promotion strategies.

Reducing Nonmarital Births and Strengthening Marriage

One strategy that straddles the divide between immediate and long-term effects is reducing nonmarital births and increasing the share of children who live with their married parents. As noted, a Brookings study has shown that if the same share of children lived with their married parents today as in 1970, poverty would fall more than 25 percent without any additional government spending. Although some analysts despair of reversing the growth in single-parent families that has afflicted the nation since roughly the 1960s, some progress has already been made. The most impressive change is the decline of teen

pregnancy by about one-third since 1991. If teen pregnancy had not declined, the number of children from birth to age six living in poverty would be 8.5 percent higher than it is today.[12] In addition, the divorce rate stopped increasing during the 1980s, and the rate of increase in the nonmarital birth rate has slowed considerably since the mid-1990s. Even so, because of changes in family composition—changes that disproportionately affect poor and minority families—the share of children in single-parent families has more than doubled since 1970.

Reversing the trend toward single-parent families would have an immediate effect in reducing poverty rates. But perhaps more important, it would also have a long-term effect on children's growth and development. A recent volume of *The Future of Children* is devoted to the importance of marriage to children.[13] The volume reflects the nearly universal view among scholars that children do better in married-couple families than in any other living arrangement. Thus, in addition to quickly reducing poverty rates, increasing the share of children in married-couple families would benefit their development over the long term and reduce the likelihood that they would be poor when they grow up. We invited Paul Amato of Pennsylvania State University and Rebecca Maynard of the University of Pennsylvania to present and analyze specific recommendations on reducing teen and unwed pregnancy and strengthening marriage.

Amato and Maynard propose programs to prevent nonmarital births by promoting abstinence among nonmarried adolescents and by improving contraceptive use among sexually active couples who are not intending to become pregnant. And they propose programs to improve the quality of marital relationships and lower divorce rates by teaching individuals and couples communication, conflict resolution, and social support skills before and during marriage.

The authors argue that an average delay of one year in the age at first intercourse among youth would lower the share of twelve- to nineteen-year-olds at risk for pregnancy and birth by about 9 percentage points. This delay, in turn, would reduce the number of teen births by about 81,000, or 24 percent a year. If only half of teens not now using contraception were to become consistent users of condoms, the pill, an injectable form of contraception, or an implant, the number of unintended births would decline by an estimated 60,000 a year, or 14 percent.

Recent trends in teen sexual activity, contraceptive use, and births suggest that a combination of existing policies and changes in the larger culture have produced favorable reductions since the early 1990s. Thus, Amato and Maynard recommend that all school systems offer health and sex education, beginning no later than middle school, with the primary message that parenthood is highly problematic for unmarried youth and young adults. They also recommend that school systems (as well as parents and community groups) educate young people about methods to prevent unintended pregnancies. Ideally, the federal government would provide districts with tested curriculum models that emphasize both abstinence and the use of contraception. All youth should understand that pregnancies are preventable and that unintended pregnancies have enormous costs for the mother, the father, the child, and society.

In addition to reducing unintended births, Amato and Maynard argue that supporting marriage is potentially an effective strategy

for fighting poverty. Research indicates that premarital education improves subsequent marital quality and lowers the risk of divorce. About 40 percent of couples now participate in some type of education program before marriage. The authors suggest doubling the overall rate from 40 percent to 80 percent by offering such programs on a voluntary basis. They also recommend that states offer mar-

In addition to reducing unintended births, Amato and Maynard argue that supporting marriage is potentially an effective strategy for fighting poverty.

riage education programs to 2 million married couples. Expanding marriage education services in this fashion could result in a decline in divorces of about 72,000 annually, which in turn would reduce by around 65,000 the number of children entering a single-parent family every year because of marital dissolution. The number of children spared the experience of divorce would accumulate annually, and after seven or eight years, half a million fewer children would have entered single-parent families through divorce. Amato and Maynard present estimates to show that these investments in premarital and marriage education programs would almost certainly be cost effective in the long run and could reduce child poverty by nearly 30 percent.

Increasing Preschool Education
Along with trying to avoid nonmarital births and increase the share of children in married-

couple families, another long-term strategy for fighting poverty is to improve education. We asked Greg Duncan of Northwestern University, Jens Ludwig of the University of Chicago, and Katherine Magnuson of the University of Wisconsin at Madison to recommend promising reforms at the preschool level aimed at improving the education of poor children.

> *Along with trying to avoid nonmarital births and increase the share of children in married-couple families, another long-term strategy for fighting poverty is to improve education.*

The proposal by Greenberg on expanding child care, noted earlier, would allow millions of children to receive subsidized child care while their parent or parents work. Although there is no sharp distinction between the usual type of care that parents select in the market, which is typically of mediocre quality, and the kind of high-quality care that boosts children's development, Greenberg's proposal would provide care that on average would be less expensive than developmental care. A common claim made by both scholars and advocates is that high-quality care can boost children's development and overcome, at least partially, the achievement gap between poor children and their more advantaged peers.[14] Model programs such as Abecedarian and Perry Preschool show that large and lasting gains from interventions during the infant and preschool years are

possible, but these gains are difficult to achieve and would be unlikely as long as most care is of average quality.[15]

Duncan, Ludwig, and Magnuson believe the nation should provide very high-quality care to disadvantaged children. They argue that early childhood is a key developmental period, when children's cognitive and socioemotional skills develop rapidly. Thus, they propose an intensive two-year, education-focused intervention for economically disadvantaged three- and four-year-olds. Classrooms would be staffed by college-trained teachers and have no more than six children per teacher. Instruction based on proven preschool academic and behavioral curricula would be provided to children for three hours a day, with wraparound child care available to working parents. Classroom teachers would engage in parent outreach when they were not teaching.

The authors estimate that the annual cost of the instructional portion of the program would be about $8,000, with supplemental child care adding as much as $4,000.[16] Their plan would make both the instructional and child care programs available to all parents, although only low-income parents would receive full subsidies; higher-income parents would pay on a sliding scale related to income. The total cost of their proposal, net of current spending, would be $20 billion a year. The authors estimate that the benefits would likely amount to several times the cost, with some of the cost saving showing up quickly in the form of less school retention and fewer special education placements and some showing up later in the form of less crime and greater economic productivity. They estimate that their program would reduce participants' future poverty rates between 5 percent and 15 percent by increasing their future schooling, ultimately leading to higher productivity and earnings.

Improving Public Education

Even as most researchers and analysts agree that high-quality preschool would boost children's development over the long term, researchers also believe that effective public education could augment preschool gains if poor and minority children received higher-quality instruction. Children living in poverty tend to be concentrated in low-performing schools staffed by ill-equipped teachers. They are especially likely to leave school before earning a high school diploma and to leave without the skills necessary to earn a decent living in a rapidly changing economy.[17]

In his article Richard Murnane of Harvard University describes three complementary sets of initiatives that the federal government could take to improve the education of impoverished children and increase the chances that they will escape poverty in the long run. All three sets of initiatives are designed to improve the operation of the standards-based educational reforms enacted in the No Child Left Behind Act of 2001 (NCLB). In particular, the initiatives will strengthen the three legs on which standards-based reforms rest: accountability, incentives, and capacity.

The federal government can improve accountability by amending the adequate yearly progress provisions of NCLB. One important change would be to focus on growth in children's skills rather than on having children meet specific test score targets. Another would be to develop meaningful goals for increasing the share of students who graduate from high school.

The second set of initiatives focuses on improving incentives for states to align high school graduation requirements with the skills needed for success after graduation and to develop voluntary interdistrict school choice programs that attract both low-income urban students and more affluent suburban students to study together. The third set of initiatives builds the capacity of schools to educate low-income children well and the capacity of state departments of education to improve the performance of failing schools and districts. Competitive matching grants would support the development of programs to improve teaching and leadership in high-poverty schools, as well as programs to serve high school students who do not fare well in conventional high school programs.[18]

The annual cost of these federal education initiatives would be approximately $2 billion. Some of the funds could be taken from money now allocated to the federal compensatory education program, which has not systematically improved the academic achievement of the disadvantaged students to whom it was originally targeted.[19]

Helping Very Poor Mothers

If all our proposals for reducing poverty were implemented, and were moderately successful, several million families would still remain in poverty—and would likely be more disadvantaged than those who escaped poverty. The article by Rebecca Blank of the University of Michigan focuses on the appropriate policy response to single mothers who face multiple disadvantages and have difficulty finding or holding a full-time job. Some highly disadvantaged women now remain on welfare, although this population is shrinking. Meanwhile, studies show that the number of single mothers who are neither working nor on welfare has grown significantly over the past ten years, and especially since 2000. Such "disconnected" women now make up between 20 and 25 percent of all low-income single mothers, and reported income in these families is extremely low. These women often report multiple barriers to work, including low education, health problems, or a history of domestic violence or substance abuse. Counting both longer-term welfare recipients and disconnected women, Blank estimates that about 2.2 million women who head families are not able to find jobs or are unsuccessful in holding them; almost 4 million children live in these economically challenged families.

Blank proposes a Temporary and Partial Work Waiver Program to provide greater employment assistance to highly disadvantaged women, as well as economic support. The program would recognize that some women may be able to work only part time or may be temporarily unable to work. It would supplement their earnings while also offering referral to services that address some of their work barriers. The support would be only temporary, and women would be regularly reassessed for their readiness to return to work or work more hours. Such a program would require intensive case management, regular reassessment, and referral to mental health and substance abuse services, job training, and subsidized child care. The program could piggy-back on state Temporary Assistance to Needy Families (TANF) programs, serving their most disadvantaged populations while also bringing in women who are currently outside the TANF system. Blank estimates the cost of her proposal at roughly $2.8 billion, although some of these dollars are already being spent as part of the TANF program.

Probably the greatest challenge emerging from the welfare reforms of the mid-1990s is the problem of the so-called "hard to employ" population. Current TANF programs are not well designed to serve these women, many of whom have very limited earnings and no access to public assistance. Blank's proposal suggests an approach that addresses the problems of highly disadvantaged women who cannot easily move into full-time employment and need greater assistance and support than are provided by traditional work-welfare efforts.

A Strategy for Success

The fact that the nation has made only modest progress against poverty over the past three decades does not mean that progress is impossible. As the decline in poverty among female-headed families during the 1990s shows, poverty can be reduced substantially. The success of welfare reform also suggests a general strategy for cutting poverty further—namely, by a judicious use of sticks and carrots to encourage or require responsible behavior by individuals and to reward responsible behavior with increased income or opportunity. Progress in the battle against poverty is also more likely if the nation can improve the education of poor children who currently fall behind their more privileged peers during the preschool years and never catch up. The articles in this volume, written by some of the nation's top scholars, outline eight specific proposals that, following this general strategy, have a high likelihood of reducing poverty. Many of the proposals are expensive. But poverty is expensive too: it drains resources from the nation while simultaneously depriving it of human capital that would increase productivity and reduce social problems. Investments in these proposals, which could be financed out of savings from cuts in other government spending, are certain to produce numerous benefits in the long run.

Notes

1. John Cochran, "New Perspectives on Poverty," *Congressional Quarterly Weekly*, October 23, 2006, pp. 2802–09; Julie Kosterlitz, "Social Policy: The Katrina Experiment," *National Journal*, November 5, 2005, pp. 3436–42; Jason DeParle, "Liberal Hopes Ebb in Post-Storm Poverty Debate," *New York Times*, October 11, 2005, p. A1.

2. Jonathan Gruber and Gary Engelhardt, "Social Security and the Evolution of Elderly Poverty," in *Public Policy and the Income Distribution*, edited by Alan Auerbach, David Card, and John Quigley (New York: Russell Sage Foundation, 2006), pp. 259–87.

3. For further analyses of economic factors influencing poverty rates, see Hilary Hoynes, Marianne Page, and Ann Stevens, "Poverty in America: Trends and Explanations," Working Paper 11681 (Cambridge, Mass.: National Bureau of Economic Research, October 2005).

4. Adam Thomas and Isabel Sawhill, "For Love and Money? The Impact of Family Structure on Family Income," *Future of Children* 15, no. 2 (Fall 2005): 57–74; Hoynes, Page, and Stevens, "Poverty in America: Trends and Explanations" (see note 3).

5. Ron Haskins and Isabel Sawhill, "Work and Marriage: The Way to End Poverty and Welfare," Welfare Reform and Beyond Brief 28 (Brookings, September 2003); Isabel Sawhill and Adam Thomas, "A Hand Up for the Bottom Third: Toward a New Agenda for Low-Income Working Families," Working Paper (Brookings, May 2001).

6. Not all government spending counts in the calculation of income when the official poverty rate is calculated. But even if we use alternative Census Bureau definitions of poverty that include more government benefits in the definition of income, poverty has still increased in the face of the huge increase in government spending.

7. Nicholas Eberstadt, "Why Poverty Doesn't Rate" (Washington: American Enterprise Institute, September 2006).

8. Fred Doolittle and Suzanne Lynn, *Working with Low-Income Cases: Lessons for the Child Support Enforcement System from Parents' Fair Share* (New York: MDRC, 1998).

9. Leighton Ku and Matthew Broaddus, "Coverage of Parents Helps Children, Too" (Washington: Center on Budget and Policy Priorities, October 20, 2006).

10. Isabel Sawhill, "Introducing the Issue," *Future of Children* 16, no. 2 (Fall 2006): 3–17; Isabel Sawhill, "Opportunity in America: Does Education Promote Social Mobility?" Future of Children Policy Brief (Fall 2006).

11. Pamela Morris, Lisa Gennetian, and Greg Duncan, "Effects of Welfare and Employment Policies on Young Children: New Findings on Policy Experiments Conducted in the Early 1990s," *Social Policy Report* 19, no. 2 (2005); Lisa A. Gennetian and others. *How Welfare and Work Policies for Parents Affect Adolescents: A Synthesis of Research* (New York: MDRC, 2002); Ron Haskins, *Work over Welfare: The Inside Story of the 1996 Welfare Reform Law* (Brookings, 2006).

12. Kasia O'Neill Murray and Wendell E. Primus, "Recent Data Trends Show Welfare Reform to Be a Mixed Success: Significant Policy Changes Should Accompany Reauthorization," *Review of Policy Research* 22 (2005): 301–24.

13. Sara McLanahan, Elisabeth Donahue, and Ron Haskins, "Introducing the Issue," *Future of Children* 15, no. 2 (Fall 2005): 3–12.

14. Christopher Jencks and Meredith Phillips, eds., *The Black-White Test Score Gap* (Brookings, 1998); Cecilia Rouse, Jeanne Brooks-Gunn, and Sara McLanahan, "Introducing the Issue," *Future of Children* 15, no. 1 (Spring 2005): 5–14.

15. Frances Campbell and others, "Early-Childhood Programs and Success in School: The Abecedarian Study," in *Early Care and Education for Children in Poverty*, edited by W. Steven Barnett and Sarane Spence Boocock (State University of New York, 1998), pp. 145–66; Frances Campbell and others, "Early Childhood Education: Young Adult Outcomes from the Abecedarian Project," *Applied Developmental Science* 6, no. 1 (2002): 42–57; and Lawrence J. Schweinhart and others, *Lifetime Effects: The High/Scope Perry Preschool Study through Age 40* (Ypsilanti, Mich.: High/Scope Press, 2005).

16. The additional cost of wraparound care would not increase the expense of the Duncan-Ludwig-Magnuson proposal if the child care proposal advanced by Mark Greenberg were implemented.

17. Paul E. Barton, "One Third of a Nation: Rising Dropout Rates and Declining Opportunities" (Princeton, N.J.: Educational Testing Service, February 2005).

18. For a detailed proposal of a program to improve teaching in high-poverty schools, see Ron Haskins and Susanna Loeb, "A Plan to Increase the Quality of Teaching in American Schools," Future of Children Policy Brief (Spring 2006).

19. Marvin Kosters and Brent Mast, *Closing the Education Achievement Gap* (Washington: AEI Press, 2003).

Rewarding the Work of Individuals: A Counterintuitive Approach to Reducing Poverty and Strengthening Families

Gordon L. Berlin

Summary

Gordon Berlin discusses the nation's long struggle to reduce poverty in families with children, and proposes a counterintuitive solution—rewarding the work of individuals.He notes that policymakers' difficulty in reducing family poverty since 1973 is attributable to two intertwined problems—falling wages among low-skilled workers and the striking increase in children living with a lone parent, usually the mother. As the wages of men with a high school education or less began to decline, their employment rates did likewise. The share of men who could support a family above the poverty line thus began to decline—and with it the willingness of low-income women to marry the fathers of their children. Because the U.S. social welfare system is built around the needs of poor families with children—and largely excludes single adults who are poor (and disproportionately male)—it creates disincentives to work and marry for some families, aggravating these larger trends.

Berlin proposes a new policy that would partially overcome the low wages and income of poorly educated males and second earners in two-parent households by using the earned income tax credit (EITC) to supplement the earnings of all low-wage workers aged twenty-one to fifty-four who work full time—regardless of whether they have children or whether they are married. By conditioning the benefit on full-time work and by retaining the existing family-based EITC program while treating EITC payments as individual income rather than as joint income for income tax purposes, the policy would restore equity to the American social compact without distorting incentives to work, marry, and bear children. The largest benefits by far would accrue to two-parent households in which both adults can work full time.

Because the policy would carry a large price tag—nearly $30 billion a year when fully implemented—Berlin says that a prudent next step would be to test this strategy rigorously in several states over several years, preferably using a random assignment design.

www.futureofchildren.org

Gordon L. Berlin is president of MDRC. He wishes to thank Sheldon Danziger and Frank Levy for generously sharing their ideas and suggestions; and Ron Haskins, John Hutchins, Charles Michalopoulos, Cynthia Miller, Wendell Primus, Belle Sawhill, Timothy Smeeding, and Robert Solow for their many insights and helpful comments on earlier drafts. He is indebted to Andy Sum and the Center for Labor Market Studies for the Current Population Survey eligibility and cost estimates.

Between the end of World War II and 1973, the share of Americans living in poverty fell by half. But since 1973 the overall poverty rate has remained largely unchanged. Why didn't poverty continue to decline? Falling wages and increasing rates of lone parenting are the two principal explanations. Economic changes led to stagnant and declining wages at the bottom of the wage distribution, especially among men with a high school diploma or less, and demographic changes saw a near doubling of the fraction of all families with children that were headed by a single parent.[1]

The problems of falling wages and single parenthood are intertwined. As the wages of men with a high school education or less began to tumble, the employment rates of these men also fell, and, in turn, the share who could support a family above the poverty line began to decline—and with it the professed willingness of low-income mothers and fathers to marry.[2] Because the U.S. social welfare system is built around the needs of poor families with children—and largely excludes single adults who are poor (and disproportionately male)—it creates disincentives to work and marry for some, aggravating these larger trends. Although recent changes have reduced marriage penalties in the tax and transfer system, some do remain, particularly when both spouses in a married-couple family have similar earnings.

A strategy that used the federal earned income tax credit (EITC) to supplement the earnings of all low-wage workers aged twenty-one to fifty-four who work full time— whether they have children or not and whether they marry or not—would counter three decades of wage stagnation and persistent poverty, with significant positive corollary effects on employment and parental child support. By conditioning the benefit on full-time work, by targeting individuals regardless of their family status, by keeping the existing EITC for families with children in place, and by calculating EITC eligibility on the basis of individual income (as Canadians and Europeans do) rather than joint income for tax filing purposes, this earnings-based supplement would restore equity to the American social compact while minimizing the distortion of incentives to work, marry, and bear children.

Although it might seem counterintuitive to reduce poverty and strengthen families by rewarding individuals, focusing on individuals may have substantial advantages over traditional strategies to reduce poverty, especially given the underlying causes of poverty and the investments made to date in supporting families with children. This strategy rewards work in the formal economy, it reduces the disincentive to marry while restoring the incentive for parents to live (and parent) together, it creates social policy parity between poor men and women and between parents and childless individuals, and it helps noncustodial fathers in low-wage jobs meet their child support obligations. Importantly, the largest benefits would accrue to two-parent households when both adults can work full-time. Some 21 million low-wage married individuals and another 16 million single individuals would receive an EITC payment under this plan.

The annual cost of this policy, estimated to be between $29 billion and $33 billion, is equal to 4 percent of the $750 billion in *extra* income received each year by the top 10 percent of earners as a result of the pronounced shift in the nation's income distribution that has occurred since 1975—or about one-third

Figure 1. Trends in Earnings for Production Workers, 1947–2004, and in Poverty, 1959–2004

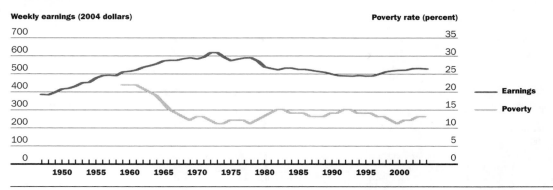

Source: Bureau of Labor Statistics, U.S. Census Bureau.

of the annual tax reduction for the top 1 percent of the income distribution as a result of the Jobs and Growth Tax Relief Reconciliation Act of 2003. A prudent next step would be to rigorously evaluate a limited demonstration of this idea to determine if the benefits in increased work effort, marriage rates, and child support payments—as well as reduced criminal activity and poverty among low-income men and their families—exceed the costs.

Explaining Several Decades of Persistent Poverty

During the 1950s and 1960s, the U.S. economy grew robustly, and poverty rates declined. By contrast, the national poverty rate remained largely unchanged throughout the 1980s and 1990s, despite several sustained periods of economic growth. Why?

Low Wages, High Unemployment: Relentless Recession

The explanation for today's persistent poverty begins with low wages. During the twenty-five years following the end of World War II, earnings marched steadily upward. By 1973, the real weekly earnings of private sector, nonfarm, nonsupervisory production workers stood at $650, more than 60 percent higher

than in 1947. As earnings rose, the poverty rate plummeted—falling from 22 percent in 1960 to 11 percent by 1973.[3] But by 2004, in a startling reversal, the average production worker's weekly earnings had fallen to $528 (in inflation-adjusted dollars), a nearly 20 percent decline.[4] As a result, officially measured poverty stopped falling and it has hovered between 11 and 13 percent ever since (see figure 1).

What caused this abrupt shift in fortunes? Until 1973, the postwar economy as measured by gross domestic product grew robustly, as did productivity—what a worker could produce in an hour—and these gains translated into rapidly growing wages, earnings, and incomes. People at the low end of the income distribution experienced the largest proportional gains. Unexpectedly, the up-escalator economy ground to a halt after 1973. Output per worker slowed to less than 1 percent a year, and wages and earnings fell. In the face of these declining economic prospects, two-parent families maintained their standard of living by having fewer children and sending both parents into the workforce. Even as the economy recovered from a steep recession during the early 1980s, job growth resumed, but with little or no wage growth for those at

Figure 2. Real Annual Earnings for Men across the Wage Distribution in 1979 and 2004

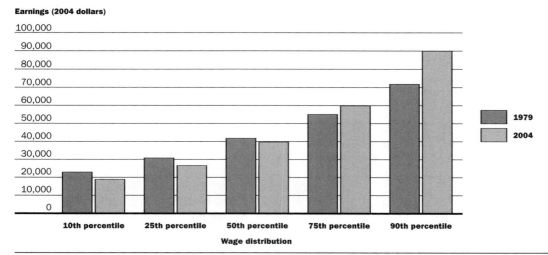

Earnings (2004 dollars)

Source: Author's tabulations of data on men aged 25 years and older who worked full time from the U.S. Census Bureau's Current Population Surveys (CPS), 2005.

the bottom. In addition, a new skills bias began to dominate the labor market, creating high-paying jobs that required a college degree or better and lots of low-paying jobs that required no more than a high school diploma and often less. As a result, economic inequality—the gap between the richest and poorest Americans—widened during the 1970s and 1980s, as earnings for those with college accelerated, while wages for those at the bottom fell in step with the loss of high-paying blue-collar jobs; figure 2 shows the disparity in earnings gains between 1979 and 2004 for high-wage and low-wage men.[5]

For a brief, shining moment during the "roaring nineties," increasing wages at the bottom of the wage distribution and declining child poverty appeared to promise that 1960s-like earnings growth would be restored. But that hope was dashed by the 2001 recession. Signaling trouble for all workers, the growth in earnings of college graduates slowed during the 1990s and fell thereafter. The sources of growing inequality changed accordingly—earnings continued to rise at

the very top but fell for middle-earners, even as lower-wage workers held their own.[6]

Further underscoring the stark reality that low-wage work and the relentless recession it signifies are here to stay, the Bureau of Labor Statistics projects that 46 percent of all jobs in 2014 will be filled by workers with a high school diploma or less. The bulk of these jobs—janitor, food service, retail sales, laborer, child care provider, home health aid—are expected to offer either low or very low pay.

The second important part of the poverty story is declining employment rates among men, particularly men of color. Over the same period that wages were falling, employment rates among men were also tumbling—down a startling 20-plus percentage points between 1970 and 2000 for men with a high school education or less and roughly 7 percentage points for those with some college.[7] By contrast, as a result of economic necessity, changing norms, and the rise of the service sector, women's employment rates rose dra-

Table 1. Change in the Employment Rates of Young Black Men, by Age and Educational Status, 1992–2000

Percent

Age and educational status	Employment rate		Absolute change
	1992	2000	
Enrolled in school			
Ages 16–24	22.5	29.4	6.9
Ages 16–19	17.4	22.8	5.4
Ages 20–24	35.8	46.7	10.9
Not enrolled in school, ages 20–24			
All levels of education	62.2	66.2	4.0
Less than high school diploma	41.6	48.4	6.8
High school diploma only	64.2	66.7	2.5
Some college, no bachelor's degree	73.8	79.6	5.8
College graduate	85.7	88.1	2.4

Source: Analyses by the Center for Labor Market Studies, Northeastern University.

matically as more and more women entered the labor market.

Why have men's employment rates been declining? For some men, employment became less attractive as blue collar jobs evaporated and wages fell.[8] The strong economy of the 1990s offers a reverse proof: as wages at the bottom rose, the employment rates of white, black, and Hispanic young men stabilized and began to grow. Even the employment rates of black men aged sixteen to thirty-four rose between 1992 and 2000, as did the rates for young black men (sixteen to twenty-four) with a high school diploma or less (see table 1). But once the boom years were over, the employment rates of black men resumed their downward trend; following the 2001 recession they plunged much as they did during the 1991 recession.[9] While the reasons for the dismal position of young black men in the labor market are complex (and include racial discrimination and inadequate basic skills and education, as well as the behavioral changes documented by Lawrence Mead in

his article in this volume), a key part of the explanation is the interaction among low wages, the rewards of illegal activity, and strict drug laws, which have resulted in as many as 30 percent of all young black men (and 90 percent of black male high school dropouts) becoming entangled with the criminal justice system.[10] Incarceration appears to have its own, independent effect, further worsening and tainting future employment prospects for all ex-prisoners.[11]

In sum, past success in reducing poverty depended on growing employment and wages for those at the bottom of the earnings distribution. Today, instead, earnings are stagnant. The decline of unions and the power of workers to bargain for higher wages, the reduction in jobs covered by unemployment insurance, and congressional reluctance to increase the minimum wage—thus allowing inflation to erode its value over time—undoubtedly further exacerbated these trends. Without earnings growth, the ability of men without a college education to support a family diminished, making them, in turn, less attractive as marriage partners, according to many experts.[12] Indeed, among men aged twenty-five to fifty-four with a high school diploma or less in 2003, a quarter of whites, a third of blacks, and two-fifths of Hispanics did not earn enough to support a family of four above the poverty line.[13]

Rising Single Parenthood and Declining Marriage

These tectonic economic shifts coincided with inexorable erosion in the cultural norms associated with marriage and out-of-wedlock childbearing. Today, nearly half of all marriages end in divorce, a phenomenon that knows few class distinctions, and a third of all births occur out of wedlock. As a result, the share of all families headed by a single parent has nearly doubled from 13 percent in 1959 to 26 percent today. As one disheartening consequence, more than half of all American children will likely spend part of their childhood growing up in a single-parent family. Many will be poor; the poverty rate for single-parent, female-headed families with children under age eighteen is about five times higher than the rate for married couples (38 percent as against 7 percent in 2004)—in part because a single mother is more likely to have limited education and skills and thus low wages, and in part because she is trying to support her family on one income rather than two. Although the reasons why this is so are still hotly debated, evidence convincingly demonstrates that, as a group, children who grow up in single-parent families have diminished life prospects, faring worse on a wide range of economic, social, emotional, and cognitive outcomes than similarly situated children who grow up in two-parent families.[14]

Cohabiting couples, a rapidly growing family type that now accounts for about 40 percent

of all nonmarital births, typically have more resources than single-parent households. But they are still more likely to be poor than married-couple families, and they are often unstable—about a quarter of cohabiters split within a year of the birth of a child.[15] Interviews with so-called "fragile families" near the time of birth suggest that many of these couples expect to marry.[16] Few will do so.

Even though marriage rates in low-income communities are uncommonly low, marriage remains an ideal for the poor and near poor, as for all Americans. In surveys and ethnographic interviews, poor men and women aspire to the emotional and social benefits of marriage. At the same time, they consistently cite economic barriers (unemployment, low wages, involvement with the criminal justice system) and relationship issues (principally infidelity) as primary reasons for not marrying.[17] In their ethnographic account of poor women in Philadelphia, Kathy Edin and Maria Kefalas find keen support for marriage but trepidation that it will add another mouth to feed without a commensurate increase in resources.[18] Lending support to these statements, as shown in figure 3, marriage rates for men (including African American men) generally rise as earnings go up—although this is somewhat less so for Hispanic men (not shown).[19]

Moreover, the link between earnings and marriage persists even after controlling for race, ethnicity, age, education, and other variables.[20] Indeed, one study of unmarried couples who recently had a child together found that the likelihood of subsequent marriage increased as men's annual earnings rose.[21] Nevertheless, the decline in men's earnings is but one of a complex web of factors, including changing cultural norms and the increasing economic independence of

Figure 3. Marriage Rates of Men Aged 22 to 30 Years, by Annual Earnings, 2004

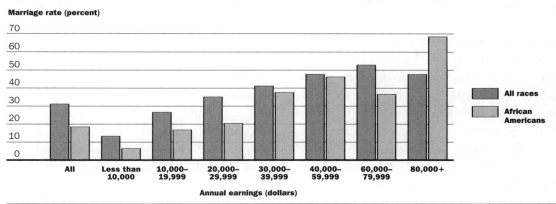

Source: Tabulations of the 2005 CPS by the Center for Labor Market Studies, Northeastern University.

women, that have altered the now outmoded model of marital specialization that pegged men as breadwinners and women as homemakers. Together, these factors have boosted the number of female-headed households, increasing in turn the number of families living in poverty.

Tax and Transfer Penalties

America's social welfare system was designed almost exclusively to meet the needs of poor families with children—a majority of which are now female-headed, single-parent households. Today, the bulk of these benefits support parents when they work. Outside of food stamps, few comparable work supports are available for childless individuals; indeed, the only public systems that focus predominantly on able-bodied men who are not living with children are criminal justice and child support enforcement. Adding insult to injury, by treating income jointly, the tax system penalizes some couples when they do marry, especially couples who earn like amounts and have combined annual earnings between $20,000 and $30,000.[22] As they begin to lose eligibility for food stamps and health benefits, such as Medicaid and the State Children's Health Insurance Program,

and cross over to the phase-out range of the earned income tax credit, they can lose as much as a dollar in benefits for every dollar increase in income.[23] In a vicious cycle, once people are married, the same high cumulative marginal tax rates penalize additional work effort.

Policymakers have taken several important steps over the past decade to reduce the disincentive to work and marry—for example, by increasing the generosity of the EITC for married couples, time-limiting welfare receipt, toughening up child support enforcement, and requiring fathers to live with children and jointly report income when claiming the EITC. As a result, some poor families are better off if they marry now, but penalties remain for others. As David Ellwood explains, any program targeted at "low-income working families, where low income is based on the combined income of the family, . . . [will create] incentives for a working single parent to remain single."[24] Nevertheless, available evidence is mixed about exactly how these disincentives have affected work or marriage, with earlier studies finding no effects and more recent studies finding some effects, especially for working, unmarried couples where both parents earn similar amounts—the group facing the largest penalties.[25]

Although it is daunting to try to measure precisely the effects of tax and transfer policies on behavioral decisions, in the end a low-income working mother is left to make an unfathomable and discomfiting decision about marriage—weighing the uncertain contribution of a potential spouse against the relative certainty of the benefit package she would lose. Fairness argues at the very least for "do no harm" tax policies that maintain an even playing field for all.

Strategies That Work: Earnings Supplements as a Response to Low Wages

Given these discouraging labor market trends, the changing social norms that led to high rates of single parenting, and the distorted incentives resulting from the briar patch of overlapping benefit programs and cumulative high marginal tax rates, one might reasonably ask: can government successfully intervene to raise incomes and reduce poverty? Encouragingly, a reliable body of evidence demonstrates that work-based earnings supplements—such as the EITC—can be an effective strategy for boosting employment and earnings, and reducing poverty, without distorting work incentives.

The "Make Work Pay" Experiments

Concerned that low-wage work simply did not pay relative to welfare, the State of Minnesota, the New Hope community group in Milwaukee, and two provinces in Canada began to experiment during the 1980s with new approaches designed to increase the payoff from low-wage work. All provided work incentives in the form of monthly cash payments to supplement the earnings of low-wage workers. The payments were made only when people worked, and the amount of each month's cash payment depended on the amount of each month's earnings. Minnesota targeted welfare recipients, relied on the welfare benefit system to make payments, and supplemented both part-time and full-time work, while the Canadian and New Hope programs targeted welfare recipients and all low-income people, respectively, operated as independent entities, and rewarded only full-time work of thirty hours a week or more.

The results were encouraging. The mostly single mothers who were offered earnings supplements in these large-scale, rigorous studies were more likely to work, earned more, had more income, and were less likely to be in poverty than those in control groups who were not offered supplements.[26] At their peak, these employment, earnings, and income gains were large—reaching 12 to 14 percentage point increases in employment rates, about $200–$300 more per quarter in earnings, and $300–$500 more in quarterly income. The earnings supplements also had a secondary benefit for children. Preschool-age children of participating parents did better academically than like children in the control group, in large part because their parents had higher incomes and they were more likely to attend high-quality, center-based child care programs.[27] The largest and only persistent effects on adults were found for the most disadvantaged participants, particularly high school dropouts without recent work history and with long spells on welfare. For this group, the employment and earnings effects continued through the end of the follow-up period—six years in the Minnesota project—implying that early work experience could provide a lasting leg up in the labor market for more disadvantaged populations.[28] The pattern of results also suggests that income gains—and thus the poverty reduction—

could be sustained by an ongoing program of supplements.

The findings from the programs in Minnesota and Canada speak primarily to the behavior of single mothers, raising the question of whether offering supplements to single men could have similar effects. The New Hope program did achieve modest, statistically significant gains in the number of quarters employed for men overall, as well as for single men, when cumulated over the full eight-year follow-up period—although the small number of men in the study sample (by design) makes these findings suggestive at best.[29]

Last, both the Minnesota and the New Hope programs also served two-parent families. In Minnesota, the offer of an earnings supplement led to modest reductions in quarterly employment rates and earnings, principally among the second earner, who could work less because the supplement offset the earnings loss. Cutbacks also occurred in the New Hope program initially, but these were trivial, concentrated among people who were working overtime hours that exceeded forty hours a week, and did not persist. Importantly, work reductions in the New Hope program were limited by the program's thirty-hour full-time work requirement, a feature the Minnesota program did not share.[30]

The Earned Income Tax Credit

Recognizing the contradiction of remaining poor while working in a society that values work, policymakers have used employee subsidies as an integral part of the nation's strategy for reducing poverty since the EITC was first passed in 1975 (to offset payroll taxes paid by the poor). The EITC was substantially expanded in 1986, 1990, and 1993, and today is available to all low-income workers who file tax returns. It is refundable, which

means that its benefits are paid out even when the tax filer does not owe any income taxes. More than 20 million taxpayers take advantage of the EITC each year, at a cost exceeding $34 billion, making it by far the largest cash benefit program for the poor.[31] By design, the overwhelming majority of beneficiaries are single parents supporting children.

The EITC's distinguishing feature is its status as a safety net built around work—only people with earnings can claim the credit. The amount varies by both family type and earnings. Families with two or more children can receive a maximum credit of $4,400; those with one child, $2,662; and single adults with no children, $399.[32] At its maximum, the credit provides an additional 40 cents for every dollar earned to a family with two children, effectively turning a $6.00 an hour job into an $8.40 an hour job. But this is the maximum credit for a family with two or more children, where the parent is able to earn between $11,000 and $14,400 a year. The average family receives about half of the theoretical maximum either because it earns too little to get the full credit or because it earns too much and is in the phase-down range.

Based on a comprehensive review of studies of the EITC, Steve Holt reports that it reduces family poverty by a tenth, reduces poverty among children by a fourth, and closes the poverty gap by a fifth.[33] The Census Bureau, by using a measure of disposable income that relies on revised, and still controversial, definitions of income and poverty and includes all government cash transfers (but not Medicaid or Medicare), and by subtracting both taxes paid (but adding back EITC payments) and work expenses (but not child care expenses), estimates that the 2005 poverty rate falls to 10 percent, about 2 percentage points lower than the official rate.[34] The after-tax value of the EITC probably accounts for about half of this reduction. But even so, someone who works full time (2,000 hours a year) at the 2006–07 minimum wage of $5.15 and who receives the maximum EITC credit would still have income below the 2005 poverty line of $15,577 for a family

---

The EITC can penalize marriage when both partners work—even as it rewards marriage between a nonworking single parent and a working partner.

---

of three ($10,300 in wages plus $4,400 from the EITC, or $14,700).

Nonexperimental assessments find that the EITC affects work in two ways. First, it encourages job taking, especially among single mothers (a 3 percentage point increase in the labor force participation rate of single women with children).[35] Several studies estimate that as much as a third of the increase in female labor force participation rates during the 1980s and 1990s was due to the expansion of the EITC.[36] Second, in two-parent families, it might reduce by a small amount the hours that second earners work, but there is scant evidence of a reduction in hours worked among single parents.[37]

Because the bulk of EITC benefits go to families with children and because both parents' earnings are counted when a couple is married, but only one parent's earnings count when they are not, the EITC can penalize marriage when both partners work—even as

it rewards marriage between a nonworking single parent and a working partner.[38] These penalties can be large. According to Saul Hoffman and Lawrence Seidman, a single parent working full time at the minimum wage who marries another minimum-wage earner could stand to lose $1,600, while two full-time workers (each earning $14,000), both with two children, could lose as much as $6,700 in EITC benefits.[39] Recently enacted provisions that increase the credit's value for married couples by several hundred dollars a year attempt to offset those penalties. By 2008, when those changes are fully in effect, penalties would be eliminated for most cohabiting families with incomes below 200 percent of the poverty line, but substantial penalties (averaging $1,742) would still remain for 44 percent of all cohabiting couples, mostly those with incomes between $20,000 and $30,000 a year.[40] Two-earner couples where both workers have similar earnings are especially hard hit by EITC reductions if they marry.

Weighing Alternative Strategies for Reducing Poverty
Although the EITC, as now designed, has helped to ameliorate poverty in families with children, it still leaves behind many poor and near-poor families and individuals. Additional strategies for further reducing poverty include boosting the minimum wage, investing in education and training, and rethinking the generosity, targeting, and structure of the EITC.

Minimum Wage
Both experience and empirical evidence suggest that the minimum wage can play a valuable role in raising wages and reducing poverty without severely distorting labor markets. First passed in 1938 in response to the Great Depression, the minimum wage

placed a floor under the wages of most workers and was pegged at about half the median hourly wage of nonsupervisory workers throughout the 1950s and 1960s. As of early 2007, its value had fallen to less than a third of the nonsupervisory wage, its lowest level in fifty years.[41] Both President Bush and congressional leaders have vowed to increase the minimum wage to $7.25, although if its value is not indexed to inflation, it will once again gradually erode over time.

Why are political leaders reluctant to keep up the value of the minimum wage, a cornerstone of antipoverty policy since the Great Depression? There are two primary reasons. First, raising the cost of workers reduces the profits of employers, weakens their competitive position relative to global employers, and lowers the number of employees they can hire without raising prices. Second, only one in five minimum-wage workers lives in a family with below-poverty income. Most are between sixteen and twenty-four years old and do not support families, making the minimum wage a relatively inefficient way to reduce family poverty. However, Peter Edelman, Harry Holzer, and Paul Offner, summarizing empirical work by David Card, Alan Krueger, and others, conclude that increasing the minimum wage to $7 an hour would at most result in trivial job losses in the tight labor market expected as the baby boomers begin to retire.[42] Moreover, they note that about four-fifths of the increase would accrue to people with incomes in the bottom 40 percent of the income distribution, partly as a result of upward ripple effects on nearby wages.[43] Nonetheless, reluctance to raise the minimum wage or to adjust it for inflation and concerns about targeting inefficiencies make the minimum wage alone an unreliable vehicle for addressing poverty.

Postsecondary Education

Given the steep rise in the return to higher education over the past twenty-five years—today a college graduate earns more than twice what a high school graduate earns (about $23,000 more, annually)—investing in the education and training of low-wage adults is an essential long-run alternative strategy for reducing poverty.[44] And for workers who have the necessary basic skills to succeed in postsecondary education, community college is a particularly attractive and ubiquitous option. Community colleges enroll nearly half of all college students in the United States—more than 11 million nationwide. But nearly half of all students who begin at community colleges leave before they can receive a credential, including untold thousands of students who are relegated to developmental education classes and never make it to credit-granting courses.[45] Although community colleges are actively experimenting with curricular reforms, student support services, and new forms of financial aid to address these problems, the fact remains that a large fraction of low-wage workers will not have the necessary skills to take a postsecondary route to higher earnings. And the K–12 reforms that are the subject of the article by Richard Murnane in this volume are at least a decade or two away from making a major difference in the skills of graduating seniors, who in any event constitute only a small fraction of the total workforce in any given year.

Other EITC Reforms

Over the next ten to twenty years, then, it is hard to imagine reducing poverty without finding a way to make low-wage work pay. A compelling body of evidence suggests that the earned income tax credit can be an effective way to supplement low earnings. Policymakers have three choices. They can increase the EITC for families with children, and especially for large families; increase it for married couples only; or supplement the earnings of individual low-wage workers, exempting the supplement from joint income tax filing requirements.

The first strategy moves more families with children above the poverty line but perpetuates current inequities by doing little to address the companion problems of single parenthood, the low earnings of single men and women, or marriage penalties in two-earner families. The second approach shares several of the shortcomings of the first and while it reduces marriage penalties for some, it creates new ones further up the income stream. It also asks people to marry for the money, running the risk of promoting any marriage over a healthy marriage, which has attendant risks for children and crosses a line that many find objectionable. Moreover, it fails to tackle the problem of the low wages of single adults, and places the burden on a single mother to calculate the value of a possible increase in benefits that would come with a potential marriage partner who at the moment may be underemployed and quite poor. That is asking a lot: to act on incentives, people have to understand them. Yet hardworking but still poor men would have no way of knowing— much less signaling—that their income would be 25 percent higher if they were married. That leaves the third option.

A Counterintuitive Response with a Radical Twist in Tax Policy

A bold and equitable strategy for reducing poverty would tackle the interrelated problems of men's low wages, single parenthood, and a tax and transfer system that, by giving primacy to families with children, has unintentionally distorted incentives on the margin to work, marry, and have children. An earnings supplement for individuals could accomplish

these goals by providing all low-wage workers aged twenty-one to fifty-four who work full time (thirty hours a week) with a payment approaching that of the current EITC but with a crucial, if radical, twist: payment would be based on an individual's personal income, not joint or family income, and singles would be eligible for the supplement whether or not they have children and whether or not they marry, as would second earners in a married family receiving the existing family EITC.

The credit should fall somewhere between 50 and 100 percent of the current EITC payment for families with one child.[46] For equity and simplicity, to illustrate the new credit's properties let's assume that the maximum credit is about 75 percent of the current one-child EITC. Thus, instead of the tiny $400 current annual maximum EITC payment for singles, every dollar of earnings under the new plan would be supplemented by 25 cents until earnings reached $7,800 (for a maximum credit amount of $1,950), after which the supplement would remain level until earnings reached $14,400, and it would then fall by 16 cents for every dollar of earnings until it was phased out entirely at $26,587. In effect, this policy would turn a $6 an hour job into a $7.50 an hour job. For someone who worked 1,500 hours over the course of a year, it would turn a below-poverty annual salary of $9,000 into an above-poverty salary of $11,250. Figure 4 offers another example of how this new EITC would benefit a single man working full time in a job that put him in the bottom tenth of earners. The average man in the bottom tenth of the earnings distribution earned just over $22,000 in 1979 but only around $18,000 in 2004; the new EITC would raise this to nearly $20,000.

To avoid penalizing children or couples who marry, the existing benefit structure and gov-

Figure 4. The Effect of the New EITC on the Income of Low-Earning, Single Adult Men

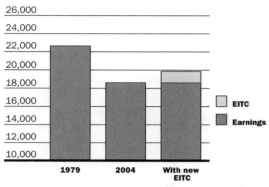

Annual income (2004 dollars)

Note: Low-earning adult men are defined as those working full time and in the bottom tenth of the annual earnings distribution.

erning rules for the one- and two-child EITC would remain in place for the primary earner in a family with children. The second earner in a married-couple family would now qualify for the new individual's credit without regard to the primary worker's earnings, essentially giving married couples the option of filing taxes individually, at least with regard to the EITC. In addition, with income treated separately, some married families with joint income that exceeds current cutoffs would now qualify for both the family and this new individual EITC. Emulating the approach to taxation used in Canada and many European countries, this strategy eliminates the marriage penalties now embedded in tax policy (at least for low-income couples claiming these EITC benefits), while also reestablishing social policy parity between men and women, and between parents and childless individuals, by bolstering the earnings position of low-wage individuals.[47]

The benefits to second earners in married or cohabiting couples would be substantial. Couples with joint earnings would each be able to receive an EITC payment, with the principal earner qualifying for the current child benefit and the second earner qualifying for this new individual EITC payment (possibly subject to an income cap of 250 percent of poverty). As figure 5 illustrates, for a two-child family in which each parent earned $14,000 ($28,000 together), the total maximum EITC payment could provide an additional $6,350—$4,400 for the existing two-child credit due one spouse plus $1,950 for the other spouse's individual credit. Note that in this example, without an income cap or a lower overall subsidy, the earnings supplement would continue, although at progressively lower amounts, until it was zeroed out when *combined* income reached $62,000.

At first blush, a subsidy that reached this far into the middle of the family income distribution would likely be politically unacceptable. But unless the earnings of families above the poverty line are subsidized to some degree, it will be very difficult to resolve the work and marriage disincentives imposed by current policy on families with similar earned income in the $20,000-and-up range that result from high—and behavior-distorting—cumulative marginal tax rates. Moreover, as the example makes clear, adopting this policy would require coordination with, and possibly rethinking, the $1,000 per child tax credit, which is now partly refundable if income exceeds $11,000 a year and is not phased out until income reaches $75,000 for a single parent and $110,000 for a married couple.[48]

Adult men and women who are not caring for children and who work full time but are still poor—a group that has been largely ignored despite their substantial work effort—would also benefit. Using data from the National Survey of America's Families, Stephen Bell and Jerome Gallagher paint a portrait of

Figure 5. The Effect of the New EITC for a Single Parent with Two or More Children Who Marries Another Low-Wage Worker

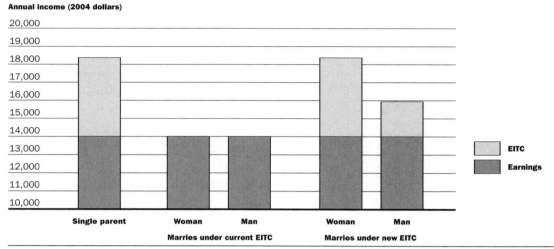

Note: Assuming that each adult earns approximately $7.00 an hour and that the man is the secondary earner.

twenty-five- to forty-nine-year-olds with incomes below 200 percent of the poverty line who are not disabled and who do not have children of their own living with them. More than three-quarters work, mostly full time, but their wages are low (90 percent make less than $10.30 an hour) and one-third have incomes below the poverty line for their family size, while another 27 percent are near poor. A quarter are noncustodial parents and a quarter live with a spouse. More than half are white men with a high school diploma or less. They receive little in the way of government assistance—only 6 percent get food stamps and only 5 percent, unemployment insurance benefits—yet they too have been hit hard by labor market changes over the past thirty years.[49]

The impact on poverty of an individually based EITC of the size proposed here would be certain, large, and immediate. Individuals who now work more than thirty hours a week and earn less than the threshold amount annually (whether married, cohabiting, or unattached) would receive an immediate supplement to help to restore earnings to pre-1973

levels, when the average high school graduate—or even a dropout—could support a family above the poverty line. Those working less than thirty hours a week, including second earners in two-parent households, would have an incentive to increase their work hours, further boosting income, promoting self-sufficiency, and reducing poverty. Finally, those not in the labor force would have added incentive to find a full-time job, which would substantially boost total income.

Reliable experimental evidence indicates that employment effects could be significant. Economists estimate that increasing the hourly wage of a low-income worker by 10 percent would boost employment between 2 and 10 percent.[50] Under this proposal, a potential minimum-wage worker, who could earn about $875 for 170 hours of full-time work per month, would be eligible for a monthly supplement of about $200. This 20 percent increase in income would be expected to increase employment rates by 4 to 20 percent.[51] Adding credence to these estimates, the make-work-pay experiments described above had similar employment, earnings, and income effects, albeit for a population of mostly single mothers. Data from all four years of follow-up from each of these programs (including the period after the supplement programs ended) indicate that employment increases ranged from 8 percent in New Hope to 19 percent among long-term welfare recipients in the Canadian Self-Sufficiency Project (SSP).[52] Intriguingly, employment effects for the most disadvantaged (those with limited education, little previous work history, and long prior spells of welfare dependency) were very large—up 56 percent in the SSP, 48 percent in Minnesota, and 25 percent in New Hope.

Less reliable observational evidence suggests that an earnings supplement could also have small but significant secondary beneficial effects on crime and marriage. Men's involvement in criminal activity might reasonably be expected to decline as their earnings rise and the opportunity cost of crime goes up. Similarly, higher earnings, together with the elimination of EITC-related tax and transfer penalties on marriage, might also lead to more co-parenting, cohabitation, and marriage. Although these secondary effects are somewhat speculative, an individually based EITC payment at the very least creates the necessary, if not sufficient, conditions to make an increase in marriage feasible when combined with a direct intervention to promote marriage of the kind proposed by Paul Amato and Rebecca Maynard in their article in this volume.[53]

Finally, by supplementing the earnings of single men in low-wage jobs and increasing their income, this plan would encourage more "on the books" work, while helping men meet their child support obligations. As in current law, single people who are parents and owe child support would have their EITC payment attached to pay their child support obligations.

Anticipating Unintended Consequences

Even as it addresses important gaps in current policy, this plan, like any tax and transfer policy reform, opens up the possibility of creating unintended consequences. Five such consequences are anticipated below.

What about the principle of "horizontal equity"? An important and long-standing principle of tax policy is horizontal equity: the tax system should treat all married couples with the same total family income similarly, regardless of the source of their income. For some families, this plan violates that principle: a family in which one spouse accounts for most of the household's earnings would receive substantially less in benefits than a family in which the earnings of both spouses are similar. Ironically, current tax policy has the opposite effect, penalizing couples when both parents' earnings are similar. The problem of unequal earners could be partly remedied by following the Canadian example, which allows the high-earning spouse to claim a credit for the not-working or low-earning spouse, a credit that declines in value as the spouse's earnings rise (see note 47).

Would there be an incentive for some people to reduce the number of hours they work? In the EITC and Minnesota programs, second earners in families were likely to reduce their work hours, especially when their earnings were in the phase-down range. Both the New Hope program and the Canadian Self-Sufficiency Project substantially alleviated this problem by conditioning the payment of earnings supplements on full-time work of at least thirty hours a week. As findings from the two projects demonstrate, a full-time work requirement has important advantages: it lowers total costs, moves people closer to self-sufficiency, and limits reductions in hours worked among those already working. However, applying a full-time "hours rule" to second earners in two-parent households, especially those with young children, would effectively penalize some for making the legitimate decision to spend more time with their children. Several modifications might help alleviate these concerns, including establishing a twenty-hour work minimum for the second earner only, creating a fifty-hour combined minimum per week for both earners, or lowering the minimum hours rule for parents with children under age three. There is also some risk of a cutback in work effort among primary earners receiving the existing EITC for families, which does not include an hours requirement. That risk is minimal, however, and could be reduced further by imposing a combined hours requirement or by making the individual EITC less generous.

Would it be feasible to administer an hours requirement? To facilitate administration of an average thirty-hour-a-week work requirement (using a monthly, quarterly, or annual accounting period), employers would have to report hours worked in at least one of two

> *A full-time work requirement lowers total costs, moves people closer to self-sufficiency, and limits reductions in hours worked among those already working.*

ways. The simplest approach would be to require employers to report monthly or quarterly hours worked on the end-of-the-year W-2 forms now given to all employees for tax-filing purposes. Then, individuals would claim the EITC as they do now, when filing their annual tax returns. Alternatively, employers could report hours worked along with the quarterly earnings report they now submit for unemployment insurance purposes on every paid employee. Several states, including Minnesota, New Jersey, Oregon, Washington, and Wyoming, already require employers to report hours worked. The unemployment insurance system would then have to share these employer reports electronically with the IRS to ensure accurate calculation of the EITC. Given that it now takes employers about five months to file wage reports, this process would have to be speeded up. Requiring employers to report hours worked would also make it possible for the government to pay the EITC quarterly instead of annually at tax time and would enable states to use hours rather than earnings to more fairly and accurately determine eligibility for unemployment insurance, a factor in the system's currently low coverage rates.

Wouldn't private employers be less likely to increase wages? An increase in public sector wage subsidies would likely make private employers less likely to raise wages. To avoid this problem, policymakers should consider indexing the minimum wage to inflation, so that it provides a floor below which wages cannot fall as the EITC expands. The higher one sets the minimum wage, the lower the cost of an EITC expansion. However, the politics of the minimum wage and its targeting inefficiencies (particularly the problem of teenage workers in affluent households) may make policymakers reluctant to expand the minimum wage much beyond $7.25 an hour nationally (although California's minimum wage will reach $8 an hour by 2008). A minimum wage increase could substantially boost wages at the bottom, but it would not address the problems of persistent poverty or of high marginal tax rates that undermine decisions about parenting and marriage. In addition, the political unpredictability of the minimum wage makes it an unreliable policy lever for supporting low-wage workers.

Wouldn't young people be lured out of school? Young people between eighteen and twenty-five have to make a range of decisions about the present value of work as measured against the future value of additional schooling. The opportunity to get a generous earnings supplement might change that calculus somewhat. Starting the supplement at age twenty-one, however, reinforces the value of postsecondary education, and the thirty-hour work requirement limits the likelihood of making payments to teens and college students who often have other means of support, although it might require the use of a four-month accounting period to avoid paying supplements to college students in the summer. Waiting until age twenty-five, as the current EITC for singles does, may unnecessarily penalize young, non-college-bound workers who are supporting families.

Eligibility and Costs

The plan affects three distinct populations. The first group is single men and women (some have children who do not live with them and others may be cohabiting). The second group is second earners in married two-parent households. The third is married couples without children (some whose children are over age eighteen and others who are just starting life as a couple). According to the eligibility criteria—age twenty-one to fifty-four, thirty hours or more of work a

week for at least twenty-six weeks in the past year (a proxy for a quarterly accounting period), individual income below $31,030—roughly 35 million *additional* people would be eligible to receive EITC payments (44 million who meet these criteria, minus the 9 million who already receive EITC payments, according to the Current Population Survey).[54] About 15 million of these newly eligible recipients would be unmarried singles; 11 million, married individuals with children under eighteen (7 million second-earner spouses and 3.8 million primary earners); and 9 million, married individuals without children under eighteen. Another 3 million, mostly single, individuals (some supporting children and some not) who now receive small EITC supplements would be eligible for a threefold increase in their EITC payment.[55] More than half of the newly eligible group is married. And somewhere between one-third and one-half are supporting children.

Two key questions remain. First, how much would this plan cost? Assuming no change in the work behavior of recipients, a rough cost estimate is $29 billion a year to supplement the earnings of *existing* full-time workers.[56] Today 35 million people are not eligible for the existing child-based EITC but work thirty hours a week or more, are struggling economically, and have earnings low enough to make them eligible for this new credit. The expected average earnings supplement of $1,000 would substantially raise their income and reduce the number of people living in poor families. What about additional costs for people moving from unemployment or part-time work to full-time jobs? Roughly 14 million potentially eligible people now work less than thirty hours a week for twenty-six weeks, and 22 million more are not working at all. Assuming a 15 percent increase in the share of part-time or part-year workers moving to full-time work, and a 10 percent increase in the number of nonworkers who take a full-time job because of the supplement, benefits would be paid to an additional 4 million people.[57] With an average supplement of $1,000, these increases would bring total costs to roughly $33 billion annually.

Second, can we afford it? Based on the size of the federal budget deficit and the enormity of the Social Security and Medicare obligations that the nation faces, the obvious answer would seem to be no. But it is also true that if the economy had continued growing at 1960s-like rates and if the distribution of income between rich and poor had been the same in 2006 as it was in 1975, then the poverty rate would be about half what it is today.[58] Instead, growth was decidedly slower during the 1970s and early 1980s and when it began accelerating significantly thereafter, the main beneficiaries were the top 10 percent of the income distribution—especially the top 0.1 percent[59]—who are accumulating unprecedented wealth (roughly an extra $750 billion annually)[60] that would, in 1975, have gone disproportionately to the bottom of the income distribution. Assuming, as most economists would, that there is nothing inherently superior, from a national investment and savings perspective, about the distribution of income in 2006 relative to 1975, a $29 billion to $33 billion tax on these very high earners that was used to supplement the income of low earners would make no discernible difference in the economic position of the United States. To put this number into perspective, it represents about one-third of the annual tax reduction for the top 1 percent of the income distribution as a result of the Jobs and Growth Tax Relief Reconciliation Act of 2003. In that case, the answer is yes, we can afford it.

Still, $29 billion to $33 billion a year is a lot of money. There are less expensive alternatives. Total costs could be halved, to $15 billion, if the subsidy rate were reduced from 25 percent to 20 percent, and further reduced to $4 billion if the rate were reduced to 15 percent. But at these lower rates, average per-person subsidy amounts fall from $1,000 per year (at the 25 percent rate) to $720 (20 percent) and $437 (15 percent), significantly reducing the plan's antipoverty benefits.[61]

Conclusion

As technological change, globalization, and other forces continue to roil labor markets in what Alan Blinder has referred to as the dawn of the Third Industrial Revolution and Frank Levy and Dick Murnane have called the New Division of Labor, all American workers face a difficult period of transition.[62] Through no fault of their own, low-wage workers have been especially hard hit over the past thirty years and appear destined to bear an even greater future burden. A decision to simply let global market forces work will likely exacerbate already high rates of inequality. Indeed, the case for growth-promoting free trade is predicated on the pledge that winners will compensate losers from a larger economic pie. Similarly, as baby boomers retire, slowing the rate of growth in the size of the labor force, economic growth may also slow, a development that adds urgency to the need to create strategies that increase labor force participation rates among men.

An earnings supplement for individuals offers a potentially promising alternative to persistent poverty, low wages, and declining employment rates among men. It is a strategy designed to tackle, in whole or in part, three interrelated issues. The first is three decades of stagnant and declining wages at the low end of the economic ladder, which have hit low-income men especially hard. The second is an enduring crisis in the share of children raised in single-parent, low-income households. And the third is a tax and transfer system that ignores men, while penalizing marriage and work on the margin.

Solid and reliable evidence demonstrates that earnings supplements have encouraged work and reduced poverty among unemployed and underemployed single parents. A strategy that redesigned EITC eligibility to give equivalency to individuals might have a similar effect on second earners and childless, low-income women and men. Indeed, the New Hope program had just such an effect on its tiny sample of single men. And by treating two-parent earnings separately rather than jointly when establishing EITC eligibility and when filing taxes, a new EITC for individuals could also be expected to increase the work effort of second earners in two-parent households, and in turn to raise the income of two-parent, two-earner families. In fact, it would immediately and substantially end poverty among individuals who are now working full time. At issue is how many nonworkers and part-time workers would be induced to find full-time work.

Moreover, if survey data and ethnographic evidence are right in suggesting that the poor share mainstream values about parenting and marriage but that the economics simply do not work for them, then equitably supplementing the earnings of individuals could also affect men's and women's decisions about childbearing, co-parenting, cohabiting, and even whether to marry. Indeed, studies simulating large increases in men's earnings predict small increases in marriage.[63]

But no matter how promising the idea, questions remain—primarily about cost and the magnitude of any behavioral changes. Would a work incentive of this size really induce second earners and single men to work more than they do now? Would single men be more likely to live with the mothers of their children, assume co-parenting roles, and even marry? Of special concern would be how an earnings supplement would affect African American men, particularly

Solid and reliable evidence demonstrates that earnings supplements have encouraged work and reduced poverty among unemployed and underemployed single parents.

whether it would increase their employment rates and make them less likely to become involved with the criminal justice system. How would it affect single women's employment, childbearing, and marriage decisions? Would the resulting poverty reductions measurably affect the well-being of children? Would the supplement unintentionally lower college-going among young people or reduce work effort among eligible higher earners who work more than thirty hours a week? What would it really cost to implement? And would the benefits justify the cost?

Because finding answers to these questions is vital, a prudent next step would be to rigorously test this strategy in several states over several years—preferably using a random assignment design and sample recruitment strategies like those used in the New Hope and similar studies.[64]

If you could do one thing to end poverty in America, what would it be? Any serious effort would have to tackle more than thirty years of falling wages, particularly for single men. An enhanced EITC for individuals, predicated on full-time work, would effectively end poverty for individuals and families who are able to work full time, while at the same time minimizing the distortions in incentives to work, co-parent, and marry that exacerbate poverty and ensure its persistence.

Notes

1. Sheldon H. Danziger and Peter Gottschalk, "Diverging Fortunes: Trends in Poverty and Inequality," in *The American People: Census 2000,* edited by Reynolds Farley and John Haaga (New York: Russell Sage Foundation, 2005), pp. 49–75; Hilary Hoynes, Marianne Page, and Ann Stevens, "Poverty in America: Trends and Explanations," Working Paper 11681 (Cambridge, Mass.: National Bureau of Economic Research, October 2005), prepared for a symposium on poverty for the *Journal of Economic Perspectives.*

2. William J. Wilson, *When Work Disappears: The World of the New Urban Poor* (New York: Knopf, 1996); Kathryn Edin and Maria Kefalas, *Promises I Can Keep: Why Poor Women Put Motherhood before Marriage* (University of California Press, 2005); Andrew Cherlin, "American Marriage in the Early 21st Century," *Future of Children* 15, no. 2 (2005): 33–55.

3. After 1973, the United States dramatically increased spending on social welfare programs, including the EITC, food stamps, and housing assistance, but these transfers are not counted in official poverty statistics. When alternative measures of poverty that include these transfers but subtract for other expenses (like payroll taxes and work-related child care costs) are used, poverty rates do decline, typically by 1 or 2 percentage points. See Constance F. Citro and Robert T. Michael, eds., *Measuring Poverty: A New Approach* (Washington: National Academies Press, 1995); and U.S. Census Bureau, *The Effects of Government Taxes and Transfers on Income and Poverty: 2004* (2006).

4. Danziger and Gottschalk, "Diverging Fortunes" (see note 1); Frank Levy, *The New Dollars and Dreams: American Incomes and Economic Change* (New York: Russell Sage Foundation, 1998).

5. Frank Levy and Richard J. Murnane, *The New Division of Labor: How Computers Are Creating the Next Job Market* (New York: Russell Sage Foundation, 2004); David H. Autor, Lawrence F. Katz, and Melissa S. Kearney, "The Polarization of the U.S. Labor Market," Working Paper 11986 (Cambridge, Mass.: National Bureau of Economic Research, January 2006); David Card and John E. DiNardo, "Skill-Biased Technological Change and Rising Wage Inequality: Some Problems and Puzzles," *Journal of Labor Economics* 20, no. 4 (2002): 733–83.

6. Autor, Katz, and Kearney, "The Polarization of the U.S. Labor Market" (see note 5).

7. Peter Edelman, Harry J. Holzer, and Paul Offner, *Reconnecting Disadvantaged Young Men* (Washington: Urban Institute Press, 2006).

8. Chinhui Juhn, "Decline of Male Labor Market Participation: The Role of Declining Market Opportunities," *Quarterly Journal of Economics* 107, no. 1 (1992): 79–122; Edelman, Holzer, and Offner, *Reconnecting Disadvantaged Young Men* (see note 7).

9. Andrew Sum and others, *Trends in Black Male Joblessness and Year-Round Idleness: An Employment Crisis Ignored* (Chicago, Ill.: Alternative Schools Network, 2004); Edelman, Holzer, and Offner, *Reconnecting Disadvantaged Young Men* (see note 7).

10. Edelman, Holzer, and Offner, *Reconnecting Disadvantaged Young Men* (see note 7); Steven Raphael, "Early Incarceration Spells and the Transition to Adulthood," in *The Price of Independence: The Economics of Early Adulthood,* edited by Sheldon Danziger and Cecilia Rouse (New York: Russell Sage Foundation, forthcoming 2007).

11. Bruce Western, "The Impact of Incarceration on Wage Mobility and Inequality," *American Sociological Review* 67, no. 4 (2002): 526–46; Raphael, "Early Incarceration Spells" (see note 10).

12. Cherlin, "American Marriage in the Early 21st Century" (see note 2); Wilson, *When Work Disappears* (see note 2); Edin and Kefalas, *Promises I Can Keep* (see note 2).

13. Danziger and Gottschalk, "Diverging Fortunes" (see note 1).

14. Paul R. Amato, "The Impact of Family Formation Change on the Cognitive, Social, and Emotional Well-Being of the Next Generation," *Future of Children* 15, no. 2 (2005): 75–96.

15. Cherlin, "American Marriage in the Early 21st Century" (see note 2).

16. Kathryn Edin and Joanna M. Reed, "Why Don't They Just Get Married? Barriers to Marriage among the Disadvantaged," *Future of Children* 15, no. 2 (2005): 117–38.

17. Earl Johnson, Ann Levine, and Fred Doolittle, *Fathers' Fair Share: Helping Poor Men Manage Child Support and Fatherhood* (New York: Russell Sage Foundation, 1999); Frank Furstenberg Jr., Kay Sherwood, and Mercer Sullivan, *Caring and Paying: What Fathers and Mothers Say about Child Support* (New York: MDRC, 1992).

18. Edin and Kefalas, *Promises I Can Keep* (see note 2).

19. Andrew M. Sum and Neal Fogg, "The Changing Economic Fortunes of Young Black Men in America," in *The Black Scholar: Journal of Black Studies and Research* 21, no. 1 (1990): 47–56; Ronald B. Mincy, ed., *Black Men Left Behind* (Washington: Urban Institute Press, 2006).

20. I am grateful to Andrew Sum of Northeastern University for this analysis.

21. Marcia Carlson, Sara McLanahan, and Paula England, "Union Formation in Fragile Families," *Demography* 41, no. 2 (2004): 237–62.

22. Gregory Acs and Elaine Maag, "Irreconcilable Differences? The Conflict between Marriage Promotion Initiatives for Cohabiting Couples with Children and Marriage Penalties in Tax and Transfer Programs," *New Federalism: National Survey of America's Families,* series B, no. B-66 (Washington: Urban Institute, 2005).

23. Adam Carasso and C. Eugene Steuerle, "The Hefty Penalty on Marriage Facing Many Households with Children," *Future of Children* 15, no. 2 (2005): 157–75.

24. David T. Ellwood, "The Impact of the Earned Income Tax Credit and Social Policy Reforms on Work, Marriage, and Living Arrangements," in *Making Work Pay: The Earned Income Tax Credit and Its Impact on America's Families,* edited by Bruce D. Meyer and Douglas Holtz-Eakin (New York: Russell Sage Foundation, 2001), p. 157.

25. Robert Moffitt, "The Effect of Welfare on Marriage and Fertility," in *Welfare, the Family, and Reproductive Behavior*, edited by Robert Moffitt (Washington: National Academy Press, 1998); Ellwood, "The Impact of the Earned Income Tax Credit" (see note 24); Acs and Maag, "Irreconcilable Differences?" (see note 22).

26. Charles Michalopoulos, *Does Making Work Pay Still Pay? An Update on the Effects of Four Earnings Supplement Programs on Employment, Earnings, and Income* (New York: MDRC, 2005).

27. Pamela A. Morris, Lisa A. Gennetian, and Greg J. Duncan, "Effects of Welfare and Employment Policies on Young Children: New Findings on Policy Experiments Conducted in the Early 1990s," *Social Policy Report* 19, no. 2 (2005).

28. Lisa Gennetian, Cynthia Miller, and Jared Smith, *Turning Welfare into a Work Support: Six-Year Impacts on Parents and Children from the Minnesota Family Investment Program* (New York: MDRC, 2005).

29. Aletha C. Huston and others, *New Hope for Families and Children: Five-Year Results of a Program to Reduce Poverty and Reform Welfare* (New York: MDRC, 2003); and unpublished eight-year follow-up survey results from the New Hope evaluation.

30. Gennetian, Miller, and Smith, *Turning Welfare into a Work Support* (see note 28), p. 51; Johannes M. Bos and others, *New Hope for People with Low Incomes: Two-Year Results of a Program to Reduce Poverty and Reform Welfare* (New York: MDRC, 1999).

31. U.S. House of Representatives, Committee on Ways and Means, *2004 Green Book: Background Material and Data on Programs within the Jurisdiction of the House Committee on Ways and Means* (2004).

32. To encourage work, the value of the credit rises steeply in the phase-in range, until a two-child family's earnings reach $11,000 ($7,800 for a single-child family and $5,200 for a childless single); then flattens in the plateau range, until earnings reach $14,400 for a two-child or a single-child family ($6,550 for a childless single); and then gradually declines to zero in the phase-down range, as earnings rise to $35,263 ($31,030 for one child and $11,750 for no child). To help reduce the marriage penalty, the phase-out income target for married couples is several thousand dollars higher than for single-parent families, which translates into a few hundred dollars more per year.

33. Steve Holt, "The Earned Income Tax Credit at Age 30: What We Know" (Brookings, February 2006); V. Joseph Hotz and John Karl Scholz, "The Earned Income Tax Credit," in *Means Tested Transfer Programs in the United States,* edited by R. Moffitt (University of Chicago Press, 2003); Robert Greenstein, *The Earned Income Tax Credit: Boosting Employment, Aiding the Working Poor* (Washington: Center on Budget and Policy Priorities, 2005); James P. Ziliac, "Filling the Poverty Gap, Then and Now," Working Paper 2003-06 (University of Kentucky Center for Poverty Research, 2004).

34. Census Bureau, *The Effects of Government Taxes and Transfers on Income and Poverty* (see note 3).

35. Nada Eissa and Jeffrey B. Liebman, "Labor Supply Response to the Earned Income Tax Credit," *Quarterly Journal of Economics* 111, no. 2 (1996): 605–37; V. Joseph Hotz, Charles H. Mullin, and John Karl Scholz, *Trends in EITC Take-Up and Receipt for California's Welfare Population, 1992–1999,* Working Paper (Institute for Research on Poverty, University of Wisconsin, Madison, 2003); Hotz and Scholz, "The Earned Income Tax Credit" (see note 33).

36. Bruce D. Meyer and Dan T. Rosenbaum, "Making Single Mothers Work: Recent Tax and Welfare Policy and Its Effects," in *Making Work Pay: The Earned Income Tax Credit and Its Impact on America's Families,* edited by Meyer and Holtz-Eakin (see note 24), pp. 69–115; Jeffrey Grogger, "The Effects of Time Limits, the EITC, and Other Policy Changes on Welfare Use, Work, and Income among Female-Headed Families," *Review of Economics and Statistics* 85, no. 2 (2003): 394–408.

37. Nada Eissa and Hilary Williams Hoynes, "Taxes and the Labor Market Participation of Married Couples: The Earned Income Tax Credit," *Journal of Public Economics* 88 no. 9–10 (2004): 1931–58; Eissa and Liebman, "Labor Supply Response to the Earned Income Tax Credit" (see note 35).

38. Acs and Maag, "Irreconcilable Differences?" (see note 22); Saul D. Hoffman and Laurence S. Seidman, *Helping Working Families: The Earned Income Tax Credit* (Kalamazoo, Mich.: W. E. Upjohn Institute for Employment Research, 2003).

39. Hoffman and Seidman, *Helping Working Families* (see note 38).

40. Acs and Maag, "Irreconcilable Differences?" (see note 22).

41. Sar Levitan, Frank Gallo, and Isaac Shapiro, *Working but Poor: America's Contradiction* (Johns Hopkins University Press, 1993); Jared Bernstein and Isaac Shapiro, *Nine Years of Neglect: Federal Minimum Wage Remains Unchanged for Ninth Straight Year, Falls to Lowest Level in More than Half a Century* (Washington: Center on Budget and Policy Priorities and Economic Policy Institute, August 2006).

42. Edelman, Holzer, and Offner, *Reconnecting Disadvantaged Young Men* (see note 7); David Card and Alan G. Krueger, *Myth and Measurement: The New Economics of the Minimum Wage* (Princeton University Press, 1995); David Neumark and William Wascher, "Comment on 'Minimum Wages and Employment: A Case Study of the Fast-Food Industry in New Jersey and Pennsylvania' by David Card and Alan B. Krueger," *American Economic Review* 90, no. 5 (1998): 1362–96.

43. Amy Chasanov, "No Longer Getting By: An Increase in the Minimum Wage Is Long Overdue," Research and Ideas Working Paper (Washington: Economic Policy Institute, 2004).

44. Sheldon Danziger and Cecilia Rouse, "Introduction," in *The Price of Independence: The Economics of Early Adulthood,* edited by Danziger and Rouse (see note 10).

45. Thomas Brock and Allen LeBlanc, *Promoting Student Success in Community College and Beyond: The Opening Doors Demonstration* (New York: MDRC, 2005).

46. Edelman, Holzer, and Offner propose an EITC for singles with a maximum value of $1,500; *Reconnecting Disadvantaged Young Men* (see note 7). Primus proposes for fathers who owe child support a credit of half the current EITC for single parents; Wendell Primus, "Improving Public Policies to Increase the Income and Employment of Low-Income Nonresident Fathers," in *Black Males Left Behind,* edited by Ronald B. Mincy (Washington: Urban Institute Press, 2006), pp. 211–48. The maximum subsidy discussed here of $2,400, about $200 a month, would restore low-end wages to closer to their 1973 level.

47. Canadians file taxes as individuals for personal income purposes, with special rules governing some forms of "taxable income" when filers are married (for example, the child care expense deduction can be claimed only by the lower-earning spouse, and refundable tax credits to benefit low-income families, such as the Child Tax Benefit and the Goods and Services Tax Credit, where eligibility is family-income based, can be claimed by either spouse). Because of these features, each tax filer is required to report the name and social insurance number of his or her spouse and the net income reported by that spouse; Revenue Canada then cross-references the two tax returns. In addition, a tax filer who has a dependent (in general, a nonworking spouse) can claim a deduction from income that decreases as the spouse's earnings increase (becoming zero at just over $8,000 in annual earnings).

48. Adam Carasso, Jeffrey Rohaly, and C. Eugene Steuerle, "Tax Reform for Families: An Earned Income Child Credit," Welfare Reform and Beyond Policy Brief 26 (Brookings, 2003); Ellwood, "The Impact of the Earned Income Tax Credit" (see note 24), p. 157.

49. Stephen H. Bell and L. Jerome Gallagher, "Prime-Age Adults without Children or Disabilities: The Least Deserving of the Poor—or Are They?" *New Federalism: National Survey of America's Family,* series B, no. B-26 (Washington: Urban Institute, 2001).

50. Chinhui Juhn, Kevin Murphy, and Robert Topel. "Why Has the Natural Rate of Unemployment Increased through Time?" *Brookings Papers on Economic Activity 1991,* no. 2: 75–142; Lawrence Katz, "Wage Subsidies for the Disadvantaged," in *Generating Jobs: How to Increase Demand for Less-Skilled Workers,* edited by Peter Gottschalk and Richard Freeman (New York: Russell Sage Foundation, 1998); Jeffrey Grogger, "Market Wages and Youth Crime," *Journal of Labor Economics* 16, no. 4 (1998): 756–91; Edelman, Holzer, and Offner, *Reconnecting Disadvantaged Young Men* (see note 7).

51. For a discussion of these effects, see Edelman, Holzer, and Offner, *Reconnecting Disadvantaged Young Men* (see note 7).

52. The Canadian Self-Sufficiency Project increased employment 19 percent, earnings 23 percent, and income 14 percent; the less generous Minnesota program increased employment 13 percent, earnings 5 percent, and income 8 percent; and the New Hope program increased employment 7 percent, earnings 5 percent, and income 5 percent.

53. It could play a similarly necessary but not sufficient role for the employment interventions that Mead proposes in his article in this volume for chronically unemployed men involved in the justice system.

54. Calculations from the 2005 March supplement of the U.S. Census Bureau's Current Population Survey (CPS) by the Center on Labor Market Studies, Northeastern University. The CPS underestimates EITC receipt, suggesting that these eligible population estimates overstate the number of eligibles.

55. Of the 58 million working Americans with income below $31,030 in 2004, 48 million worked full time (thirty hours a week or more) when they worked (44 million of whom met the thirty hours a week for twenty-six-weeks eligibility requirement), and 10 million worked part time. Twenty-three million did not work at all.

56. This assumes that individuals worked thirty hours a week or more for at least twenty-six weeks out of the year and had total income of less than $31,030. While the plan proposes a quarterly accounting period—that is, thirty hours of work per week, on average, over three months—the estimates use "worked at least twenty-six weeks in the last year" as a proxy. Current Population Survey estimates of new eligibles, prepared by the Center for Labor Market Studies, are available from the author on request. In short, net costs subtract current EITC payments as reported in the CPS. Recall that new credit parameters are a 25 percent subsidy phase-in rate until income reaches $7,800 and a 16 percent phase-down beginning at $14,400 and ending at $26,587. A 34 percent subsidy rate was used to calculate costs for married family heads, a group whose joint income was too high for the existing family EITC but who would become eligible if income were treated on an individual, not joint, basis. Because most full-time workers work full year, relaxing the "weeks worked" criterion from twenty-six weeks to five weeks only increases the total cost to $32.5 billion. The assumptions used to derive these estimates most likely result in an overstatement of the potential number of beneficiaries: people receiving disability payments or who were otherwise unable to work were not excluded; the estimates assume that all those who worked thirty hours and twenty-six weeks in the past year would qualify; no savings were calculated for any increase in work effort that might occur; and, as noted earlier, the CPS underestimates EITC receipt.

57. The Canadian Self-Sufficiency Project increased the share of nonworkers who moved to qualifying full-time work by about 7 percent, and a best estimate from both the SSP and New Hope of the effect of moving from part-time to full-time work might be in the 10–15 percent range, if one averages the effects for the applicant and recipient groups in SSP and considers the composition of the sample in New Hope.

58. Danziger and Gottschalk, "Diverging Fortunes" (see note 1).

59. Ian Dew-Becker and Robert J. Gordon, "Where Did the Productivity Growth Go? Inflation Dynamics and the Distribution of Income," Working Paper 11842 (Cambridge, Mass.: National Bureau of Economic Research, December 2005).

60. See Steven Pearlstein, "Solving Inequality Problem Won't Take Class Warfare," *Washington Post,* March 15, 2006, p. D1. Pearlstein estimates that the top 10 percent of the income distribution received an extra $750 billion as a result of its increased share of national income.

61. By comparison, Edelman, Holzer, and Offner estimate a $9.8 billion annual cost for a more narrowly targeted credit for singles that includes a maximum payment of $1,500 and has no full-time work requirement, but includes a plan to reduce marriage penalties by not counting 50 percent of the lower-earning spouse's wages when eligibility for the current family EITC is calculated. See Edelman, Holzer, and Offner, *Reconnecting Disadvantaged Young Men* (see note 7).

62. Levy and Murnane, *The New Division of Labor: How Computers Are Creating the Next Job Market* (see note 5); Alan S. Blinder, "Offshoring: The Next Industrial Revolution," *Foreign Affairs* 85, no. 2 (2006): 113–28.

63. Edin and Reed, "Why Don't They Just Get Married?" (see note 16).

64. Other examples include the SIME/DIME Negative Income Tax Experiments.

Toward a Mandatory Work Policy for Men

Lawrence M. Mead

Summary

Lawrence Mead addresses the problem of nonwork among low-income men, particularly low-income black men, and its implications for families and children. The poor work effort, he says, appears to be caused partly by falling wages and other opportunity constraints but principally by an oppositional culture and a breakdown of work discipline. Mead argues that if government policies are to increase work among poor men, they must not merely improve wages and skills but enforce work in available jobs. Using the same "help with hassle" approach that welfare reform has used successfully to increase work among poor mothers, policymakers should adapt the child support enforcement and criminal justice systems so that both actively help their clients find employment and then back up that help with a requirement that they work.

Men with unpaid child support judgments and parolees leaving prison would be told to get a job or pay up, as they are now. But if they did not, they would be remanded to a required work program where their efforts to work would be closely supervised. They would have to participate and get a private job and have their subsequent employment verified. Failing that, they would be assigned to work crews, where again compliance would be verified. Men who failed to participate and work steadily would—unless there were good cause—be sent back to the child support or parole authorities to be imprisoned. But men who complied would be freed from the work program after a year or two. They would then revert to the looser supervision practiced by the regular child support and parole systems. If their employment record deteriorated, they could again be remanded to the work program.

Mead estimates that such a program would involve as many as 1.5 million men who are already in the child support and criminal justice systems and would cost $2.4 billion to $4.8 billion a year. It is premature, says Mead, for such a program to be mandated nationwide. Rather, the best role for national policy at this point is to establish and evaluate promising model programs to see which work best.

www.futureofchildren.org

Lawrence M. Mead is professor of politics at New York University. He gratefully acknowledges comments on earlier drafts from Ron Haskins, Isabel Sawhill, Harry Holzer, Gordon Berlin, Swati Desai, and participants in the authors' conference for this volume of *The Future of Children*.

Lawrence M. Mead

The nation has successfully raised employment among poor mothers through welfare reform. The share of all poor mothers with children who worked jumped from 44 percent in 1993 to 64 percent in 1999, while the share working full time, year-round rose from 9 to 17 percent. Those figures fell back to 54 and 16 percent by 2005, partly because of the 2001 recession, but were still well above the level before welfare reform.[1]

Meanwhile, however, work levels among low-income men—many of them the absent fathers of welfare families—remain low and falling. In 2005, only 42 percent of working-aged men under the poverty line reported any employment at all, only 16 percent of them full time year-round.[2] Partly for this reason, work levels for the overall poor population have not improved. How might work levels for low-skilled men be raised in the same manner as those of welfare mothers? That is the question I address here.

The success of welfare reform in putting poor mothers to work was unprecedented. Until Congress passed the 1996 Personal Responsibility and Work Opportunity Reconciliation Act, government efforts to increase work among the poor had fallen far short of expectations. The problem, in part, was the tendency of researchers and policymakers to see the challenge too much in economic terms. Viewing poor adults as lacking in "human capital," they had sought to solve the problem by raising the skills of the poor, through education and training or by improving their incentives to work. But experience with numerous experimental welfare work programs during the 1980s and 1990s proved that it was also necessary to enforce work. Welfare reform succeeded where other programs had failed largely because it linked new wage and child care subsidies with clearer demands that people work in return for aid. That combination, plus superb economic conditions during the 1990s, propelled welfare mothers into the working world as never before.

Much of the effect of welfare reform, it is important to note, came through "diversion." As reform took hold during the 1990s, welfare mothers got a message that work was now expected of them. In response, many took jobs even before they were told to do so. Many more single mothers went to work without going on welfare at all. Change was driven by a political dynamic wider than social policy. Because of this, the impact of reform exceeded what one would have expected based on the experimental welfare work programs conducted since the 1980s.[3]

Policymakers should use a similar strategy to raise employment among poor men. For men, there is no broad benefit structure like welfare to use as a basis for promoting work, but other institutions can serve. One such is child support enforcement; another, the criminal justice system. Both are already heavily involved in the lives of many low-income men. In this article, I describe the problem of nonwork by poor men and suggest its causes, stressing male psychology. I argue that benefit-oriented solutions, such as higher wages, will not suffice. They must be combined with measures to enforce work. I outline a possible mandatory work program that would be linked to child support and criminal justice, and I propose federal demonstrations, similar to those that preceded welfare reform, to develop such programs further. Finally, I consider objections about the cost, politics, and implementation of such programs.

Table 1. Poor Men: Numbers and Share of Male Population, by Age and Race, 2005

Race/ethnicity	Ages							
	16–50		16–24		25–35		36–50	
	Number (millions)	Percent of total	Number (millions)	Percent of total	Number (millions)	Percent of total	Number (millions)	Percent of total
Total	7.3	10	2.7	15	2.1	10	2.5	8
White	5.1	9	1.9	13	1.5	8	1.8	7
Black	1.5	17	0.6	23	0.4	16	0.5	13
Native American	0.1	23	0.04	28	0.04	22	0.06	20
Asian	0.4	11	0.1	18	0.1	11	0.1	7
Hispanic	2.0	16	0.7	21	0.7	15	0.6	14

Note: Racial categories do not overlap. Native American includes American Indian and Alaska Native. Asian includes Native Hawaiian and other Pacific Islanders. Racial groups add to less than total because persons of two or more races are omitted. Hispanics are an ethnic category that overlaps the races and may draw from any of them.

Source: Author's tabulations from U.S. Bureau of the Census, 2006 Annual Social and Economic Supplement.

Nonworking Men

In 2005, 7.3 million men in the United States between the ages of sixteen and fifty—10 percent of all American men of that age—lived in poverty (see table 1). The vast majority were white, although more men who were poor for several years running would no doubt be nonwhite. The poverty rate is highest among young men, those aged sixteen to twenty-four, then falls at later ages. As they age, most men settle into regular employment, and their poverty rate declines. Each of the racial or ethnic subgroups shows the same pattern, although poverty rates run higher among blacks, Hispanics, and Native Americans at all ages than among whites or Asians.

Table 2 compares employment patterns for all men and for poor men, in the same age groups as table 1 during 2005. The contrast is dramatic. The share of poor men not working at all—50 percent—approached the share of all men working full time year-round—63 percent.[4] For all men, the share working full time was 26 percent among the youngest age group, but it surged quickly to more than 70

percent in the older categories. The share not working correspondingly plunged. But for the poor, the share working full time peaked—at only 29 percent—for men aged twenty-five to thirty-five before falling again. The share not working fell to only 38 percent for that age group before rising again to more than half for those aged thirty-six to fifty. If current trends hold, most poor men will leave the labor force well before the usual retirement age.

For all men, work increased with age for all the racial and ethnic categories, although work levels ran somewhat lower for blacks and Native Americans than the norm. But for poor men, the share not working exceeded the share employed for every group, although work levels ran conspicuously lower for blacks and higher for Hispanics than the average. Almost two-thirds of poor black men as a whole and nearly three-quarters of those aged sixteen to twenty-four reported not working at all during 2005.

The problem has grown worse in recent decades. For men under age thirty-five with

Table 2. Shares of All Men and Poor Men Working Full Time and Not Working, by Age and Race/Ethnicity, 2005

Percent

| Race/ethnicity | Ages | | | | | | | |
| | 16–50 | | 16–24 | | 25–35 | | 36–50 | |
	Working full time	Not working	Working full time	Not working	Working full time	Not working	Working full time	Not working
All men	63	16	26	36	73	9	77	9
White	65	14	28	32	75	7	79	8
Black	50	28	17	51	61	19	67	19
Native American	52	23	17	44	64	13	62	18
Asian	62	18	19	48	67	12	80	8
Hispanic	64	16	35	36	74	7	76	10
Poor men	19	50	8	58	29	38	23	52
White	23	45	10	53	35	33	27	48
Black	6	66	1	73	11	59	8	64
Native American	8	57	4	53	7	49	11	65
Asian	20	51	8	67	19	41	38	42
Hispanic	33	39	13	56	44	25	41	38

Source: See table 1. Full-time workers work full time and full year. The category of working less than full time and full year is omitted. See note to table 1 regarding racial categories.

no more than a high school education (and no longer in school), employment has fallen steadily since the 1980s. The decline in work was particularly severe for black men during the 1990s, despite the economic boom of that era.[5] The implications for family poverty are dire. Men without steady earnings seldom marry or stay married, nor are they likely to support their children.

Causes

Social scientists have two principal approaches to explaining nonwork among poor men, especially among blacks.[6] Economists typically assume that nonworking men display economizing behavior—that they are acting so as to maximize their utilities. If they are working less, then they must be responding rationally to changes in incentives or in working conditions that have made work less worthwhile or available. The other approach

is cultural; proponents interpret nonworking behavior not as economizing and rational but as dysfunctional. As they see it, nonworking men are acting counter to their own interests—and the interests of their families and society as well. Policymakers seeking solutions to the male work problem must first decide which of these viewpoints is truest to the psychology of the men. For measures to increase male work levels cannot succeed unless policymakers accurately perceive the state of mind that they seek to change.

The Economic Approach

As noted, economists assume that people will work if working is worth more to them than not working. If people who have been employed begin to work less, work must have become less valuable relative to other pursuits. Thus employment should vary directly with wages—work levels and wages should go up and down together. This is called the substitution effect. And indeed, as wages among the low-skilled (those with a high school education or less) stagnated or fell during the 1970s and 1980s, the work level of this group also fell. Economists infer that the falling wages caused falling employment: these men decided to work less because doing so had become less worthwhile.

One difficulty with this reasoning, though, is that lower wages can also generate an incentive to work more. When pay per hour is lower, workers must put in more hours to cover their financial needs; conversely, higher wages allow them to cover these needs with fewer working hours. In this case, work levels should vary inversely with wages—work levels should go up as wages go down. This is called the income effect. When wages change over time, whether the substitution or income effect will dominate is unclear a priori.

Several economists estimate that, at least for low-paid workers, the substitution effect dominates. This is why the economic approach to explaining male nonwork stresses low wages. However, these estimates rest on data before 1990.[7] During the 1990s, real wages for the low-skilled rose, especially late in the decade. Work levels for poor single mothers also rose sharply, as is consistent with the economic theory, although welfare reform and the new benefits also helped. For low-skilled black men, however, labor force participation rates continued to fall even during the 1990s, which is not consistent with the theory. Some force other than reduced pay must be driving work levels down.[8]

Some economists also argue that jobs have become less available to disadvantaged men as well as paying less. Employers, they believe, have become less patient with low-skilled workers than they once were. Pay now varies far more according to a worker's education than it once did, leaving the low-skilled worse off. Under pressure from restructuring and globalization, employers demand that low-paid employees show adaptability and produce without problems, or be replaced.[9] But this argument cannot explain why millions of unskilled immigrants from Latin America and Asia are now at work in the U.S. economy. Nor can it account for the large differences in work levels among different groups of poor men.

Yet another hypothesis is that native-born blacks have become less employable than other low-skilled groups. Economists once thought that the flood of women into the labor force during the 1970s and 1980s drove down wages and employment for young blacks, but during the 1990s there is no sign of this.[10] George Borjas argues that rapid immigration from Mexico, both legal and illegal, has depressed unskilled male wages and employment. Anecdotal evidence suggests that employers today often hire women or illegal aliens rather than native-born blacks, viewing them as more tractable. But other economists question these effects. They are in any event too small to explain the low black male work levels or their decline even in the tight labor markets of the later 1990s.[11]

One fact that used to make male nonwork seem rational is that the drug trade and other illicit activities seemed to offer better opportunities than legal but low-paid jobs. However, returns to drug selling have fallen since the 1980s. Most drug gang members today make barely more than they would in legitimate employment, while they also face high risks of violence and arrest. Drug dealing no longer seems a rational alternative to working in legal but low-paid jobs.[12]

The final explanation for nonwork offered by economists is that other types of barriers block employment for the poor. The so-called mismatch theory asserts that jobs have become less accessible to the inner-city poor, either because the jobs moved—from urban areas to the suburbs, to the South, or overseas—or because they now demand more education and skills than poor adults offer. This theory too seemed more plausible during the 1970s and 1980s, when deindustrialization was rampant, than it did during the 1990s, when legions of unskilled job seekers—immigrants as well as welfare mothers—found jobs in cities. Even in a globalizing economy, most jobs do not demand a four-year college education, and many of these jobs still pay well.[13]

The Cultural Approach

The cultural view of male nonwork is that nonworking men fail to take advantage even of the jobs they can get. Lower wages do not cause employment to fall. Rather, both low wages and low employment result from a breakdown in work discipline. Low-income men, particularly blacks, have become less reliable employees. As a result they are paid less and they also work less, either because they are fired or because they drop out of jobs. This logic is consistent with employers' loss of patience with low-skilled workers. One argument against the cultural view is that schooling levels for men—our best measure of labor quality—continue to improve, although educational standards have no doubt fallen over the past several decades.[14]

An argument in favor of culture is that the forces driving work levels down for younger blacks during the 1990s include the child support and criminal justice systems. Compared with the past, many low-skilled men today seem deterred from working because of automatic wage deductions to pay child

support or because they are incarcerated. These forces likely overwhelmed the greater disposition to work that higher wages in that decade might well have caused.[15] Although wage deductions and imprisonment could be viewed as disincentives or barriers to work, consistent with the economic approach, the behavior that generates such sanctions is not optimizing, but self-defeating.

The best evidence for the cultural theory comes from ethnographic accounts that capture the attitudes of nonworking men toward employment. If disincentives such as low wages explained the problem, we would find these men calculating carefully whether working were worthwhile. They would be complaining about low wages and demanding to be paid more, in the practical style of trade unionists who bargain over working conditions with employers.

But this is not what ethnographers find. Typically these men do not reject the work ethic; like other poor adults, they usually affirm it. Nor do they say dispassionately that working is not worthwhile. Rather, they affirm the work norm yet fail to achieve it for reasons that remain mysterious.[16] Thus, any theory of nonwork must explain why the nonworkers appear to violate their own values. For poor women, the explanation is often lack of confidence. Hence the evolution of welfare policy toward work programs that both require welfare women to work and help them to do so. For men, one explanation is temptation: the men want to do the right thing but are lured away from it by the seductions of the street, such as the drug trade.[17]

A more important explanation focuses on respect: low-income men often fail to work because doing so would violate their self-esteem. Black youth, for example, typically demand higher wages before they will work than whites with the same qualifications. Economists might say that they have a higher "reservation wage"—the wage that would induce them to accept a job. But this framing again suggests a quality of calm calculation that is lacking.[18] Actually, passion reigns. Black youth will often refuse to work for "chump change" even if it means not working at all. Or they accept jobs but then find them unrewarding or abusive. So they leave them in a huff or are fired.[19]

Low-skilled blacks feel that employers treat them as expendable, firing them at the least provocation. To the employers, however, it seems that the men simply "don't want to work." So bosses grow wary of hiring them, particularly minorities and ex-offenders. They often hire women or immigrants instead. One cannot call such preferences racist, because black employers voice the same complaints as whites.[20] Economists may say the men behave "as if" they do not find work worth their time. A psychologist would suggest rather that, out of intemperateness, they violate their own intention, which—as for other men—is to get ahead.

The men also commonly fail as husbands and fathers. Spouses expect them to work regularly to support the family, but they often refuse, or they get into drugs or crime. They do not argue that jobs pay too little to take; they simply behave badly in ways that even they disapprove of. So the women give up on them and raise their children alone.[21] Soon the authorities come looking for them, demanding child support payments or arresting them for crimes.

Male Psychology

What is the source of these rebellious patterns? One interpretation, although it is spec-ulative, appeals to frustrated male psychology. At the heart of nonwork is not economic behavior but men's hunger for "dignity" or "respect." More than most women, men typically work not just to make money but to "be somebody." The male quest is to get out front for some cause and by so doing to vindicate oneself. That drive is valuable because it motivates men's achievements, but it is also dan-

> *Lower wages do not cause employment to fall. Rather, both low wages and low employment result from a breakdown in work discipline.*

gerous unless it is harnessed to larger purposes, typically employment and the family.[22] The trouble today, of course, is that poor men's drive to succeed has often lost these ties. It now seems merely self-serving. Many men now seek respect by rejecting available jobs or by taking risks by committing crimes. By asserting themselves without performing, they earn failure rather than respect.

Selling drugs, far from being a rational option for the low skilled, exemplifies this frustrated drive for respect. Unskilled youths who go into drugs are searching for any way they can to vindicate themselves against the disapproval they feel from the society. Unfortunately, to pursue recognition in this way proves destructive for both them and their communities.[23]

This rebellious pattern often surfaces early in poor men's lives. By misbehaving, many alienate first their parents, then their teachers, and finally their employers. Each rejection makes the quest for dignity more desperate, producing further rebellion, which produces further rejection, in a descending spiral. To observers, the men seem anarchic, yet they themselves feel powerless.[24] In the middle class, by contrast, most boys learn in infancy to satisfy their parents, then their teachers and bosses, in an ascending spiral. By behaving well, they achieve success and respect while also serving others. By behaving badly, poor men never get to first base.

This perspective helps to explain one of the mysteries of poverty—why poor men seem more impaired than poor women. On average they are less employable than poor single mothers, even though the women have children to worry about. The reason may be that their lot in life is less affirming. Poor women find their identity chiefly as mothers. They typically believe they can succeed in that role, even if outside observers dissent. They have to meet community standards for their children, but they are not in direct competition with other mothers. They also have had their own mothers as role models, even if their fathers were absent.[25] For them, working is secondary. It usually poses practical problems, not a crisis of identity.

Men, by contrast, are wired to achieve self-esteem chiefly through ventures outside the home. That forces them into the labor market, a far more competitive arena than motherhood. There they are up against other men much better prepared than themselves. They often lack fathers to guide them, and government does little to help them. So their failure, at least in competitive terms, is all but inevitable. Hence the prickly defensiveness that often blocks them from working at all, to their own cost.

Among successful men, what keeps assertiveness in line is early conditioning. Most middle-class boys of all races internalize the values and lifestyles of their parents. Obeying their elders—especially their fathers—prepares them later to obey their teachers and employers. To be sure, working does not solve all their problems. They still have to struggle for adequate wages, by earning raises or promotions, or through trade union or political activity. But by becoming steady workers, they at least get a foot on the ladder.

Today's urban poverty arose chiefly because work discipline broke down in the mid-twentieth century among low-income people, especially blacks. Somehow, many parents lost their own discipline and thus their authority over children. Fathers failed to work and often disappeared. Their sons then became rootless, seeking to work but not knowing how. Paradoxically, the collapse came just as opportunities for blacks were expanding.

To a cultural interpretation, poverty reflects social disorder more than deficient opportunity. As Daniel Patrick Moynihan wrote, "a community that allows a large number of young men to grow up in broken homes, dominated by women, never acquiring any stable relationship to male authority, never acquiring any set of rational expectations about the future—that community asks for and gets chaos."[26] The chief solution to poverty then is to restore order. Government must provide some of the pressure to work that today's poor have not internalized.

Assessing the Two Views of Male Nonwork

On balance, I find the cultural view of male nonwork more persuasive. It is more true to life, and it captures the self-defeating quality of male nonwork. The economic reading is unpersuasive as long as jobs sufficient to prevent poverty appear readily available, as immigration proves. But the two theories are not completely inconsistent. Opportunity constraints may exacerbate the cultural problem.

A key issue is whether reduced opportunities generate an oppositional culture or the reverse.[27] Both may be true. To say that lousy jobs directly generate resistance to working is too simple. That view does not account for trends over time. Low-skilled work attitudes seem to have worsened since the 1960s, a period when opportunities for blacks, on balance, improved. Work behavior among black men is worse today than it was under segregation and Jim Crow. That deterioration must have causes in the broader culture, outside the labor market.[28]

Yet, to a degree bad behavior and lousy jobs may reinforce each other. Acting out undermines men's reputation with employers, driving wages and opportunities down. At the same time, low wages exacerbate a dysfunctional culture. When disadvantaged men confront the job market, they may already be unfitted for it, but low wages also dramatize their failure. This helps to trigger the cycle of rebellion and rejection, and it is this—more than low wages per se—that brings them down.

Benefit-Oriented Programs

What does this causal analysis imply about government efforts to raise male work levels? One clear implication is that merely providing better opportunities is not enough. To say that cuts against the grain of our political culture. When the political class becomes aware of any new social problem, its initial instinct is to define the sufferers as victims and seek causes outside of them. Later, as cultural causes of the problem become more evident,

the victims come to bear more onus for their difficulties. Welfare reform shows that trajectory, and nonwork among poor men is beginning to do the same.

Nonworking men have begun to get serious attention in Washington only in the past few years, since the success of welfare reform. The news media initially characterized them as oppressed by external conditions—as child support defaulters overwhelmed by their arrears or as ex-offenders without support in the community.[29] But if a failure to work reflects rebelliousness more than economic disincentives, then merely improving opportunities and services is unlikely to change much.

Confronted with male nonwork, many analysts still stress benefits. They would either pay unskilled men more to work in the jobs they can already get or give them education and training to get better positions. On the record, such programs would yield some gains, but they would not produce much steadier work, which is the main goal here. This is just what a cultural view would expect.

Wage Subsidies
One way to motivate more work might be to raise the minimum wage. At $5.15 an hour, the current minimum is below historic levels in real terms. At this writing, Congress seems likely soon to raise that figure to $7.25. The two primary objections to the increase are that it might destroy some low-skilled jobs and that most of the workers who would benefit are already above poverty, chiefly because they live in households where other people are working.

Most analysts would prefer to raise wage subsidies, which do not deter hiring and are better targeted on the low-income population. Some propose making noncustodial fathers eligible for the same generous earned income tax credit (EITC) that is now paid to custodial parents of children—as much as 40 percent of wages—provided the father pays his child support. Or they would limit the child support a poor absent father must pay, viewing it as a "tax" on earnings. Some would also expand the much smaller EITC given to single low-wage workers or create a more gen-

---

Evaluators of various experimental programs aimed at increasing employment among disadvantaged men have not found that raising wages clearly produces more work.

---

eral subsidy for all low-wage workers.[30] See, for example, the article in this volume by Gordon Berlin.

Raising wages would no doubt make poor men *better off* in some sense. They could either make more money if they worked or make the same amount by working less. But whether they would work more, which is the goal here, is doubtful. Provisions in force before the 1990s that allowed welfare beneficiaries to engage in work and still receive benefits had little effect on recipients' work behavior.[31] Federal income maintenance experiments beginning in the late 1960s also found that low-paid work effort was largely unresponsive to wages.[32] During the 1990s, the EITC appeared to increase work by single mothers, but its influence is difficult to separate from that of rising work requirements in welfare and the strong economy,

which cut in the same direction.[33] And this finding applies largely to women rather than to men.

Evaluators of various experimental programs aimed at increasing employment among disadvantaged men have not found that raising wages clearly produces more work. The Jobs-Plus program, which tested whether financial incentives and social supports would increase work rates among residents of public housing, showed some employment gains by men, but the men were mostly husbands in two-parent welfare families, not the more detached men who are at the heart of the male employment problem.[34] The New Hope project, which tested the effects of a work guarantee and work supports such as child care, increased the work and earnings of men outside families "sporadically," but the program involved benefits besides wage subsidies as well as encouragement from a capable staff.[35] One statistical study of whether black youth work more consistently when they get better jobs returned mixed findings.[36]

One risk of higher pay is that it would exacerbate the inflow of immigrants, thus creating more competitors for low-skilled men in getting jobs. That danger could be avoided only if border and administrative controls on immigration became more effective than they are now.

Raising wages might increase work over the long term, because of the interaction with culture already noted. Paying poor men more is a visible sign that society values their labor. Over time, that might reconcile some men to taking menial jobs. But in the short term, higher pay seems unlikely to overcome the fractious psychology that now undermines male work. For wage incentives to have much effect on behavior, low-skilled men would first have to become more committed to working steadily. At that point they would start behaving more like trade unionists who bargain over their conditions of work. Higher wages alone cannot produce that shift. Today the chief value of higher pay may be political—in reconciling liberal leaders and opinion makers to the need for work enforcement.

Education

Most disadvantaged men do badly at school. Many drop out, and few earn more than a high school diploma. Because their skills are poor, their pay is low. How might policymakers help them stay in school longer, acquire better skills, and thus merit higher pay? Most schools in low-income areas function poorly. Government has recently tried to improve them by imposing outside standards, as in the No Child Left Behind Act of 2001, and by promoting choice and competition among schools. Another approach has been to create small high schools that focus on work rather than college. But because teachers unions often oppose these measures, progress by this route will be slow.

The alternative is compensatory programs that promote learning outside of the schools. Intensive preschool programs can raise employment and depress unwed pregnancy and crime in the later lives of students. Recently, some after-school programs for at-risk teenagers have shown promising effects on education and health.[37] But these benefits come from a few small, high-quality experiments. The programs probably could not be expanded to a wider population and realize the same gains. The national Head Start program has not shown the impacts achieved by the most noted preschool pilot programs. And even if the programs were effective at scale, their benefits would be long delayed. Compensatory programs have too remote a

tie to adult employment for them to be the primary solution to the male work problem.

Training

The final benefit-only approach to the work problem has been to train low-skilled workers after they leave school.[38] With exceptions noted below, these programs have had much smaller impacts than the work programs that transformed welfare. An evaluation of the Job Training Partnership Act (JTPA) during the 1990s found only slight earnings gains for adults—smaller for men than women—and losses for youth.[39] One reaction is that the programs are simply underfunded.[40] Another explanation—more plausible in my view—is that the clients commonly lack the raw ability to raise their skills by much. The only way to elevate their wages, then, will be through regulating or subsidizing wages, as suggested above.[41]

But voluntary training has also failed to accomplish much because of the widespread misconception that the main barrier to work is low skills. In fact, it is work discipline. When men are poor in America, it is usually because they do not work consistently at *any* job, not because they earn too little. That has been apparent since the 1960s.[42] What trainers really need to instill in disadvantaged men, if they can, is the personal organization to get and stick with the jobs that they can already get. If men show discipline, then employers will teach them specific skills. That commitment is what immigrants typically show today, as their native-born competitors often do not. So like education, improved training can make only a limited contribution to solving the male work problem.

The Need for Structure

The record suggests strongly that opportunity-oriented measures alone can do little to improve men's work effort because they fail to confront the oppositional culture described above. Nonworking men must comply with legitimate demands to work, however hard that is, before they can expect to earn the success and respect they crave. They must accept the old-fashioned view that the best expression of male dignity is to do a legitimate job, however lowly, rather than not to do it. Only this can halt the current negative cycle, where resistance begets failure. Only this can begin a positive cycle, where work discipline yields steadier employment and advancement.

How to cause that shift is the great question. The answer suggested by welfare reform is that government must enforce work as well as promote it. Work must become an obligation and not a choice. Programs must link help and hassle. As the editors put it in introducing this volume, government must use both carrots and sticks. New benefits can help, but they must be tied to requirements bearing on the clients. Some chance for success—some respect—must be offered up front. But there must also be demands to work steadily at the jobs offered or available, backed up by some kind of sanction.

Directive Programs

To be effective, programs to increase employment among nonworkers must be directive. They must tell their clients clearly that they are expected to work. Programs framed as incentives or as additions to human capital leave work too much as a choice. Welfare reform mandated work for welfare mothers as a condition of aid. The most successful welfare work programs use case managers to check up on clients to be sure they fulfill their obligations, a style I call paternalist.[43] And in the policy areas just mentioned, the most successful programs have been the most directive.

Among innovative high schools designed to increase employment, the one clear success has been Career Academies, a form of school-within-a-school where teachers engage small groups of students in a family-like setting. Instructors set high standards and then help youth attain them with more sustained and personalized attention than they get in the usual high school. This approach significantly improves students' earnings and employment.[44] The most successful training program has been Job Corps, which places disadvantaged youth in a prep-school-like setting, away from home, where they are closely supervised; it too raises both earnings and employment.[45] Similarly, the National Guard Youth Challenge Corps sends disadvantaged youth to a military base for five months, followed by a year of mentoring by National Guard members. The youth begin as dropouts, but 73 percent of those who finish the program have gotten high school diplomas or a GED.[46]

All these programs are for youth. Government has so far failed to generate comparable structures for adult men. Such programs must be both more supportive and more demanding than traditional training. Rather than just impart skills, they must address the troubled relations that disadvantaged men often have with employers. The program itself must exemplify a constructive relationship between the worker and authority, trading acceptance for performance.

A model might be the Center for Employment Training, a noted training organization for adults in San José, California. Local employers work closely with CET to define well-paying jobs they need to fill. The program then prepares trainees, most of whom are Hispanic, to take the jobs with full-day sessions that mimic actual work. The key appears to be offering real opportunities, while keeping clients under strong pressure—with help from the surrounding Hispanic community—not to waste their opportunity. Unfortunately, CET has not proven to be replicable in other locations.[47]

The Military Model

The limitation of all these programs, including CET, is that they are voluntary and cannot literally enforce work. Clients can walk away from them without losing anything else of value. The programs thus depend on informal suasions to maintain involvement. How could men be *required* to work in the same manner as welfare mothers?

Some observers have seen the military as a possible answer. Hugh Price, a close observer of black youth, remarks on the power of military service to straighten out other blacks he knew growing up who never connected with school. The army imposed discipline while also offering advancement to soldiers who performed. It taught what society wants all youth to learn—that "if you do a job well, you get ahead." During the late 1980s, after conditions for ghetto youth had sharply deteriorated, another expert opined that it might be time to "conscript them for their own good."[48]

The military achieves exactly the sublimation of male assertiveness mentioned above. The "four-star general," as Daniel Moynihan wrote in the "Moynihan Report," expresses the "very essence of the male animal," which is "to strut." The military offers blacks an arena for advancement where equal opportunity is stiffly enforced. Black entry into the military has historically been high. But once in the military, many youth find that officers act like the fathers they never had, demanding compliance with rules and orders.[49] So the effect on black recruits can be salutary.

But relatively few blacks tested well enough to qualify for the army even in 1965, when the draft was still in force. Even fewer can do so today, when the military is volunteer and seldom admits high school dropouts. Some studies find that black men who serve in the military do indeed have better postservice work records than blacks who do not serve, but black enlistment is no longer unusually high.[50] To combine opportunity with a work requirement, then, policymakers must adapt other large institutions that already exert authority over many low-income men.

Child Support Enforcement

One such structure is child support enforcement. Traditionally, low-income fathers have viewed that system as one-sided, biased in favor of single mothers and interested in fathers only for their money.[51] As noted, child support withholding seems to have driven down employment among low-skilled young black men. But conceivably the system could also promote employment, to the benefit of both the men and child support collections.

In 2003, among the 3 million poor single mothers, only 60 percent had a child support order and only 36 percent received any payment.[52] Child support problems were most serious among black men. In 2003, 68 percent of black births occurred outside marriage, much the highest rate for any race. Probably a quarter of black men aged sixteen to twenty-four—and half of those aged twenty-five to thirty-four—are noncustodial fathers.[53] Government has made far more progress in establishing support orders than in getting poor fathers to pay up.[54] In 2003, about 1 million absent fathers owed child support to poor families yet paid either nothing or less than they owed.[55] These are the men for whom irregular employment is likely to be part of their problem.

Past Programs

Middle-class absent fathers are relatively easy to locate, they usually have enough income to pay their judgments, and they cannot easily abscond. The low-income father is tougher to find and has less to lose by evading support. And if he is located, family courts have difficulty determining his ability to pay. He may claim to be jobless and destitute, but how can judges be sure? They can tell him to get a job, but they cannot verify whether he does.

Child support enforcement programs emerged to solve this problem. Judges now can remand nonpaying fathers to a work program, with the mandate to attend the program or pay up, on pain of going to jail. This obligation can be monitored, so the father cannot evade it. If he is in fact working surreptitiously, the work program will conflict with his job, forcing him to admit his earnings and pay support. If he really is jobless, the program can help him get a job. Thus help is combined with hassle.

During the 1990s, the Parents' Fair Share (PFS) demonstration in seven sites around the country offered low-income nonpaying fathers reduced support orders along with employment and other services. In return, they were required either to pay their judgments or to attend the program. Low-income cases were also reviewed more intensively. The program increased the share of clients paying support and the amount they paid, largely through "smoke-out" effects—participation revealed unreported jobs, forcing fathers to pay up. The fathers also valued the attention they received from the job clubs and support groups provided. But PFS registered no clear gains in the fathers' employment or earnings.[56] Children First, a similar program in Wisconsin, recorded similar results.[57]

Critics say that Parents' Fair Share intervened in the child support problem too late, after the fathers had left the families and reneged on support. Better, if possible, to prevent breakup in the first place. The Fragile Families and Child Wellbeing Study found that most unwed parents plan to stay together at the point their child is born, although most split up within a year or two. "Fragile family" programs attempt to build that relationship through a range of services, but without requiring work.[58] The Responsible Fatherhood and Partners for Fragile Families demonstrations were conducted in nine states during the late 1990s and early 2000s with government and foundation funding. Some Responsible Fatherhood sites showed encouraging gains in employment, earnings, and child support payment by fathers, but no experimental evaluations were done to attribute these gains clearly to the program.[59] Without the requirement of work, positive impacts are probably unlikely.

Adding Mandatory Work

A more promising course is for child support enforcement programs to require work. The employment side of Parents' Fair Share was underdeveloped. The program made clear that clients had to participate or pay up, but not that they had to work. Employment was framed largely in passive and economic terms. It was seen not as an obligation, but as a benefit provided through services such as job search. PFS banked heavily on arranging on-the-job training (OJT) for many of its clients. This proved difficult to do, in part because much of the funding had to come from the Job Training Partnership Act. JTPA often doubted that PFS fathers could satisfy employers and refused to fund them.[60]

If PFS had included a more clear-cut work requirement, it might have generated both more smoke-out effects and more employment gains. A work test would change PFS's requirement from "participate or pay up" to "work *and* pay up." Clients would have to get a job or work in one arranged by the program for twenty or thirty hours a week for a specified number of months, on pain of incarceration. Out of their earnings they would also pay their judgments. Once they were working and paying steadily, they could qualify for training to enhance wages. That is the sequence typical of the more successful welfare work programs.[61]

Many absent fathers fall behind on their support payments, in part because their judgments are not reduced when they are unemployed or in prison. These arrearages provide a further need—and opportunity—to enforce work. Some share of the arrearages owed to government might be forgiven for each month or year that a father pays his judgment. The effect would be to convert much of his monetary debt into a work obligation.[62] The rationale is that society benefits when the father works, not just when he pays money. Working generates favorable spillovers for poor families and communities, aside from the income it provides.

Adding work enforcement would broaden the child support mission beyond collecting support to getting fathers to work. Some new benefits and programs would be needed, but would make it possible to enforce both work and support payment more effectively.

Criminal Justice

The second important authority structure for low-income men is the criminal justice system. Ex-offenders leaving prisons need work to rebuild their lives. Traditionally correction systems have sought mainly to incarcerate offenders. Work programs aimed at this group have not achieved much, but they could be

revamped to promote successful reentry and reduce recidivism.

During the 1960s and 1970s, as more poor mothers went on welfare, more poor men committed criminal offenses, and crime rates soared. The nation responded by sending more offenders to prison for longer terms. Rates of incarceration went on increasing even

Many absent fathers fall behind on their support payments, in part because their judgments are not reduced when they are unemployed or in prison.

during the 1990s, after crime rates had started to fall. More than 2 million people are now in prison or jail. The problem is most severe among blacks: probably 30 percent of young black men have criminal records. Crime also overlaps substantially with the child support problem: probably 70 percent of male offenders are also noncustodial parents.[63]

As more men enter prison, more also leave. Around 630,000 men now exit the prisons annually—four times more than in 1978. Few convicts learn meaningful skills while in prison, and few reliably reintegrate into the community upon their release. Recidivism runs high. Thirty percent of released men are arrested again for new offences within six months; two-thirds within three years.[64]

Ex-offenders must reconnect with families, handle various health problems, and find housing. Failure at any of these hurdles can drive them into homelessness or addiction, or back into crime. In the long run, however, whether they stay free depends more than anything else on whether they work steadily.[65] Just as for other men, success—or failure—at work stands at the center of their lives.

Past Programs

Criminal justice has few successful model programs on which to draw. During the 1970s, vocational programs in prisons appeared to have no effect on recidivism, prompting the conclusion that "nothing works." Later assessments have been more positive, but even the better programs reduce recidivism by only 8 to 17 percent, and only a minority of inmates receives remediation in prison.[66] Prison-based rehabilitation appears to achieve little, in part because it takes place inside the walls, removed from the conditions ex-offenders face out in the society.

Work programs for convicts outside the walls would appear more promising, but experimental programs have not yet shown effects comparable to those of work programs in welfare. Ex-offenders were one of several groups served by the National Supported Work Demonstration run by the Manpower Demonstration Research Corporation (MDRC) during the late 1970s. This study placed disadvantaged job seekers in positions created in local nonprofit agencies. It improved employment for welfare mothers and former drug addicts, but not for ex-offenders or youth. The ex-offenders did increase their work while they were in the program, but they also left quickly, after which the effect dissipated.[67] During 1991–94 a program for convicts on work release in Washington State failed to reduce recidivism or costs, although it did help a minority of men transition from prison.[68]

The parole system oversees convicts who leave prison before their sentences end. Parole officers typically require clients to meet with them once or twice a month and to take drug tests, among other rules. These requirements look like the sort of oversight that has generated strong impacts in welfare work programs. Yet by itself parole does not reduce recidivism. Even intensive supervision serves mainly to detect more violations of parole conditions such as drug use.[69] Some experts have concluded—adapting a phrase from welfare reform—that we must "end parole as we know it."

In 2005 the Bush administration funded Ready4Work, a set of seventeen voluntary demonstration programs aimed at prisoner reentry. One goal was to involve faith-based groups. Because the programs are service-oriented and do not enforce participation, they presume a motivated client.[70] Perhaps they will do some good, but they are unlikely to produce significant change. Nor can any effect be proven, because no experimental evaluations are planned.

Improving Work Enforcement

Work programs for ex-offenders can be improved. The chief focus of parole supervision has been to detect parole violations. Changing clients' work behavior has been secondary. To affect recidivism, a new program must combine parole with demands that clients participate in programs aimed at their problems. To promote employment, supervision must be targeted much more specifically on working, and it must be more immediate. The supervisor must monitor actual work or job search and must have some quick way to reward good behavior and penalize bad.[71] The precedent is drug programs, where swift and certain, not severe, punishment is what promotes compliance.[72]

Besides better supervision, a second necessity is help in finding work. Low-paid jobs clearly are available, and most ex-offenders already find them on their own. But their work rates fall with time, and unemployment runs high.[73] Most employers admit their reluctance to hire former convicts.[74] The danger is that some reentering offenders will take too long to find work, become discouraged, and return to crime. So a reentry work program must ensure work for its clients in some way. Equally, it must deny to men who might resist taking menial positions the excuse that jobs are unavailable. Christopher Jencks has argued that if jobs could be guaranteed to the jobless adults of the ghetto, community pressure on them to go to work would become far more effective.[75]

But did not guaranteed jobs for ex-offenders fail in the past work programs just mentioned? Yes, but National Supported Work was voluntary. Those ex-offenders had finished their sentences and were no longer under correctional authority. In the program I am proposing they would be on parole and would have to work or return to prison. The difference from the Washington State work release program, which was mandatory, is that supervision would be far more work-focused.

A third element needed is orientation to the demands of working. Even if training is not generally effective, men who have lived behind bars need some instruction about the demands of the workplace. Fourth, they need some help dealing with other problems in their lives, such as health, housing, and relations with their families. A reentry work requirement should thus initially be part time, allowing time to address these other problems. In both New York City and Wisconsin, mandatory work assignments for welfare mothers have been less than full time, to accommodate remediation activities.

America Works

One program combining these four elements is the Criminal Justice Program run by America Works (AW) in New York City.[76] America Works here applies to men the same private-sector approach to work placement that it has used successfully with welfare mothers. Ex-offenders are given an intensive orientation, lasting up to six weeks, on getting a job and working, including interviewing, dress, and behavior. They are then placed by sales representatives in private firms that recruit low-skilled labor from AW. Once placed, AW "corporate representatives" visit the clients on the job, talk to the employers, and help to work out any problems that the new hires may have.

Thus, work is arranged and overseen, although jobs are found privately rather than created. Clients also receive preparation for work and help in working out difficulties. America Works is financed largely through incentive payments. In the evaluation in New York described below, AW receives $1,160 from New York State for each initial job placement, then $2,088 for each placement that lasts at least ninety days, then a final $464 for each that lasts six months or more, for a total of $3,712. In its first year, 2001, the Criminal Justice Program placed 78 percent of the clients who completed its orientation in jobs. Of these, 44 percent held their jobs for at least ninety days.

The program serves not only parolees who are referred to it but also other ex-offenders who choose the program themselves, food stamp recipients (who also face a work test), and men from New York City's child support enforcement program. A version of the program serving only ex-offenders is now being evaluated experimentally by Public/Private Ventures. In this version, the orientation will be given to clients in prison, before they leave to come to the program in New York.

Center for Employment Opportunities

An alternative model is offered by the Center for Employment Opportunities (CEO), also in New York City.[77] Parolees come to CEO from the state prison system. After receiving several days of preemployment instruction, they are assigned to work crews that CEO maintains through its Neighborhood Work Project (NWP). There they do maintenance and repairs for local government agencies. Their attendance, performance, and comportment are monitored daily, and they are also paid daily, which meets their need for immediate income. Pay is $6.75 an hour, the New York State minimum wage. Clients work full time, four days a week.

On the fifth day, they report to a Vocational Development Program (VDP), where they work with a "job coach" who instructs them on job interviewing and helps them straighten out personal problems that could interfere with working. After two weeks in NWP, they also see a job developer, who lines up interviews for them with private employers. Clients stay in NWP as long as is needed to get a regular job, with a limit of seventy-five days. After placement, they are followed up at thirty, sixty, ninety, and one hundred and eighty days. CEO's job retention rate at six months has been about 40 percent, and it has recently begun tracking retention over a year.

CEO sells its programs to state parole officers in the city as a way to keep their parolees employed. It also serves youth returning from the state Shock Incarceration program (boot camp), as well as some offenders leav-

ing city jails. It is funded mostly by the parole system, the agencies that hire its work crews, and other government agencies. It costs CEO $33,220 a year to provide a slot in its community work crews. Since an average of six clients will hold a slot in a year, the cost per client is only $5,537. Furthermore, these costs are largely defrayed by the income CEO earns from the agencies that employ its crews. The net cost is only $3,219 per slot, or $536 per client.[78]

The core program—NWP and VDP serving state parolees—is one of four now being assessed in MDRC's Enhanced Services for the Hard-to-Employ evaluation. In addition, the Joyce Foundation has begun to evaluate a similar transitional work program for ex-offenders at five sites in the Midwest.

Both CEO and AW arrange and oversee work, while providing work orientation and casework. But AW does not regard transitional jobs as necessary, whereas CEO does. America Works believes that only placing clients with regular employers can prepare them to work, that creating jobs in government is a waste of time and money. If clients fail, and some do, AW gets them further positions until they succeed. CEO, by contrast, sees a need for supported work. Ex-offenders must function for some period under conditions where serious work demands are made but standards are more lenient than in regular jobs, and supervisors accept a mentoring role.

Even if one accepts the need for transitional jobs, the CEO positions seem short, lasting at most seventy-five days. Positions in other work guarantee programs have lasted six months to a year or more, in part because more time was thought necessary to instill work discipline.[79] Longer assignments might improve job retention after clients move on to private jobs. On the other hand, longer positions cost more, and many clients placed in public jobs for enforcement purposes leave them quickly. Average tenure in a government job is far less than the assignment. CEO finds that whether a client can succeed at work is usually settled well before seventy-five days.

A Possible New Program

To sum up the discussion thus far: the nation faces a serious social problem because of low work levels among poor men, particularly blacks. This problem appears due partly to falling wages and other opportunity constraints, but principally to an oppositional culture and a breakdown of work discipline. The solution is partly to improve wages and skills, but more importantly to enforce work in available jobs. That suggests the same "help with hassle" approach as succeeded in welfare reform. Policymakers might adapt the child support and criminal justice systems to help enforce employment among men. Each system must both assist and require its clients to work. But experimental programs have not yet shown the clear effects on employment seen in welfare work programs.

Localities with serious poverty appear to need a mandatory work facility to which low-income men could be referred if they persistently failed to work despite a work obligation. This includes low-skilled men in arrears on their child support and ex-offenders on parole who do not maintain employment.[80] The program would be funded and run jointly by the local child support agency (or family court) and the parole system. A joint program should permit economies of scale because the clienteles overlap.

Men with unpaid child support judgments and parolees leaving prison would be told to get a job or pay up, as they are now. But if they did not, say, within sixty days, they would be remanded to a required work program where their efforts to work would be more closely supervised. There they would have to participate and get a private job within, say, sixty days, with subsequent employment verified. Failing that, they would be assigned to work crews on the CEO model, where again compliance would be verified.

Localities with serious poverty appear to need a mandatory work facility to which low-income men could be referred if they persistently failed to work despite a work obligation.

Jobs would pay the regular wage (if private) or the minimum wage (if public). The program would deduct child support from the pay of men who owed it, but would also help them arrange offsetting public benefits, perhaps including enhanced wage subsidies. Men who failed to participate and work steadily would—unless there were good cause—be sent back to the child support or parole authorities to be imprisoned. But men who complied would be freed from the work program after a year or two. They would then revert to the looser supervision practiced by the regular child support and parole systems. If their employment record deteriorated, they could again be remanded to the work program.

The clientele for the proposed program could include the estimated 1 million child support defaulters (see above) plus prison parolees whose work problems are serious enough to warrant closer supervision. Because more than half of parolees quickly get jobs on leaving prison, but then tend to slack off on their work effort, the share of parolees with serious work problems is probably more than half. There were 784,000 parolees nationwide at the end of 2005.[81] Assume 60

> *Because more than half of parolees quickly get jobs on leaving prison, but then tend to slack off on their work effort, the share of parolees with serious work problems is probably more than half.*

percent, or 470,000, have significant work problems. Thus, around 1.5 million cases might be subject to the new work program.[82]

America Works serves ex-offenders at a cost of $1,160 for each case placed in a job plus $2,088 for each placement that lasts at least ninety days. Seventy-eight percent of clients reached the first milestone, 44 percent of these the second (I omit the further payment for jobs lasting at least six months). Applying these figures to 1.5 million total cases yields a cost of about $2.4 billion a year. For the Center for Employment Opportunities to serve the same population would cost $3,219 per slot, after deducting revenues from expenses, or $4.8 billion annually.[83] That figure—twice AW's—reflects the higher cost of public employment programs.[84] Both figures are conservative in that they assume no diversion effects. But if the new program were well-

implemented—a big if—it might cause some nonworking men to go to work voluntarily, thus reducing the population to be served. The precedent is welfare reform.

A Federal Demonstration

Such a program probably would raise child support collections. Whether it would increase work or reduce recidivism is still unclear. Thus, it should not yet be mandated nationwide. Rather, the best role for national policy currently is to promote the kind of program development that lay behind welfare reform. During the 1980s, early studies by MDRC, chiefly in San Diego, established that mandatory work programs tied to welfare could raise the employment and earnings of welfare mothers substantially. Then during the 1990s, further studies showed that welfare work programs were more effective if they stressed work in available jobs rather than education and training. That evidence came partly from MDRC's evaluation of Greater Avenues for Independence (GAIN) in California, but mainly from its National Evaluation of Welfare to Work Strategies (NEWWS), a federal study of eleven welfare work programs around the country conducted in the mid-1990s.[85] The requirements to participate in work programs and to "work first" were essentially the policies instituted by welfare reform in the later 1990s.

In welfare work, the first stage of program development was funded largely by states and foundations, the second by the federal government. The same approach might work well for men's programs. The first stage might include Parents' Fair Share plus the evaluations of AW, CEO, and the Joyce programs that are now under way. PFS, although less successful than the early welfare work programs, taught important lessons about how to promote work among child support defaulters. The current projects, largely privately funded, may well do the same for work among ex-offenders.[86] Then, assuming these studies show potential, the second stage would be a federal comparative evaluation of different strategies for men's programs, similar to NEWWS.

The cost of such studies appears manageable.[87] The PFS evaluation cost $12 million to $15 million. The NEWWS evaluation covered eleven programs over thirteen years (1989–2002) and cost about $30 million. But costs in these studies were inflated by the surveys used to track results and by the NEWWS studies of child and family effects. A study of men's work programs without these dimensions, which simply used unemployment insurance reporting to track work effects, should cost much less. The current MDRC assessment of CEO will cost $4 million to $5 million over six or seven years. The AW and Joyce studies together cost around $6 million.

However, the welfare work studies typically did not fund the program being studied, only its evaluation. The services and benefits were already defrayed largely by welfare and other existing programs. A men's program could well involve benefits not now provided, such as transitional jobs, and the evaluation would have to fund these as well as the research. Then again, transitional jobs can also generate revenue, as in the CEO program noted above, offsetting some of their cost.

Federal funding for men's programs is already substantial. For 2005, the Bush administration proposed $300 million for prison reentry programs, leading to the $22.5 million being spent on Ready4Work. For 2006 it proposed adding a further $75 million. Reauthorization of welfare reform in 2006

included $50 million for responsible fatherhood programs. But, as noted, the administration's emphasis is on involving faith-based and other community organizations, not on evaluating the success of the programs. Thus, it is doubtful that anything systematic will be learned about what works. Future appropriations should fund a research structure, like NEWWS, that can help settle the best model for work enforcement for men.

Objections

Aside from the expense of evaluations, skeptics might raise several objections to addressing the male work problem through mandatory work programs.

Cost

Could government afford to create the work programs needed to enforce work by men, even if they proved effective? Government jobs are costly. That was one reason why welfare reform largely placed recipients in jobs in the private sector. Only Wisconsin and New York City invested heavily in public positions. In New York, work experience jobs cost $43 million in 1999, or about $1,400 per filled slot per year excluding child care.[88] Such expense might be particularly difficult for child support. That system currently costs government more to run than it saves in welfare costs, although economies in other programs may offset these losses.[89]

The costs of an AW- or CEO-style program taken to scale—$2.4 billion or $4.8 billion a year—are not inconsiderable, but they are far lower than the costs of welfare reform. The expense would also be offset by several benefits or economies. One is higher child support collections, though these are difficult to calculate because PFS—the closest evaluation of such a program—did not include a cost-benefit analysis. Another saving would be in incarceration, which is enormously expensive. On average, American states spent $25,487 to house each prison inmate in 2005.[90] Savings here would hinge on whether and how far work programs reduced recidivism, thus allowing ex-offenders to be released earlier. Prison savings are the chief reason to think that mandatory work programs could be affordable.[91] Finally, higher work levels would translate into hard-to-estimate reductions in other social problems (welfare, unwed pregnancy, foster care) and their costs. These cost issues imply that further evaluations of men's work programs, including those now under way, should include cost-benefit as well as impact assessments.

Politics

Would it be politic to create new programs for nonworking men? Many authors note that nonworking men are the most feared and least popular of all the poor. They are not viewed as "deserving," like the working poor or the elderly, nor do they care for innocent children as welfare mothers do. But to suggest that this negative view bars government from helping them is to misunderstand public attitudes. While the voters do disapprove of the way many poor people live, they still support helping them, provided programs promote good behavior. The desire to save money is secondary, contrary to what many academics believe.[92] Welfare reform is enormously popular simply because it promotes work. The billions spent on child care, health care, and wage subsidies to accomplish that end more than outweighed the savings from caseload reductions, yet no objections were raised.

Proposals for men's work programs must be carefully framed. The main reason to support them cannot be that the men are unfortunate, or that the community would benefit in practical ways if they went to work, such as

through lower crime, although both things are true. Still less can government seem to be negotiating with the nonworkers over the terms on which they will work, as might appear if they were offered only higher wages or wage subsidies. Rather, work policies must offer nonworkers the same terms as other low-skilled people who already work. Above all, programs must directly affirm the work norm. They must demand work of men in the same direct way that welfare did for its recipients, and there must be clear gains in work. Past programs that tried to do that were popular, and improved programs for men could also be.[93]

Implementation

The greatest practical obstacle to my proposals probably is that most child support and corrections agencies, which would be the means to enforce work, do not now regard employment as a central goal. One reason child support has not seriously addressed the work problem is that its routines are modeled on middle-class absent fathers who usually have the means to pay their judgments. Child support agencies thus tend to assume that nonpaying fathers can pay if pressed. This view fails to credit the serious employment and income problems faced by about a third of the nonpayers. Parents' Fair Share found it difficult to work closely with child support personnel because they were reluctant to ease pressure on the men.[94] More recently, some child support agencies have done more to help disadvantaged fathers pay their judgments.

Another implementation problem is that child support usually lacks welfare's ability to mandate work on its own authority. Typically, the agency cannot remand a father to a work program without a judicial order. Roughly half the states have experimented with work programs for child support defaulters, most of them with enforcement aspects like PFS. But the programs appear small and largely separate from the main child support operation.[95]

Corrections agencies, for their part, see their mission as punishing offenders, not helping them succeed after they leave prison. The parole system exists to enforce parole rules. It insists that parolees work, as that is among the rules in most states. But officers typically see achieving work as the convicts' responsibility rather than their own. Neither prison nor parole focuses on what happens to men after they leave supervision. This mind-set is one reason why supported work programs for prisoners failed during the 1960s and 1970s. The current experimental work programs for ex-offenders report similar problems working with parole officers today. To solve the work problem, as well as reduce recidivism, the corrections system must be made more accountable for how its clients turn out.[96]

In the short term, the implementation problem can be minimized by keeping work programs separate from ordinary child support and corrections operations. The work mission would be vested in a separate organization that was optimized around it. Child support and corrections still have the power to incarcerate, the final sanction behind getting the men to participate and work. But they would be moved into the background, their authority invoked only as a last resort.

In the end, however, fundamental change can occur only when the regular child support and corrections agencies fully incorporate the work mission. This was what happened with welfare reform. The idea of putting welfare mothers to work was pioneered in experimental programs, but then mainstream welfare adopted that goal as its own. In the extreme case—Wisconsin—welfare was entirely rebuilt around employment. Only then did the world change for welfare families, producing the large diversion effects seen in the past decade.[97] Similarly here, nonworking men will probably not take available jobs in visibly higher numbers until child support and corrections agencies consistently press them to do so. When they do, on the welfare precedent, many nonworking men will go to work voluntarily, not only those immediately subject to sanctions. As with welfare reform, work effects could be much larger than program evaluations under the old conditions might suggest.

Administrative change, in turn, finally rests on politics. Successful work programs must first be developed, but then they must be implemented across the country by politicians and administrators who believe in them. That means not just driving new bureaucratic routines down to the ground, but changing expectations in the culture. Elected leaders, speaking for the public, must credibly state that work will now be seriously expected of men with debts to society. Work will also be newly rewarded. The community will share with jobless men the burdens and the benefits of change. The goal of the new work programs is not to blame or to exclude jobless men. Rather, it is to change lives and integrate the jobless into society. If that commitment is clear, on past precedent the poor will respond and work levels will rise.

Notes

1. Data from the U.S. Bureau of the Census, March Current Population Survey, for the years after the indicated years.

2. U.S. Bureau of the Census, *Annual Social and Economic Supplement,* March 2006, table POV22.

3. Lawrence M. Mead, *Government Matters: Welfare Reform in Wisconsin* (Princeton University Press, 2004), chap. 9; Jeffrey Grogger and Lynn A. Karoly, *Welfare Reform: Effects of a Decade of Change* (Harvard University Press, 2005), pp. 171–72.

4. Admittedly, poverty is often endogenous to nonwork. To a large extent, that is, poverty and nonwork measure the same thing. Nevertheless, not all poor men are nonworking, and there are revealing differences among subgroups.

5. Harry J. Holzer, Paul Offner, and Elaine Sorensen, "Declining Employment among Young Black Less-Educated Men: The Role of Incarceration and Child Support," *Journal of Policy Analysis and Management* 24, no. 2 (Spring 2005): 330–33.

6. For what follows, I am indebted to a meeting of experts on the men's problem that I convened at New York University in December 2004 with support from the Center for Civic Innovation at the Manhattan Institute. My interpretation, however, is my own and should not be attributed to the other participants or to CCI, MI, or their funders.

7. In technical terms, the elasticity of labor supply with respect to wages is positive. The estimates come from Chinhui Juhn, Kevin M. Murphy, and Robert H. Topel, "Why Has the Natural Rate of Unemployment Increased over Time?" *Brookings Papers on Economic Activity, 1991,* no. 2: 75–142; Lawrence F. Katz, "Wage Subsidies for the Disadvantaged," in *Generating Jobs: How to Increase Demand for Less-Skilled Workers*, edited by Richard B. Freeman and Peter Gottschalk (New York: Russell Sage, 1998), chap. 1; and Jeff Grogger, "Market Wages and Youth Crime," *Journal of Labor Economics* 16, no. 4 (October 1998): 756–91. My thanks to Harry Holzer for these sources.

8. Harry J. Holzer and Paul Offner, "Trends in the Employment Outcomes of Young Black Men, 1979–2000," in *Black Males Left Behind*, edited by Ronald B. Mincy (Washington: Urban Institute Press, 2006), chap. 2.

9. Ronald F. Ferguson, "The Working-Poverty Trap," *Public Interest*, no. 158 (Winter 2005): 71–82.

10. George J. Borjas, "The Demographic Determinants of the Demand for Black Labor," in *The Black Youth Employment Crisis*, edited by Richard B. Freeman and Harry J. Holzer (University of Chicago Press, 1986), chap. 5; Rebecca M. Blank and Jonah Gelbach, "Are Less-Educated Women Crowding Less-Educated Men Out of the Labor Market?" in *Black Males Left Behind*, edited by Mincy (see note 8), chap. 5.

11. George J. Borjas, "The Labor Demand Curve Is Downward Sloping: Reexamining the Impact of Immigration on the Labor Market," *Quarterly Journal of Economics* 118, no. 4 (November 2003): 1335–74. Borjas estimates that high school dropouts lost 5 percent of wages to immigration over the 1980s and 1990s. For the debate about the issue, see Roger Lowenstein, "The Immigration Equation," *New York Times Magazine*, July 9, 2006.

12. Steven D. Levitt and Sudhir Alladi Venkatesh, "An Economic Analysis of a Drug-Selling Gang's Finances," *Quarterly Journal of Economics* 115, no. 3 (August 2000): 755–89. My thanks to Peter Reuter for helping me interpret this research.

13. Peter Edelman, Harry J. Holzer, and Paul Offner, *Reconnecting Disadvantaged Young Men* (Washington: Urban Institute Press, 2006), pp. 28–30.

14. Holzer and Offner, "Trends in the Employment Outcomes of Young Black Men" (see note 8), p. 24.

15. Holzer, Offner, and Sorensen, "Declining Employment among Young Black Less-Educated Men" (see note 5), pp. 333–47. My thanks to Harry Holzer for helping me interpret these trends.

16. Lawrence M. Mead, *The New Politics of Poverty: The Nonworking Poor in America* (New York: Basic Books, 1992), pp. 139–40.

17. Elijah Anderson, "The Story of John Turner," *Public Interest*, no. 108 (Summer 1992): 3–34; Mark Kleiman, "Coerced Abstinence: A Neopaternalist Drug Policy Initiative," in *The New Paternalism: Supervisory Approaches to Poverty*, edited by Lawrence M. Mead (Brookings, 1997), chap. 6.

18. Harry J. Holzer, "Black Youth Nonemployment: Duration and Job Search," in *Black Youth Employment Crisis*, edited by Freeman and Holzer (see note 10), chap. 1.

19. Alford A. Young, "Low-Income Black Men on Work Opportunity, Work Resources, and Job Training Programs," in *Black Males Left Behind*, edited by Mincy (see note 8), pp. 150–58. For an early statement of this culture, see Elliot Liebow, *Tally's Corner: A Study of Negro Streetcorner Men* (Boston: Little, Brown, 1967). For a later and more hostile statement, see Orlando Patterson, "A Poverty of the Mind," *New York Times*, March 26, 2006.

20. Joleen Kirschenman and Kathryn M. Neckerman, "'We'd Love to Hire Them, but . . .': The Meaning of Race for Employers," in *The Urban Underclass*, edited by Christopher Jencks and Paul E. Peterson (Brookings, 1991), pp. 203–32.

21. Kathryn Edin and Maria Kefalas, *Promises I Can Keep: Why Poor Women Put Motherhood before Marriage* (University of California Press, 2005), chaps. 2–4.

22. Harvey C. Mansfield, *Manliness* (Yale University Press, 2006); Francis Fukuyama, *The End of History and the Last Man* (New York: Free Press, 1992), chaps. 13–19.

23. Philippe I. Bourgois, *In Search of Respect: Selling Crack in El Barrio*, 2nd ed. (Cambridge University Press, 2003); Elijah Anderson, *Code of the Street: Decency, Violence, and the Moral Life of the Inner City* (New York: Norton, 1999).

24. Frank E. Furstenberg Jr., Kay E. Sherwood, and Mercer L. Sullivan, *Caring and Paying: What Fathers and Mothers Say about Child Support* (New York: MDRC, July 1992).

25. Edin and Kefalas, *Promises I Can Keep* (see note 21), pp. 135–36, 177–79.

26. Daniel P. Moynihan, "A Family Policy for the Nation," *America* (September 18, 1965), p. 283.

27. Edelman, Holzer, and Offner, *Reconnecting Disadvantaged Young Men* (see note 13), p. 24.

28. Mead, *New Politics of Poverty* (see note 16), pp. 147–55.

29. Blaine Harden, "'Dead Broke' Dads' Child Support Struggle," *New York Times*, January 29, 2002, p. A19; and Erik Eckholm, "Help for the Hardest Part of Prison: Staying Out," *New York Times*, August 12, 2006, pp. A1, A12.

30. Edelman, Holzer, and Offner, *Reconnecting Disadvantaged Young Men* (see note 13), chaps. 5–6; Wendell Primus, "Improving Public Policies to Increase the Income and Employment of Low-Income Nonresident Fathers," in *Black Males Left Behind*, edited by Mincy (see note 8), pp. 226–37; Edmund S. Phelps, *Rewarding Work: How to Restore Participation and Self-Support to Free Enterprise* (Harvard University Press, 1997).

31. Robert Moffitt, "Incentive Effects of the U.S. Welfare System: A Review," *Journal of Economic Literature* 30, no. 1 (March 1992): 13–19.

32. Gary Burtless, "The Work Response to a Guaranteed Income: A Survey of Experimental Evidence," in *Lessons from the Income Maintenance Experiments: Proceedings of a Conference Held in September 1986*, edited by Alicia H. Munnell (Boston: Federal Reserve Bank of Boston, n.d.), pp. 22–52. Wage subsidies do not appear promising, Burtless concludes, because "the labor supply functions estimated in the experiments are vertical or backward-bending" (p. 48).

33. The best known of several studies is Bruce D. Meyer and Dan T. Rosenbaum, "Welfare, the Earned Income Tax Credit, and the Labor Supply of Single Mothers," *Quarterly Journal of Economics* 116, no. 3 (August 2001): 1063–114. One may also doubt whether the claimed EITC effect actually occurred, as field observers of welfare reform did not hear that the credit caused welfare mothers to go to work. More likely, mothers went to work because of welfare reform and then received EITC as a windfall. See Mead, *Government Matters* (see note 3), pp. 175–81.

34. Howard S. Bloom and others, *Promoting Work in Public Housing:The Effectiveness of JOBS-Plus: Final Report* (New York: MDRC, March 2005), chapter 4.

35. Greg J. Duncan, Aletha C. Huston, and Thomas S. Weisner, *Higher Ground: New Hope for the Working Poor and Their Children* (New York: Russell Sage Foundation, 2007), pp. 62–63.

36. Higher wages reduced absenteeism, but special skills, if demanded by a job, increased it. See Ronald Ferguson and Randall Filer, "Do Better Jobs Make Better Workers? Absenteeism from Work among Inner-City Black Youths," in *Black Youth Employment Crisis*, edited by Freeman and Holzer (see note 10), chap. 7.

37. These include Big Brothers Big Sisters, Children's Aid Society-Carrera, and the Quantum Opportunities Program.

38. Here and below I rely heavily on Robert Lerman, "Helping Out-of-School Youth Attain Labor Market Success: What We Know and How to Learn More" (Washington: Urban Institute, 2005).

39. Howard S. Bloom and others, *The National JTPA Study: Title II-A Impacts on Earnings and Employment at 18 Months* (Bethesda, Md.: Abt Associates, May 1992).

40. Robert J. LaLonde, "The Promise of Public Sector-Sponsored Training Programs," *Journal of Economic Perspectives* 9, no. 2 (Spring 1995): 149–68.

41. James J. Heckman, "Doing It Right: Job Training and Education," *Public Interest*, no. 135 (Spring 1999): 86–107.

42. Lloyd Ulman, "The Uses and Limits of Manpower Policy," *Public Interest*, no. 34 (Winter 1974): 97–98.

43. Lawrence M. Mead, "Welfare Employment," in *The New Paternalism*, edited by Mead (see note 17), chap. 2; Mead, *Government Matters* (see note 3), chap. 8.

44. James J. Kemple with Judith Scott-Clayton, *Career Academies: Impacts on Labor Market Outcomes and Educational Attainment* (New York: MDRC, March 2004).

45. John Burghardt and others, *Does Job Corps Work? Summary of the National Job Corps Study* (Princeton, N.J.: Mathematica, June 2001).

46. Hugh Price, "Foreword," in Edelman, Holzer, and Offner, *Reconnecting Disadvantaged Young Men* (see note 13), p. xvi. Of course, such outcomes do not establish impact. The program is now being evaluated by MDRC.

47. Lerman, "Helping Out-of-School Youth" (see note 38), pp. 22–4.

48. Price, "Foreword" (see note 46), pp. xiv–xv.

49. U.S. Department of Labor, Office of Policy Planning and Research, *The Negro Family: The Case for National Action* (March 1965), pp. 16, 40–43.

50. Joshua D. Angrist, "Estimating the Labor Market Impact of Voluntary Military Service Using Social Security Data on Military Applicants," *Econometrica* 66, no. 2 (March 1998): 249–88; Meredith A. Kleykamp, "College, Jobs, or the Military? Enlistment during a Time of War," *Social Science Quarterly* 87, no. 2 (June 2006): 272–90; idem, "A Great Place to Start? The Effect of Prior Military Service on Hiring" (Lawrence, Kan.: University of Kansas, Department of Sociology, February 2007).

51. Furstenberg, Sherwood, and Sullivan, *Caring and Paying* (see note 24); Earl S. Johnson and Fred Doolittle, "Low-Income Parents and the Parents' Fair Share Demonstration" (New York: MDRC, June 1996).

52. U.S. Bureau of the Census, Current Population Survey, April 2004, child support microdata file, table 4.

53. U.S. Bureau of the Census, *Statistical Abstract of the United States: 2005* (2005), p. 67; Edelman, Holzer, and Offner, *Reconnecting Disadvantaged Young Men* (see note 13), p. 25.

54. U.S. House of Representatives, Committee on Ways and Means, *2004 Green Book: Background Material, and Data on the Programs within the Jurisdiction of the Committee on Ways and Means* (March 2004), pp. 8.69–8.77.

55. This figure is the difference between the 1,582 million poor single mothers who were owed child support in 2003 and the 562,000 who received full payment. See Bureau of the Census, CPS child support microdata file (see note 52).

56. Fred Doolittle and others, *Building Opportunities, Enforcing Obligations: Implementation and Interim Impacts of Parents' Fair Share* (New York: MDRC, December 1998); John M. Mar inez and Cynthia Miller, *Working and Earning: The Impact of Parents' Fair Share on Low-Income Fath s' Employment* (New York: MDRC, October 2000). There were, however, some impacts on employment and earnings for the more disadvantaged fathers, those without a high school diploma or recent work experience.

57. Ron Blasco, *Children First Program: Final Evaluation Report* (Madison, Wis.: Department of Workforce Development, November 2000).

58. Wade F. Horn and Isabel V. Sawhill, "Fathers, Mothers, and Welfare Reform," in *The New World of Welfare: An Agenda for Reauthorization and Beyond*, edited by Rebecca M. Blank and Ron Haskins (Brookings, 2001), pp. 425–27; Irving Garfinkel, "Child Support in the New World of Welfare," in *The New World of Welfare*, edited by Blank and Haskins, pp. 452–53.

59. Jane C. Venohr, David A. Price, and Tracy Griffith, "OSCE Responsible Fatherhood Programs: Client Characteristics and Program Outcomes" (Denver: Policy Studies, September 2003).

60. Doolittle and others, *Building Opportunities* (see note 56), chap. 2; John Wallace and Stuart Yeh, "Employment Component for the Parents' Fair Share Demonstration" (New York: MDRC, July 1991); telephone discussion with Fred Doolittle, April 3, 2006.

61. Cynthia Miller and Virginia Knox, *The Challenge of Helping Low-Income Fathers Support Their Children: Final Lessons from Parents' Fair Share* (New York: MDRC, November 2001), pp. 12–16.

62. Primus, "Improving Public Policies" (see note 30), pp. 238–39. Such an arrangement could apply only to child support debt owed to government, not to debts owed to the family, unless the mother agreed.

63. Jeremy Travis, *But They All Come Back: Facing the Challenges of Prison Reentry* (Washington: Urban Institute Press, 2005), p. 3; Edelman, Holzer, and Offner, *Reconnecting Disadvantaged Young Men* (see note 13), p. 25; Holzer, Offner, and Sorenson, "Declining Employment" (see note 5), p. 334, n. 10.

64. Travis, *But They All Come Back* (see note 63), pp. 34, 94.

65. Joan Petersilia, *When Prisoners Come Home: Parole and Prisoner Reentry* (Oxford University Press, 2003), p. 112.

66. Robert Martinson, "What Works? Questions and Answers about Prison Reform," *Public Interest*, no. 35 (Spring 1974): 22–54; Travis, *But They All Come Back* (see note 63), pp. 107–08, 160–62, 168–71; Petersilia, *When Prisoners Come Home* (see note 65), pp. 175–84, 246–47.

67. Board of Directors, Manpower Demonstration Research Corporation, *Summary and Findings of the National Supported Work Demonstration* (Cambridge, Mass.: Ballinger, 1980).

68. Travis, *But They All Come Back* (see note 63), pp. 171–74; Petersilia, *When Prisoners Come Home* (see note 65), p. 99.

69. Amy L. Solomon, Vera Kachnowski, and Avinash Bhati, "Does Parole Work? Analyzing the Impact of Postprison Supervision on Rearrest Outcomes" (Washington: Urban Institute, March 2005); Joan Petersilia and Susan Turner, "Intensive Probation and Parole," *Crime and Justice: A Review of Research* 17 (1993): 281–335.

70. Joshua Good and Pamela Sherrid, "When the Gates Open: Ready4Work: A National Response to the Prisoner Reentry Crisis" (Philadelphia: Public/Private Ventures, October 2005); and Linda Jucovy, "Just Out: Early Lessons from the Ready4Work Prisoner Reentry Initiative" (Philadelphia: Public/Private Ventures, February 2006).

71. Interview with Jeremy Travis, in New York, N.Y., on July 20, 2006; Petersilia and Turner, "Intensive Probation and Parole" (see note 69), pp. 313–15.

72. Kleiman, "Coerced Abstinence" (see note 17). Here and in the remainder of this subsection, I largely follow Travis, *But They All Come Back* (see note 63), pp. 173–76, 179–82.

73. Travis, *But They All Come Back* (see note 63), pp. 162–64; Petersilia, *When Prisoners Come Home* (see note 65), p. 119.

74. Harry J. Holzer, Steven Raphael, and Michael A. Stoll, "How Do Employer Perceptions of Crime and Incarceration Affect the Employment Prospects of Less-Educated Young Black Men?" in *Black Males Left Behind*, edited by Mincy (see note 8), chap. 3.

75. Christopher Jencks, *Rethinking Social Policy: Race, Poverty, and the Underclass* (Harvard University Press, 1992), pp. 127–28.

76. This account is based on an interview with Peter Cove and Lee Bowes, the managers of America Works, in New York, N.Y., on July 6, 2006; and on William B. Eimicke and Steven Cohen, "America Works' Criminal Justice Program: Providing Second Chances through Work" (New York: Manhattan Institute, November 2002).

77. The following is based on an interview with Mindy Tarlow, executive director of CEO, on February 22, 2006; and on Center for Employment Opportunities and MDRC, *The Power of Work: The Center for Employment Opportunities Comprehensive Prisoner Reentry Program* (New York: Center for Employment Opportunities, March 2006), and other CEO materials.

78. Data from the Center for Employment Opportunities.

79. These programs would include the National Supported Work Demonstration, the public jobs components of welfare reform in New York City and Wisconsin, and also the government jobs created under the Comprehensive Employment and Training Act (CETA) in the 1970s.

80. A third possible population would be single men receiving general relief, a nonfederal aid program found in some localities, notably New York City. This group is often subject to work requirements already. See Cori E. Uccello and L. Jerome Gallagher, *General Assistance Programs: The State-Based Part of the Safety Net* (Washington: Urban Institute, January 1997).

81. Travis, *But They All Come Back* (see note 63), pp. 162–63; Bureau of Justice Statistics, *Probation and Parole in the United States, 2005* (U.S. Department of Justice, November 2006).

82. The child support and parolee numbers are at a point in time; many more individuals than this would cycle through these statuses over a year. Around 630,000 ex-offenders leave the prisons annually, a number not far different from the 784,000 parolees in 2005, implying that parole is largely short-term. But the stock at a point in time determines the number of slots needed and thus the scale of the program.

83. AW's cost = (0.78 ° 1.5 million ° \$1,160) + (0.78 ° 0.44 °1.5 million ° \$2,088) = \$2.43 billion. CEO's cost = \$3,219 ° 1.5 million = \$4.83 billion.

84. Reassuringly, the per-slot costs for both AW and CEO fall within the range found for 1980s-era work experience programs for welfare recipients. See Thomas Brock, David Butler, and David Long, "Unpaid Work Experience for Welfare Recipients: Findings and Lessons from MDRC Research" (New York: MDRC, September 1993).

85. James Riccio, Daniel Friedlander, and Stephen Freedman, *GAIN: Benefits, Costs, and Three-Year Impacts of a Welfare-to-Work Program* (New York: MDRC, September 1994); and Diana Adams-Ciardullo and others, *How Effective Are Different Welfare-to-Work Approaches? Five-Year Adult and Child Impacts for Eleven Programs* (New York: MDRC, December 2001).

86. The CEO study has joint federal government and foundation funding.

87. The following discussion and cost estimates draw on conversations with researchers at MDRC and officials at the U.S. Administration for Children and Families.

88. Jason A. Turner and Thomas Main, "Work Experience under Welfare Reform," in *New World of Welfare*, edited by Blank and Haskins (see note 58), pp. 299–302. Per-slot costs were below those estimated for AW and CEO because they include only the incremental expense of adding workers to an ongoing agency. The AW and CEO costs include more for supervision and overhead.

89. U.S. House of Representatives, *2004 Green Book* (see note 54), pp. 8.65–8.69; Maureen A. Pirog and Kathleen M. Ziol-Guest, "Child Support Enforcement: Programs and Policies, Impacts, and Questions," *Journal of Policy Analysis and Management* 25, no. 4 (Fall 2006): 944, 977–78. Child support's total revenues are about four times its costs, but collections go largely to cases outside welfare.

90. Bureau of Justice Statistics, "State Prison Expenditures, 2001" (U.S. Department of Justice, June 2004), p. 3. I indexed the 2001 figure of $22,650 to $25,487 in 2005 dollars, using the unadjusted Consumer Price Index for all urban consumers.

91. Hugh B. Price, "Transitioning Ex-Offenders into Jobs and Society," *Washington Post*, April 10, 2006.

92. Martin Gilens, *Why Americans Hate Welfare: Race, Media, and the Politics of Antipoverty Policy* (University of Chicago Press, 1999), chaps. 2, 8; Fay Lomax Cook and Edith J. Barrett, *Support for the American Welfare State: The Views of Congress and the Public* (Columbia University Press, 1992).

93. Travis, *But They All Come Back* (see note 63), pp. 182–83.

94. Ronald B. Mincy and Elaine J. Sorenson, "Deadbeats and Turnips in Child Support Reform," *Journal of Policy Analysis and Management* 17, no. 1 (Winter 1998): 44–51; Doolittle and others, *Building Opportunities* (see note 56), chap. 2.

95. Office of Child Support Enforcement, "Child Support and Job Projects for Fathers by State" (U.S. Administration for Children and Families, July 27, 2006); conversation with Rob Cohen, U.S. Administration for Children and Families, August 11, 2006.

96. Travis, *But They All Come Back* (see note 63), pp. 174, 330; Petersilia, *When Prisoners Come Home* (see note 65), pp. 172–74; Heather MacDonald, "How to Straighten Out Ex-Cons," *City Journal* 13, no. 2 (Spring 2003): 24–37.

97. Mead, *Government Matters* (see note 3), chap. 9.

Next Steps for Federal Child Care Policy

Mark Greenberg

Summary

In Mark Greenberg's view, a national child care strategy should pursue four goals. Every parent who needs child care to get or keep work should be able to afford care without having to leave children in unhealthy or dangerous environments; all families should be able to place their children in settings that foster education and healthy development; parental choice should be respected; and a set of good choices should be available.

Attaining these goals, says Greenberg, requires revamping both federal child care subsidy programs and federal tax policy related to child care. Today subsidies are principally provided through a block grant structure in which states must restrict eligibility, access, or the extent of assistance because both federal and state funds are limited. Tax policy principally involves a modest nonrefundable credit that provides little or no assistance to poor and low-income families.

Greenberg would replace the block grant with a federal guarantee of assistance for all families with incomes under 200 percent of poverty that need child care to enter or sustain employment. States would administer the federal assistance program under a federal-state matching formula with the federal government paying most of the cost. States would develop and implement plans to improve the quality of child care, coordinate child care with other early education programs, and ensure that child care payment rates are sufficient to allow families to obtain care that fosters healthy child development. Greenberg would also make the federal dependent care tax credit refundable, with the credit set at 50 percent of covered child care costs for the lowest-income families and gradually phasing down to 20 percent as family income increases.

The combined subsidy and tax changes would lead to a better-coordinated system of child care subsidies that would assure substantial financial help to families below 200 percent of poverty, while tax-based help would ensure continued, albeit significantly reduced, assistance for families with higher incomes. Greenberg indicates that the tax credit expansions are estimated to cost about $5 billion a year, and the subsidy and quality expansions would cost about $18 billion a year.

www.futureofchildren.org

Mark Greenberg is executive director of the Task Force on Poverty for the Center for American Progress, while on leave from the Center for Law and Social Policy. In preparing this paper, he benefited from assistance by Indivar Dutta-Gupta and Avi Perry and conversations with and comments from Gina Adams, Helen Blank, Ajay Chaudry, Dave Edie, Danielle Ewen, Julia Isaacs, Joan Lombardi, Elaine Maag, Hannah Matthews, Anne Mitchell, Adele Robinson, and Louise Stoney, as well as the comments of Ron Haskins, Isabel Sawhill, and participants in the Brookings Institution seminar. Arloc Sherman generated an enormously helpful set of numbers for the cost estimates. The author is solely responsible for the analysis and recommendations and for the assumptions used in estimating costs.

Any national strategy to substantially reduce poverty should address child care for low-income working families. Affordable child care helps parents enter and sustain employment. Assistance with child care costs helps families increase their disposable incomes. Higher-quality care is linked with improved outcomes for children.

Although child care policy should address the needs of poor families, it should be designed to help a much larger group of Americans. Families across the income spectrum need stable, affordable, quality child care, and addressing their needs should not be viewed principally as a poverty or welfare issue. Child care simultaneously provides a work support for parents and an early education experience for children. Policymakers must be mindful of this dual role.

A national child care strategy should reflect four goals. Every parent who needs child care to get or keep work should be able to afford care that does not leave the children in unhealthy or dangerous environments. Every family should be able to place its children in settings that foster education and healthy development. Every family should be able to choose among child care providers. For parental choice to be meaningful, a set of good choices should be available to all families.

U.S. child care policy fails to meet these goals. Current policy has two principal components: tax-based assistance to middle- and higher-income families and block grant funding to states to assist lower-income families. The only federal entitlements to child care assistance are those provided through the tax code, the vast majority of which go to middle- and upper-income families. Only a small fraction of the low-income children who are eligible for assistance through the federal block grant framework receive it. The nature and extent of that assistance varies widely from state to state and often fails to provide families access to the safe and developmentally appropriate care that is likely to be available to higher-income families. In many states, working families face waiting lists or can access care only through the welfare system. Low-income families who receive no assistance pay greater shares of their income than do higher-income parents but purchase less expensive care.

A better approach would restructure both tax and nontax policy as part of an overall national child care strategy. Congress should expand the Child and Dependent Care Tax Credit (CDCTC) and replace the existing block grant structure with a new federal-state matching structure to guarantee subsidy assistance to families with incomes below 200 percent of the official poverty line. A guarantee of child care assistance that does not depend on a family's state of residence, or on its welfare status, or on whether the funding for the year had been exhausted would promote work, ensure better care for children, and reduce poverty among working families.

Such a guarantee would improve families' ability to purchase care, but it would not, in itself, ensure the availability of good choices for all families. Simply increasing families' purchasing power will not ensure an adequate supply of care in lower-income communities, increase the educational qualifications and compensation of child care teachers, or promote the development of a coordinated early education system. Ensuring the availability of good choices to all parents will require a combination of demand and supply strategies. Thus, each state should be charged with developing and implementing a strategic plan to improve the quality of care available to families and with coordinating child care with other programs and activities in its early education system. The federal government should provide dedicated funding to support these efforts.

Low-Income Families, Work, and Child Care

Most of the nation's 13.5 million low-income families with children (those with household income below 200 percent of the poverty line) include a full-time, year-round worker.[1] In two-thirds of the nation's 5.7 million poor families with children (those with household income below the poverty line), a family member worked during the year; in one-third, a family member worked full-time, year-round.[2] The share of poor children in families with a year-round full-time worker grew substantially during the 1990s and despite some fall-off since 2000 remains well above the share during the early 1990s.[3]

Low-income working families are less likely to pay for child care than are higher-income families. When they do pay, they purchase less expensive care, but pay a much larger share of their income for it.[4] They are much less likely to use center-based care. Within each type of care, they pay considerably less than higher-income families do. On a per-hour basis, families with incomes above $75,000 pay more than twice as much for care as families with incomes of $10,000 or less and about 60 percent more than families with incomes between $10,001 and $30,000.[5]

Most low-income working families do not receive child care assistance. Federal law permits states to use their federal child care block grant funds to provide subsidy assistance to families with incomes below 85 percent of state median income. Almost all states

elect to set lower eligib U.S. Department of He: vices (HHS) has estimat children eligible under subsidies in 2003.[6] HH 12 percent of children eligible under federal law received subsidy assistance in 1999, but thereafter it ceased reporting the share of federally eligible children who received child

---

Families across the income spectrum need stable, affordable, quality child care, and addressing their needs should not be viewed principally as a poverty or welfare issue.

---

care assistance. The Center for Law and Social Policy estimated that 14 percent of federally eligible children—about one in seven—received child care assistance in 2000.[7]

The lack of child care assistance has adverse effects on families and lowers the likelihood that parents can sustain employment. Parents lacking child care assistance may go into debt, return to welfare, choose lower-quality and less stable child care, lose time from work, or be forced to choose between paying for child care and paying for rent or clothes.[8] Although researchers have not experimentally evaluated how providing child care assistance affects parental employment, a set of studies has found that low-income parents who receive help meeting child care costs are more likely to get and keep work. One research summary reported that "while employment and subsidy use are inherently in-

..d, each influencing the other, mothers ..o use subsidies appear more likely than ..er low-income mothers to: work at a job, work more hours, work standard schedules, sustain employment, [and] earn more."[9]

Child care subsidies increase family disposable income by freeing up dollars that would otherwise go for child care. Providing a subsidy to offset a family's child care costs does not in itself affect poverty under official measures, because noncash benefits are not treated as income and work expenses are not considered in determining the number of families in poverty. But Isabel Sawhill and Adam Thomas have estimated that if child care expenses were considered, an additional 1.9 million people, including more than 1 million children, would be considered poor.[10]

By lowering prices, subsidies can improve access to higher-quality care. A National Academies report found that "the quality of child care is likely to have important consequences for the development of children during the early years and middle childhood," and that because of the amount of time children spend in child care, "child care provides an important opportunity to promote [children's] healthy development and overall well-being."[11] The report noted, "In comparison to their higher income peers, children of low-income families appear more likely to receive poor-quality child care and less likely to receive excellent quality child care, especially in the early years."[12] Although higher cost does not ensure higher-quality care, it is often at least a prerequisite as many characteristics of higher-quality care, including better-trained teachers, smaller class sizes, and lower adult-child ratios, are more costly.[13] Low-income parents are more likely than higher-income parents to cite cost or affordability as a key factor in choosing child care arrangements.[14]

Higher-quality care is associated with better child outcomes on a range of key school-readiness dimensions, including "basic cognitive skills (language and math) and children's behavioral skills in the classroom (cognitive/attention skills, sociability, problem behaviors, and peer relations), both of which are important factors in children's ability to take advantage of the opportunities available in school."[15] In their article in this volume, Greg Duncan, Jens Ludwig, and Katherine Magnuson note that new scientific research documents lifelong consequences from early brain development, as well as the importance of "earlier foundational skills" on which "complex cognitive capacities are built," and cite evidence that high-quality intensive early education programs can improve children's life chances. Most child care available today does not reach the quality of such intensive programs. Nevertheless, researchers at the Institute for Research on Poverty have concluded, "Children who attend higher-quality child care settings . . . display better cognitive, language, and social competencies on standardized tests."[16] The Cost, Quality, and Outcomes in Child Care Centers Study, which began in 1993, was a longitudinal study of children in four states, and was designed to examine the influence of typical center-based child care on children's development. The study population was limited to children in families that had elected center-based care. The study found that "the quality of children's experiences in typical child care centers affects . . . their readiness for school," with higher quality associated with improved math and language abilities, as well as social skills.[17]

Child care subsidies appear to promote access to center-based care. The National Academy of Sciences reported, "Both experimental and correlational studies have found that center-type experiences are associated with higher scores on cognitive and language assessments, particularly for 3- and 4-year olds."[18] Poor children particularly benefit from access to center care, but low-income children are less likely to be in center-based care than are their higher-income peers.[19] However, low-income children receiving child care subsidies are more likely than other low-income children to participate in center-based care arrangements.[20]

Federal Child Care Policy and Funding: A Summary

Although a wide range of federal programs support early care and education in some manner, federal child care policy has two principal components: tax provisions and block grant funding to states.[21] The tax and block grant provisions differ in eligible population, type of care paid for, amount of assistance, delivery mechanism, and virtually every other policy dimension.

The major federal tax provisions relating to child care are the Child and Dependent Care Tax Credit and exclusions from income for benefits under dependent care assistance programs (DCAPs). The CDCTC is a tax credit for a portion of child and dependent care expenses for children under age thirteen or for dependents of any age who are mentally or physically unable to care for themselves. In 2006, the maximum credit was 35 percent of the first $3,000 of qualifying expenses for one child or dependent or $6,000 for two or more qualifying children or dependents. No family qualifies for the maximum credit because of the way the provision interacts with tax rates and other credits. As income rises, the credit gradually declines to cover 20 percent of qualifying expenses (at income levels of $43,000 and higher). In 2005, a total of 6.3 million tax units claimed

the CDCTC with an average benefit of $529. The CDCTC cost $2.7 billion in 2006.[22]

The CDCTC is not refundable: a family's credit cannot exceed the amount of its income tax liability. As a result, the credit provides almost no benefit to lower-income families. In 2005, families with incomes below $20,000 received an estimated 0.6 percent of CDCTC benefits, while two-thirds of the benefits went to families with incomes exceeding $50,000.[23] A single parent paying for child care for two children would not benefit from the credit unless her earnings reached about $21,500.

Dependent care assistance programs allow an exclusion from taxable income for employer contributions toward child and dependent care benefits. The amount of the exclusion is limited to $5,000 per family per year. Benefits may take several forms, but the most common is a salary reduction plan in which employees may set aside up to $5,000 from annual pretax earnings for work-related child or dependent care expenses. The program cost an estimated $810 million in lost federal revenue in 2006.[24]

The DCAP structure provides little or no benefit to lower-income families. Because it allows only an exclusion from taxable income, families with no tax liability receive no benefit from the provision. Moreover, because it reduces taxable income, it provides the most assistance to higher-income families with higher marginal tax rates.[25]

The largest source of federal child care subsidy funding for low-income families is the Child Care and Development Fund. CCDF involves a complex mix of federal and state funding.[26] A state can also transfer up to 30 percent of its Temporary Assistance for Needy

Families (TANF) funds to its CCDF program. It must spend most of its CCDF funds on subsidy assistance for families with incomes below 85 percent of state median income. A state must also spend at least 4 percent of its CCDF funds to promote the quality of child care. Quality expenditures can benefit all families, including those who do not qualify for CCDF subsidies. State CCDF programs must meet

---

Federal child care subsidy funding grew rapidly after the enactment of the 1996 welfare law, but the rapid growth ended early in this decade.

---

federal "parental choice" requirements. Under the federal requirements, families must have the option of receiving a voucher that can be used with an eligible provider, and state policies and requirements cannot expressly or effectively exclude any category of care or type of provider. Federal law also provides that state payment rates must be sufficient to ensure "equal access" to child care services comparable to those provided to families not eligible to receive child care assistance under CCDF or other programs. Most CCDF assistance (85 percent in 2005) is delivered through vouchers, with the remainder provided through contracts with providers (11 percent) or cash to families (4 percent).

The TANF block grant is the other principal federal source of low-income child care assistance. Under TANF, each state qualifies for an annual block grant. A state's TANF grant may be used for cash assistance for low-income families and a wide array of other benefits and services. Total federal funding to

all states is $16.8 billion a year. States must also spend a specific amount of state funds (known as the "maintenance of effort" requirement) to avoid being penalized. A state may "directly spend" an unlimited amount of TANF funds for child care for "needy" families—that is, families that meet the state's definition of low-income. It may directly spend TANF funds whether or not it also transfers TANF funds to CCDF. When a state directly spends TANF funds for child care, it may, but need not, follow CCDF rules concerning eligibility, parental choice, and quality.

Federal child care subsidy funding grew rapidly after the enactment of the 1996 welfare law, but the rapid growth ended early in this decade. Total child care spending across CCDF, TANF, and related state funds reached $12.3 billion in 2003 and fell to $11.7 billion in 2005.[27] The Deficit Reduction Act of 2005 increased federal funding by $200 million a year. Thus it will eventually not be possible to sustain current spending and service levels unless federal funding is increased or states spend new state funds.

The Department of Health and Human Services has estimated that 2.2 million children were assisted through CCDF, TANF, and a small amount of Social Services Block Grant funding in 2005, down from a peak of about 2.45 million children earlier in the decade. Those children represent a small share of the 15.7 million children who were eligible for CCDF assistance in federal fiscal year 2000 (the most recent year for which data are available).

Goals and the Limits of Current Policy

Measuring the effectiveness of current child care policies and evaluating the strengths and weaknesses of alternatives necessarily depend on one's goals. My own view, noted above, is that a sound national child care policy should have four goals: every parent who needs child care to enter or sustain employment should be able to afford care that does not risk leaving children in unhealthy or dangerous environments; all families should have the opportunity to have their children in settings that foster education and healthy development; parental choice should be respected; and good choices should be available to families.

The current U.S. policy structure falls far short of meeting these goals. Rather than ensuring assistance to all families who need child care to go to or sustain work, current policy offers aid to only a small minority of low-income families. Even those receiving subsidies may not be able to place their children in care that fosters education and healthy development.

The tax system provides a small entitlement to middle- and upper-income families, but no help to the poorest families. In theory, the CDCTC could provide up to $2,100 to a family with child care costs of or exceeding $6,000. In reality, the credit is small in relation to child care costs, wholly unavailable to poor families, and provides little help to other low-income families. For example, Leonard Burman and his colleagues have calculated that in 2005, because of the CDCTC's interaction with other credits and effective tax rates, a single-parent family with $6,000 of countable expenses would qualify for no credit at an income of $21,000; for a credit of $810 at an income of $25,000, and for a maximum credit of $1,560 at $33,000.[28]

Subsidy policy principally relies on providing block grants to states and letting them design their own policies to ration these funds. Overall, about one in seven children eligible for CCDF assistance receives it. Coverage is probably most extensive for families receiving or leaving TANF assistance and least extensive for working families without any recent welfare connection.[29] Because available funding is not sufficient to serve all those eligible under federal law, states must make choices about how to allocate their funds. There are large variations across states concerning who is eligible for assistance and how much assistance eligible families receive.[30] For example, in 2006 a family of three was ineligible for assistance in fifteen states if it had income of $25,000; in contrast, in eight states, a family of three with income exceeding $35,000 could still be eligible for assistance. State eligibility thresholds ranged from 110 percent to 284 percent of the poverty line and from 34 percent to 89 percent of state median income. Within their state-established eligibility rules, some states serve all eligible families, while others have closed doors or have established waiting lists for categories of eligible families. In 2006, eighteen states reported waiting lists or frozen intake for nonwelfare families.

Provider payment rates are an important dimension of child care policy because they affect whether families will be able to choose from a broad range of providers in the local market and pay for higher-quality care. Some states set payment rates high enough to meet provider charges in much of the local market, but most do not. In 2006 nine states were basing their rates on relatively recent (2004–05) market rate surveys and paid providers at or above the 75th percentile for the local market. In contrast, ten states had not updated their maximum reimbursement rates for providers since 2001 or earlier.

Family copayment rules are another important dimension of policy. Copayment levels affect the amount of family income available for all other costs of living after child care expenses. Setting a copayment level too high may affect whether families participate in the subsidy system. In 2006 a family of three with one child in care and income at the poverty level had no required copayment in four states but faced a copayment exceeding $100 a month in eleven states. In 2005 the mean copayment for families with copayment obligations was 10 percent of family income or higher in six states and 3 percent of family income or lower in another six.[31]

Just as there is variation in child care policies across states, in some cases there is variation within states. Although most states have uniform state policies, three states leave key determinants of eligibility, such as income thresholds, to local discretion.

It is hard to see a rationale for a national policy that leaves virtually every major policy decision about the provision of child care assistance for low-income families to state discretion and results in such wide variation across states. One might argue that child care should be viewed as analogous to TANF—that is, a lump sum federal payment accompanied by a set of broad goals and state discretion to design policies to effectuate the goals. The analogy is flawed. The goal of TANF is not to ensure that an eligible population receives a needed service—to the contrary, federal law has encouraged states to reduce the number of families getting assistance. A key rationale for TANF's structure was the virtue of allowing for flexible funds and experimentation to help policymakers learn "what works." However, in child care, it is doubtful that the nation is learning anything valuable by allowing diverse approaches to eligibility and assistance. Instead, the result is an inequitable patch-work in which families with the same needs are treated differently from state to state and within states, in which many low-income working families receive no help, and in which states are constantly forced to make difficult trade-offs between coverage, adequacy of payment rates, quality, and affordability.

Moreover, the existing structure does not ensure that families have access to care that promotes the health and development of children. Although the law provides that families receiving subsidy assistance should have "equal access" to the care available to higher-income families, it also states that families have no right to seek enforcement of this requirement. The Department of Health and Human Services has said that it will presume that a state's payment rates are sufficient to provide equal access if, based on a market rate survey, the state's payments to providers are set at a level high enough to give families access to 75 percent of local providers or slots. Most states, however, do not meet this standard, and the federal government has never taken action against a state for failure to do so.

A Better Way

Policymakers should restructure current tax and subsidy policy to guarantee child care assistance to low-income families within a broader framework that helps all families attain access to care that promotes the health and development of children. To that end, I propose a combination of expanded tax credits, a direct subsidy system with a guaranteed eligible population instead of the current block grant structure, and a federal early care and education strategy fund to support state efforts to improve quality and develop coordinated early care and education systems in states.

These recommendations are grounded in the premise that there is no fundamental difference between the conditions facing families just below and just above the poverty line and that a very large group of families faces the challenge of affording high-quality child care. Accordingly, policies to help low-income families should be designed in ways that do not create arbitrary differences among families with similar needs. In advancing their commitment to end child poverty, policymakers in the United Kingdom have articulated a principle of "progressive univeralism," which has been defined as providing "support for all and more help for those who need it most, when they need it most."[32] A framework of progressive universalism seems particularly appropriate in the context of child care, where the stresses and challenges faced by low-income families are also faced by a far broader group of middle- and higher-income families.

Expand the Child and Dependent Care Tax Credit

The CDCTC should be made refundable, expanded to cover at least 50 percent of allowable expenditures for lower-income families, and indexed for inflation. Making the credit refundable would extend its benefits to the lowest-income families and ensure that all eligible families could receive the full amount for which they qualify. Making a greater share of a family's child care spending subject to the credit would both defray expenses and help families purchase higher-cost care. Leonard Burman, Elaine Maag, and Jeffrey Rohaly estimate that a refundable credit would provide benefits to 1.5 million more households and would expand the share of benefits going to tax units with incomes below $20,000 from less than 1 percent under current law to almost 26 percent.[33] They estimate that making the CDCTC re-

fundable, expanding the top credit rate from 35 percent to 50 percent, indexing it for inflation, and making a set of related technical changes would cost approximately $25 billion over five years.

If the CDCTC were larger and refundable, could all subsidy assistance be provided through the tax system? The United King-

---

The CDCTC should be made refundable, expanded to cover at least 50 percent of allowable expenditures for lower-income families, and indexed for inflation.

---

dom has implemented a refundable child care credit that covers the first 80 percent of eligible expenses up to £300 (about $580) a week for families with two or more children, with the credit gradually phasing down as income rises.[34] The idea of a unified tax-based approach is attractive, but it presents a range of difficulties. It is appealing because it would enable all families to receive help through a single, universal, nonstigmatized system, without waiting lists or closed intake and without extreme variations across states. Moreover, as the earned income tax credit (EITC) experience has shown, national and local outreach could promote participation and employer awareness.

But even a larger and refundable CDCTC could not fully substitute for direct assistance to families. First, the CDCTC expansion proposed here would not provide a large enough credit to substitute fully for direct subsidy assistance. If the credit were raised to 50 percent and made refundable, the maximum credit would be $1,500 for one child, $3,000 for two or more children. By contrast, CCDF payments to providers (including family co-payments), which are often criticized as inadequate, averaged $4,236 in 2005, with large variations based on age of child, hours of care, type of care, and geographical location.[35] Child care costs in much of the nation far exceed CCDF levels.[36]

Even if the CDCTC were made larger, it could not be the principal vehicle for helping many lower-income families unless its structure allowed for advance payment. Current block grant–based subsidies are typically provided monthly, with provisions to address changes in family circumstances and emergency needs. By contrast, unless alternative provisions were designed, a family's CDCTC credit for a year would be determined at the end of the tax year and paid in the subsequent year in a lump sum. Families would need to pay the full costs of care on their own throughout the year and rely on partial reimbursement in the next year. Many families would likely opt for the least costly care, which could also be the least reliable and of lower quality.

Some form of advance payment structure would be essential in order for tax credits to be a practical means to provide child care assistance to low-income families. The EITC has an advance payment option but it is rarely used, for a number of reasons. For a start, many beneficiaries are unaware of the option. Other reasons include its complexity, the need for employer participation, fear of subsequent tax liability, and the preference of many families for the "forced savings" of the once-a-year lump sum. Families might be more likely to use an advance payment op-

tion for child care, because they would likely be more interested in getting ongoing help to meet costs throughout the year. Still, the EITC experience highlights the need to develop an advance payment structure that families would view as a practical option. Moreover, developing an advance payment structure for the CDCTC could be even more difficult than developing an effective one for the EITC, because the family's eligibility for the CDCTC would turn on both income and child care costs; it is unclear whether such a structure could be effectively implemented through employers or another delivery mechanism would be needed.

The difficulties that an advance payment structure presents should not preclude efforts to develop one. Indeed, as interest grows in expanding refundable tax credits, it will be important to develop a more viable advance payment structure for a range of tax credits.[37] Absent such a structure, tax credits could not effectively substitute for much of the existing child care subsidy system.

A Guarantee of Child Care Assistance to Low-Income Working Families

Instead of the current block grant structure, federal law should provide for a guarantee of child care assistance to working families with incomes below 200 percent of poverty—about $34,340 for a family of three and $41,300 for a family of four in 2007. States would administer the guarantee through a federal-state matching structure. Families would be required to make a copayment toward the cost of the care, with the copayment increasing with income. States would pay the remainder of the cost of care. Payment rates would be adequate to ensure that low-income families had access to a range of choices, including high-quality, developmentally appropriate care. At the same time, each state would have a responsibility to act to improve the quality of choices available to all families.

A case can be made for different choices regarding each detail of the guarantee. However the details are resolved, the starting point should be the need to shift from a block grant structure with no articulable national policy to a national policy that ensures child care assistance with high-quality choices for all eligible low-income families.

A threshold question is whether having a guarantee, or entitlement, is good policy. The answer should turn on the nature and terms of the benefit. On the one hand, for example, few people question the appropriateness of entitlements to Social Security benefits, the earned income tax credit, or K–12 public education. On the other hand, a principal focus of the 1996 welfare reform law was to end the entitlement to cash assistance for low-income families. The objection to the cash assistance entitlement was that it encouraged behavior that society wished to discourage. Here, the opposite is the case. The nation should have an interest in ensuring that the need for child care is never a barrier to getting a job and that working families can purchase good care without spending a large share of their income to do so. Moreover, the nation already has entitlements to child care assistance, albeit small ones, for higher-income families; this proposal would extend entitlements to all families.

A guarantee of child care assistance for eligible families has important advantages over a block grant structure. First, it would provide a clear, simple, powerful message: if you work, you will have help paying for child care. Second, it would ensure that no working family would ever be compelled to leave a child alone or in an unsafe environment simply because of financial necessity. Third, it would ensure that all families had the opportunity to have their children in enriching environments while parents were working. Fourth, it would ensure that families in identical situations would not be treated differently simply because of the state in which they lived or the time of year in which they applied for assistance. Fifth, it could help bring the nation closer to achieving two other broad goals—that no family should ever be worse off by going to or remaining in work and that working families should have enough income to support a decent standard of living. The existing block grant structure does not ensure that any of these goals are met.

One argument against a guarantee is that in a world of limited resources, difficult choices must be made about allocating scarce dollars, and states and localities are better able than the federal government to make those judgments. Moreover, with broad discretion in use of funds, states can test a range of approaches to the parameters of their subsidy systems in order to determine the most effective ways to use limited resources. The reality is that it would be far better to have a national debate about those choices and to provide sufficient funding to serve the population defined as needing assistance, rather than to provide states with a lump sum of money and direct them to develop rationing rules.

A related argument is that entitlements of any sort put government spending on "autopilot" because there is a risk that spending will simply increase without Congress's ever considering whether the growth in spending is desirable. Here, the two principal reasons why spending might grow more than anticipated would be if more parents entered employment or more eligible families sought and benefited from assistance. Neither should be a troubling result.

Who should be guaranteed assistance? First, it is important to ensure that help is available for families receiving TANF, but it would be a serious error to limit guarantees to families receiving or leaving TANF. It is contrary to basic principles of equity to create a structure in which families can receive child care assistance only by entering the welfare system. Second, although the lowest-income families need the most help, assistance should be phased out gradually as income increases. Parents should not need to fear that working additional hours or getting a raise will make their families worse off because of loss of child care assistance. Moreover, under a subsidy structure providing for a gradual phase-out of assistance combined with an expanded CDCTC, families losing direct assistance would still qualify for refundable tax credits of up to $1,500 to $3,000.

This proposal would guarantee child care assistance to all working families with incomes below 200 percent of poverty and to families engaged in work activities while receiving TANF assistance. As under current law, states could use funds to provide child care assistance to other low-income families involved in education or training, but the federal guarantee would not extend to these families. An eligibility threshold of 200 percent of the poverty line is consistent with the growing body of research that recognizes this as a reasonable measure of low-income status and with evidence that families with incomes below 200 percent of poverty pay a far greater share of their income for substantially less costly care than higher-income families do.

A 200 percent standard is lower than maximum current CCDF eligibility. In 2006 (under HHS income guidelines) 200 percent of poverty for a family of four was $40,000, while 85 percent of the national median income for four was $56,966. As a practical matter, only three states set their CCDF income levels that high, but this proposal posits that it would be better to ensure assistance to the eligible population below 200 percent of poverty than to have a higher eligibility threshold while states are unable to serve large numbers of qualifying families. Thus, federal matching funds should be available for states that elect to provide assistance to families with incomes up to 85 percent of the state median, but the federal guarantee should be limited to families with income below 200 percent of poverty.

Under the proposal, all working families receiving subsidy assistance would be required to make a copayment toward the cost of care, subject to limited state waiver authority. Current HHS guidelines recommend that copayments not exceed 10 percent of income. However, higher-income families spend only 6.5 percent of their incomes on care, and even 6.5 percent seems excessive for poor families. Under current state policies, most states waive copayments for at least some families in poverty, ten states waive copayments for all families below poverty, and only four states require copayments for all families in poverty.[38] Under this proposal, families would face a copayment of 3 percent of their income below the poverty line and 10 percent of any income that exceeds the poverty line. With such a structure, families approaching 200 percent of poverty would face an average copayment requirement of about 6.5 percent of income, the same share as higher-income families pay for care.

The proposal would maintain the role of states in administering child care subsidies, for several important reasons. First, maintaining the state role would allow for timely ongoing assistance and adjustments for changing circumstances during the year. Second, states are currently responsible for subsidy administration and quality initiatives, and subsidy policy can function as an important vehicle for promoting quality. For example, states can act to improve quality through provider registration, training, and support; by connecting families with resource and referral agencies; by implementing quality-rating systems; and by contracting for types of care. Moreover, as states develop prekindergarten and early education models, they can use their subsidy systems in efforts to develop full-day, year-round services.

Federal and state governments would continue to share in the cost of subsidized care under this structure. Under current law, federal funds represent, on average, 57 percent of block grant–related funding and state matching rates vary, based on state per capita income. It would be reasonable to retain a federal-state cost-sharing relationship, though an argument can be made for increasing the federal share. Whatever rate is established, each state's match rate could apply to all spending, substituting for the complex rules that apply under current law.

Implementing a guarantee would require decisions about how to establish the amount of subsidy assistance for families. Current CCDF regulations are based on the premise that a payment rate sufficient to pay for 75 percent of available care in a community is adequate to ensure that families receiving assistance get "equal access" to care comparable to that received by families with incomes above the subsidy level. As noted, most states do not set payment rates that high. It is not clear how effective the 75th percentile standard is as a benchmark for equal access, as there appears to be virtually no research comparing the characteristics of care above and below the 75th percentile. The idea of "meeting the market" as the way to set payments for child care is in some ways flawed, because current care often falls short of desired quality standards, and providers wanting to upgrade facilities or raise teacher edu-

---

It is contrary to basic principles of equity to create a structure in which families can receive child care assistance only by entering the welfare system.

---

cation or compensation are constrained by what parents can pay. Moreover, basing payments on characteristics of local markets may mean paying lower rates in poorer communities where families are least able to afford more expensive care.[39]

One possible approach would draw on an important variant of the 75th percentile framework. In recent years, many states have developed quality-ratings systems that categorize child care providers according to specific quality benchmarks; higher-rated providers qualify to receive higher state payments.[40] Quality-ratings systems have been a significant step forward in state efforts to promote child care quality. They recognize the importance of parental choice, while providing valuable information to providers and families about markers of higher-quality care and creating incentives for providers to raise the quality of care. In establishing a child care guarantee, policymakers should consider requiring that all states use quality-ratings systems and pay at least the 75th percentile within each band of the state's rating system. For example, a state with a four-star rating system would need to have payments for four-star care that were high enough to pay for at least 75 percent of four-star care. This approach would ensure that families could purchase a significant share of care within the highest-rated band, while at the same time making clear that states need not pay for the most expensive care in the lowest-rated bands.

This approach is not the only possible way to set subsidy rates, and others should be considered. The key principle, however, is that to ensure that families have access to high-quality care it is not sufficient to simply meet current market costs, which are constrained by families' inability to pay, particularly in low-income areas. Rather, subsidy payment rules should be designed so that payments are high enough to ensure that participating families have effective access to high-quality care among their choices.

An Early Care and Education Strategy Fund

Although expanding families' capacity to purchase care would likely spur important market responses, a comprehensive strategy should address supply as well as demand. Federal policy should encourage and support state efforts to raise quality and to foster the coordination of early care and education. As noted, under current law states must spend at least 4 percent of their CCDF funds on quality initiatives, including those directly seeking to raise quality, as well as initiatives on health and safety monitoring, consumer education, and resource and referral activities. In some communities, simply expanding

demand may lead to increases in supply. In others, states will likely need to provide assistance and support to develop supply. Current compensation levels for child care teachers are far too low to permit providers to recruit and retain highly educated teachers. Raising payment rates can help but is not likely to solve the problem by itself. And as states expand prekindergarten efforts, it will be essential not only to develop mechanisms to help child care programs meet higher standards and become prekindergarten providers but also to promote coordination between child care and prekindergarten programs to provide year-round, full-day opportunities for families. Therefore, along with a guarantee of care, federal law should require each state to develop and implement a strategic plan to improve the quality of care for all families and to address cross-program coordination. Federal funding should support these efforts.

Thus, instead of the current requirement that states spend at least 4 percent of federal funds for quality, I propose creating a federal Early Care and Education Strategy Fund, established initially at $2 billion a year—about twice current state spending on quality.[41] States could use these funds for the same range of activities for which they spend their quality dollars under the existing block grant structure.[42] Funds would also be available for each state to develop and implement a strategic plan to improve the quality of care available to all families in the state and for state efforts to coordinate child care, Head Start, prekindergarten, and other programs into a comprehensive early care and education system for children from birth to age five.

Costs and Effects

As described earlier, the cost of expanding the Child and Dependent Care Tax Credit and making it refundable is in the range of

$25 billion over five years. Overall, I estimate that annual new costs for the guarantee and the Early Care and Education Strategy Fund are in the range of $18 billion. However, costs of the guarantee are very sensitive to a number of key assumptions, including average costs of care, numbers of potentially eligible families, and take-up rates.

I assume in this article that assistance under the guarantee would cost an average of $5,000 per child before family copayments. The cost is averaged between younger and older children, across various types of care, and across states. In 2005, average payments to providers under CCDF were $4,236 per child, including CCDF payments and family copayments. Given the limited data and range of potential costs, further development of the proposal would benefit from exploration among states, researchers, and others of the likely unit costs of the proposal.

What would the guarantee cost? If it were extended to all working families with incomes below 200 percent of poverty and to welfare families engaged in work activities, subject to the proposed copayment structure, with an average cost of $5,000 per child and an estimated 50 percent take-up rate, and with a $2 billion Early Care and Education Strategy Fund, I estimate annual costs in current dollars of about $30 billion a year. This would mean net new costs of about $18 billion above current costs of about $12 billion a year. That expenditure would provide subsidy assistance to about 3 million low-income working families; it would also provide assistance to families in TANF work activities and maintain services to other groups eligible under current law, such as other families in education and training, protective services cases, and older children who were incapacitated or under court supervision. Under cur-

rent law, the federal government pays an average of 57 percent of CCDF costs; if the federal share were to remain the same, new federal costs would be in the range of $11 billion a year.

Different assumptions or parameters lead to different cost estimates. For example, assuming an average cost of $7,000 per child would

---

Federal policy should encourage and support state efforts to raise quality and to foster the coordination of early care and education.

---

raise costs by about $10.6 billion. Imposing no copay against income below the poverty line would raise costs by about $1.4 billion. If the take-up rate were 5 percentage points higher or lower than the 50 percent estimate, costs could increase or decrease by nearly $2 billion.

Costs would also depend on whether the services and benefits available to families and children improve in other ways. Such improvements would present their own costs, but would likely reduce the costs of a child care guarantee and expansion of the CDCTC. For example, virtually every other developed nation provides paid parental leave for parents with very young children.[43] A policy of paid parental leave in the United States would allow parents to stay home during the early months of a child's life and take full advantage of their rights under the Family and Medical Leave Act; it would also reduce the "residual" costs of a child care guarantee and of the CDCTC. Similarly, recent research has found that children in the Early Head Start Program performed better on measures of cognition, language, and social-emotional functioning than their peers who did not participate in the program.[44] Making Early Head Start available to more children would likely reduce child care costs. In recent years, states have expanded prekindergarten programs for three- and four-year-olds; expanding such programs, particularly if full day, would lower residual child care costs for affected children.[45] Expanding after-school programs such as those funded through the 21st Century Community Learning Centers framework would both increase family options and reduce the need for child care outside school hours.[46]

As noted, increasing access to child care and helping families afford higher-quality care would have a range of significant benefits for children. It would also raise employment and reduce poverty. Analysts at the Urban Institute have modeled the employment and poverty-reducing effects of a proposal similar to this one, in connection with estimating the effects of a set of recommendations by the Center for American Progress Task Force on Poverty.[47] In doing so, they used a modified definition of poverty, drawn from the recommendations of the National Academy of Sciences, that subtracted child care expenses from income in measuring poverty. The Urban Institute, after reviewing the research on employment effects of child care subsidies, drew on that research to estimate that implementing the proposal would raise employment rates by 8 percentage points for unmarried parents and 3 percentage points for married parents with employed spouses, resulting in an additional 1.2 million married and 0.7 million unmarried workers. With those employment effects, the analysts estimated that implementing the proposal would

reduce the number of people in poverty by 2.7 million—about an 8 percent decline. The number of children in poverty would fall by 1.5 million—about a 14.5 percent decline. The poverty gap—that is, the total dollar amount by which those in poverty fall below the poverty line—would fall by $6.5 billion (in 2003 dollars) at a net cost to government of about $17.1 billion (in 2003 dollars). Thus, in addition to reducing poverty, the proposal would provide substantial benefits to other low-income families with incomes above the poverty line.

Criticisms and Responses

This proposal may face two very different sets of critics. One set will likely assert that it is not needed, is not the best use of scarce resources, and is too expensive. The other set will contend that it does not do enough: it leaves too many families with only modest tax-based assistance, does not ensure that high-quality care will be available to all, and still leaves significant gaps in coordination between tax and subsidy policy.

The first set of critics may contend that there is no need to expand assistance because working parents are "getting by" using their current paid or unpaid arrangements, so that much of any expansion would simply provide a "windfall" by defraying existing expenses or encourage the "monetizing" of informal relationships. Expanding assistance, however, has multiple goals: promoting employment, offsetting expenses, and supporting healthy child development. A substantial body of research finds that increasing subsidy assistance would increase the likelihood and stability of employment.[48] As noted, the Urban Institute has estimated that a similar proposal would result in 1.9 million additional working parents and a 14.5 percent reduction in child poverty. Expanding disposable income for low-income working families appears clearly desirable. Policymakers could avoid the risk of monetizing informal relationships by making such relationships ineligible for compensation, but doing so would seem a significant intrusion into parental choice. Although it is difficult to estimate reliably the extent to which enhanced capacity to purchase care would translate into higher-quality care, there is reason to believe the proposal would further that goal, too.

A second, related, objection may be that given the importance of promoting high-quality early education and school readiness, the next available dollars should be used for prekindergarten or intensive high-quality early education programs rather than for child care. However, child care and early education should not be viewed as separate and unrelated entities. Child care for young children is necessarily early education, and public policy can improve its effectiveness as such; in light of the importance of promoting and supporting parental work, it is essential to ensure that child care settings can also be high-quality early education settings. State expansions of prekindergarten programs do not obviate the need for child care. Prekindergarten programs are not typically structured as full-day, year-round, and the most common state model for prekindergarten includes child care centers and other community-based settings as delivery sites.[49] As prekindergarten programs expand, the issue is not whether they substitute for child care but rather how the two can be coordinated and integrated. Given that the most ambitious prekindergarten proposals rarely involve more than two years of classroom setting or full-year, full-day programming, policymakers necessarily must address how to ensure that safe, healthy, developmentally appropriate settings are available and afford-

able to families during the years and times when children are not in prekindergarten settings.

The third related objection may be that the proposed costs are too high, given other pressing national priorities. As noted, the benefits of the proposal would be substantial, and encouraging greater and more stable

---

Although it is difficult to estimate reliably the extent to which enhanced capacity to purchase care would translate into higher-quality care, there is reason to believe the proposal would further that goal, too.

---

labor force participation while advancing school readiness and child well-being could yield important long-run savings. It is difficult to see how to bring down costs substantially other than by doing less—for example, assisting fewer families or reducing spending per family. Another way to reduce costs would be to limit implementation to a demonstration project in a set of states or to restructure the proposal as a state option. For example, states that agreed to meet its terms could qualify for open-ended federal matching funds for implementation. A demonstration program could provide lessons about costs, participation, and behavioral effects, but would delay implementation of national policy, perhaps by five to ten years. Providing for a state option could let the political process work in each state and allow for grad-

Mark Greenberg

ual national implementation but could result in even greater inequities than there are in the current structure.

Finally, just as the proposal may be criticized for doing too much, it may also be criticized for not doing enough. If the guarantee were limited to families with incomes below 200 percent of poverty, families with higher incomes would have only modest tax-based assistance despite their high child care costs. The proposed expansion of the CDCTC will still pay only a small fraction of the costs that many families face. The guarantee framework and expanded funding for the Early Care and Education Strategy Fund may be far short of what is needed for supply-building and quality-improvement activities. Phasing out direct subsidy assistance at 200 percent of poverty still results in a significant loss of assistance for many families as their income reaches and exceeds the cutoff; providing a refundable tax credit reduces but does not eliminate the severity of that loss.

I agree that the proposal falls short of fully addressing many concerns about the affordability, accessibility, and quality of care for low- and moderate-income families. It seeks to strike a set of balances, but if additional funding were available it would be possible to do more to address these concerns. As to coordinating subsidy and tax policy, there is an inherent tension because subsidy assistance is based on a percentage of family income and tax credits are based on a percentage of costs. The gulf between the two will be greatest for families that receive the greatest benefit from subsidies—that is, those in high-cost areas, with younger children, or with several children. This proposal does not solve the problem, though it does move toward a better-coordinated national framework.[50]

Conclusion: Toward a National Child Care Strategy

In the period leading up to enactment of the Deficit Reduction Act of 2005, congressional discussion of child care policy was largely limited to disputes about whether the "right" level for additional block grant funding was zero, $1 billion, or another figure. Much of the discussion was confined to the estimated costs of meeting work participation requirements for TANF recipients. The national debate about next steps for child care policy should be broader, beginning with a shared vision of good child care choices for all families. To turn that vision into reality, it is important to focus on how to ensure that all families have access to child care assistance with good choices of care available as the nation moves toward developing a more comprehensive framework of early care and education. A low-income guarantee, a federal Early Care and Education Strategy Fund, and expanded tax assistance for all families could bring us closer to that goal.

Notes

1. In this article, "low-income" refers to having income below 200 percent of the official poverty line, and "poor" refers to having income below 100 percent of the poverty line. In 2005, among the 13.5 million families with related children under age eighteen and incomes below 200 percent of poverty, 84 percent reported some work during the year, and 56 percent had at least one full-time year-round worker. Analysis drawn from U.S. Bureau of the Census, Current Population Survey, *Families with Related Children under 18 by Number of Working Family Members and Family Structure*, 2005, Annual Demographic Survey, Annual Social and Economic Supplement POV07 (2006), pubdb3.census.gov/macro/032006/pov/new07_200_01.htm (August 31, 2006).

2. In 2005, among the 5.7 million poor families with related children under eighteen, 68 percent reported some work during the year and 30 percent had at least one full-time year-round worker. Analysis drawn from Bureau of the Census, Current Population Survey (see note 1).

3. The share of poor children with a full-time, year-round working parent grew from 19.9 percent in 1992 to 35.4 percent in 2000; the share was 32.1 percent in 2005. Velma W. Burke, Thomas Gabe, and Gene Falk, *Children in Poverty: Profile, Trends and Issues*, Report for Congress RL32682 (Congressional Research Service, updated January 16, 2007).

4. In 2002, according to the Survey of Income and Program Participation (SIPP), among working families with employed mothers and children under age fifteen, 28 percent of low-income families paid for care, compared with 39 percent of families that were not low-income. Among those paying for care, low-income families paid an average of $68 a week, representing 15 percent of their incomes; in contrast, higher-income families paid $104, representing only 6.5 percent of their incomes. U.S. Bureau of the Census, *Who's Minding the Kids? Child Care Arrangements: Winter 2002* (October 2005); and detailed tables available at www.census.gov/population/www/socdemo/child/ppl-177.html (August 3, 2006). For concerns and cautions about the use of SIPP child care data, see Douglas J. Besharov, Jeffrey S. Morrow, and Anne Fengyan Shi, "Child Care Data in the Survey of Income and Program Participation (SIPP): Inaccuracies and Corrections" (Welfare Reform Academy, University of Maryland, 2006). Data from the 1999 National Survey of America's Families (NSAF) show higher percentages of families paying for care than those from SIPP; like SIPP, they show that lower-income families pay less, but a higher share of their incomes, for care. According to 1999 NSAF data, 42 percent of low-income families paid for child care, compared with 51 percent of higher-income families. Low-income families paid an average of $53.54 weekly, representing 14 percent of their incomes; in contrast, higher-income families paid $76.38, representing only 7 percent of their incomes. Among the 38 percent of poor families with child care expenses, the average expense was $52.39 a week, an average of 18 percent of parental earnings. See Linda Giannerelli, Sarah Adelman, and Stephanie Schmidt, *Getting Help with Child Care Expenses* (Washington: Urban Institute, 2003).

5. See National Center for Education Statistics, *Child Care and Early Education Arrangements of Infants, Toddlers, and Preschoolers: 2001* (U.S. Department of Education, November 2005), table 6-B.

6. Assistant Secretary for Planning and Evaluation, Office of Human Services, "Child Care Eligibility and Enrollment Estimates for Fiscal Year 2003," Policy Issue Brief (April 2005).

7. U.S. Department of Health and Human Services News, *New Statistics Show Only Small Percentage of Families Receive Child Care Help* (December 6, 2000); Jennifer Mezey, Mark Greenberg, and Rachel

Schumacher, *The Vast Majority of Federally-Eligible Children Did Not Receive Child Care Assistance in FY 2000* (Washington: Center for Law and Social Policy, 2002).

8. See studies summarized in Hannah Matthews, *Child Care Assistance Helps Families Work: A Review of the Effects of Subsidy Receipt on Employment* (Washington: Center for Law and Social Policy, 2006).

9. Stephanie A. Schaefer, J. Lee Kreader, and Ann M. Collins, *Parent Employment and the Use of Child Care Subsidies: Literature Review* (Child Care and Early Education Research Connections, April 2006). See also David Blau, "Child Care Subsidy Programs," in *Means-Tested Transfer Programs in the United States,* edited by Robert A. Moffitt (University of Chicago Press and National Bureau of Economic Research, 2003), pp. 443–516; Rachel Connelly and Jean Kimmel, *The Effect of Child Care Costs on the Labor Force Participation and Welfare Recipiency of Single Mothers: Implications for Welfare Reform* (Kalamazoo, Mich.: W. E. Upjohn Institute, rev. March 2001); Matthews, *Child Care Assistance* (see note 8).

10. Isabel Sawhill and Adam Thomas, *A Hand Up for the Bottom Third: Toward a New Agenda for Low-Income Working Families* (Brookings, May 2001).

11. National Academies, *Working Families and Growing Kids* (Washington, 2003), p. 135, and p. 64, citing Joan Lombardi, *Time to Care: Redesigning Child Care to Promote Education, Support Families, and Build Communities* (Temple University, 2003).

12. National Academies, *Working Families and Growing Kids* (see note 11), p. 4.

13. For an overview of determinants of child care quality, see J. Lee Kreader, Daniel Ferguson, and Sharmila Lawrence, *Infant and Toddler Child Care Quality*, Research-to-Policy Connections 2 (New York: National Center for Children in Poverty, August 2005). For more on why higher-quality care tends to be more expensive and out of the reach of lower-income families, see Linda Giannerelli and James Barsimantov, *Child Care Expenses of America's Families* (Washington: Urban Institute, 2000); Karen Schulman and Gina Adams, *The High Cost of Child Care Puts Quality Care out of Reach for Many Families* (Washington: Children's Defense Fund, 1998); and National Academies, *Working Families and Growing Kids* (see note 11), pp. 56–63. Accredited child care facilities often "can cost as much as $5,000 more a year than non-accredited care"; National Association of Child Care Resource and Referral Agencies (NACCRRA), *Breaking the Piggy Bank: Parents and the High Price of Child Care* (Arlington, Va., 2006).

14. In one set of recent focus groups, more than two-thirds of parents mentioned cost as a primary concern when choosing child care arrangements; NACCRRA, *Breaking the Piggy Bank* (see note 13).

15. Ellen S. Peisner-Feinberg and others, *The Children of the Cost, Quality, and Outcomes Study Go to School: Executive Summary* (University of North Carolina at Chapel Hill, June 1999). For an overview of research on the effects of quality early child care on children, including upon entering school, see National Academies, *Working Families and Growing Kids* (see note 11), pp. 105–22.

16. Deborah Lowe Vandell and Barbara Wolfe, *Child Care Quality: Does It Matter and Does It Need to Be Improved?* (University of Wisconsin, Institute for Research on Poverty, November 2000).

17. Peisner-Feinberg and others, *The Children of the Cost, Quality, and Outcomes Study Go to School* (see note 15).

18. National Academies, *Working Families and Growing Kids* (see note 11), p. 134.

19. On the benefits to poor children, see E. S. Peisner-Feinberg and others, *The Children of the Cost, Quality, and Outcomes Study Go to School* (see note 15). A British study of preschool attendance found that "for the most disadvantaged groups . . . the experience of longer duration and higher quality is likely to be particularly important in reducing the social class attainment gap, although it can be seen that all SES groups show significant benefit from attending pre-school in relation to attainment in Reading and Mathematics." Kathy Sylva and others, *Social Class Differences in the Effects of Pre-School on Children's Academic Performance at Age 7* (University of London, November 2005).

20. Jeffrey Capizzano and Gina Adams, *Children in Low-Income Families Are Less Likely to Be in Center-Based Child Care* (Washington: Urban Institute, November 2003). Also, lower-income employed mothers with children from birth to age five are less likely to use child care centers than higher-income mothers. National Academies, *Working Families and Growing Kids* (see note 11), p. 44. Fifty eight percent of children receiving Child Care and Development Fund subsidies participate in center-based care arrangements. U.S. Department of Health and Human Services, "FFY 2005 CCDF Data Tables (Preliminary Estimates)," www.acf.hhs.gov/programs/ccb/data/ccdf_data/05acf800/table3.htm. A study comparing children receiving subsidies for child care with those on waiting lists found that the former were more likely to be in a formal licensed child care center. It also found that subsidies for low-income mothers seem to result in "more stable care, ease of finding care, and satisfaction with care [which] suggest that subsidy mothers were less psychologically stressed about child care issues compared to mothers on waiting lists." Fred Brooks, "Impacts of Child Care Subsidies on Family and Child Well-Being," *Early Childhood Research Quarterly* 17 (2002): 498–511.

21. The Government Accountability Office (GAO) has reported that "sixty-nine federal programs provided or supported education and care for children under age 5 in fiscal year 1999." However, the GAO found that of $9 billion in nontax spending identified in its report, $8 billion came from three sources: the Child Care and Development Block Grant, the Temporary Assistance for Needy Families Block Grant, and the Head Start Program. U.S. Government Accountability Office, *Early Education and Care: Overlap Indicates Need to Assess Crosscutting Programs*, GAO/HEHS-00-78 (April 2000); for an update finding that the number of programs remained at sixty-nine in 2005, see U.S. Government Accountability Office, *Update on Prekindergarten Care and Education Programs*, GAO-05-678R (June 2, 2005). Although the present article emphasizes the importance of coordinating Head Start and child care, it does not treat Head Start as a federal child care program, since the principal purpose of Head Start is to promote the school readiness of low-income children without regard to their parents' work status or need for child care.

22. Office of Management and Budget, *Analytical Perspectives, Budget of the United States of America, Fiscal Year 2007* (2006).

23. Leonard Burman, Elaine Maag, and Jeffrey Rohaly, *Tax Subsidies to Help Low-Income Families Pay for Child Care* (Washington: Urban-Brookings Tax Policy Center, June 2005).

24. Office of Management and Budget, *Analytical Perspectives* (see note 22).

25. Another small ($10 million) provision lets employers claim a tax credit of up to 25 percent of qualified expenses for employee child care and 10 percent of qualified expenses for child care resource and referral services, up to $150,000 a year.

26. Mark Greenberg, Joan Lombardi, and Rachel Schumacher, *The Child Care and Development Fund: An Overview* (Washington: Center for Law and Social Policy, June 2000).

27. Annual federal CCDF funding (not counting transferred TANF funds) grew from $2.2 billion in 1996 to $4.8 billion in 2002 but then remained flat until it was increased to $5 billion in the Deficit Reduction Act of 2005. Combined TANF transfers and direct spending peaked at $4 billion in 2000 and declined to $3.2 billion in 2005. Hannah Matthews and Danielle Ewen, *Child Care Assistance in 2004: States Have Fewer Funds for Child Care* (Washington: Center for Law and Social Policy, 2005); analysis of FY 2005 CCDF and TANF use of funds by Center for Law and Social Policy.

28. Burman, Maag, and Rohaly, *Tax Subsidies to Help Low-Income Families* (see note 23).

29. U.S. Government Accountability Office, *Child Care: Recent State Policy Changes Affecting the Availability of Assistance for Low-Income Families,* GAO 03-588 (May 2003); U.S. Government Accountability Office, *Child Care: Additional Information Is Needed on Working Families Receiving Subsidies,* GAO-05-667 (June 2005).

30. Except as noted, data on cross-state policy variation are drawn from Karen Schulman and Helen Blank, *State Child Care Assistance Policies 2006: Gaps Remain, with New Challenges Ahead* (Washington: National Women's Law Center, September 2006).

31. Child Care Bureau, "FY 2005 CCDF Data Tables, Preliminary Estimates," table 17, www.acf.hhs.gov/programs/ccb/data/ccdf_data/05acf800/table17.htm.

32. H. M. Treasury, *Pre-Budget Report 2003: The Strength to Take the Long-Term Decisions for Britain: Seizing the Opportunities of the Global Recovery* (London, 2003).

33. Burman, Maag, and Rohaly, *Tax Subsidies to Help Low-Income Families* (see note 23).

34. See H. M. Treasury, *Choice for Parents, the Best Start for Children: A Ten Year Strategy for Childcare* (London, December 2004).

35. Child Care Bureau, "FY 2005 CCDF Data Tables, Preliminary Estimates," table 15, www.acf.hhs.gov/programs/ccb/data/ccdf_data/05acf800/table15.htm.

36. NACCRRA, *Breaking the Piggy Bank* (see note 13).

37. See, for example, Lily L. Batchelder, Fred L., Goldberg Jr., and Peter Orszag, *Reforming Tax Incentives into Uniform Refundable Tax Credits* (Brookings, August 2006).

38. See National Child Care Information Center, "Child Care and Development Fund Report of State Plans FY 2006–2007," sec. 3.5.3, www.nccic.org/pubs/stateplan2006-07/part3.pdf.

39. See discussion in Gina Adams and Monica Rohacek, "More than a Work Support? Issues around Integrating Child Development Goals into the Child Care Subsidy System," *Early Childhood Research Quarterly* 17 (2002): 418–40.

40. Child Care Bureau, *Quality Rating Systems and the Impact on Quality in Early Care and Education Settings* (U.S. Department of Health and Human Services, 2005); National Child Care Information Center, *Quality Rating Systems and the Impact on Quality in Early Care and Education Settings* (Fairfax, Va., November 2006).

41. In 2005 states spent a reported $920 million on a range of program quality activities. See U.S. Department of Health and Human Services, "2005 CCDF State Expenditure Data," www.acf.hhs.gov/programs/ccb/data/expenditures/05acf696/fy05_overview_allyears.htm.

42. Under current law, in addition to providing subsidies, states can use child care block grant dollars for activities to provide consumer education, increase parental choice, and improve the quality and availability of child care. Activities can include resource and referral efforts, helping providers meet health and safety and other standards, improving the monitoring of compliance with and enforcement of standards, providing training and technical assistance to providers, and improving salaries and other compensation for child care staff. *Code of Federal Regulations*, vol. 45, sec. 98.51. There is an additional set of earmarked quality-related funds.

43. Janet Gornick and Marcia Meyers, *Families That Work: Policies for Reconciling Parenthood and Employment* (New York: Russell Sage Foundation, 2003).

44. Administration for Children and Families, *Preliminary Findings from the Early Head Start Prekindergarten Follow-Up* (U.S. Department of Health and Human Services, April 2006).

45. W. Steve Barnett and others, *The State of Preschool: 2005 State Preschool Yearbook* (National Institute for Early Education Research, 2005).

46. Afterschool Alliance, *21st Century Community Learning Centers: A Foundation for Progress* (2006).

47. The recommendation is described in Center for American Progress Task Force on Poverty, *From Poverty to Prosperity: A National Strategy to Cut Poverty in Half* (Washington, 2007). The details of the Urban Institute's modeling are presented in Linda Giannerelli, Laura Wheaton, and Joyce Morton, *Estimating the Anti-Poverty Effects of Changes in Taxes and Benefits with TRIM3* (Washington: Urban Institute, 2007).

48. The research finds positive effects of child care subsidies on employment, but does not provide a consistent picture of the size of the effect. See, for example, Erdal Tekin, "Child Care Subsidies, Wages, and Employment of Single Mothers" (Georgia State University, August 2005), which finds that a 50 percent reduction in the cost of child care would result in a 3.8 percentage point increase, and 5.4 percent increase, in employment among single mothers; Bong Joo Lee and others, *Child Care Subsidy Use and Employment Outcomes of TANF Mothers during the Early Years of Welfare Reform: A Three-State Study* (Chapin Hall Center for Children at the University of Chicago, September 2004), which finds that among single mothers who were receiving TANF or who had recently left TANF during the early years of welfare reform (1997–99), child care subsidies increased employment retention over a two-year study period by 25 to 43 percent, depending on the state; Sandra K. Danziger, Elizabeth Oltmans Ananat, and Kimberly G. Browning, "Child Care Subsidies and the Transition from Welfare to Work," Working Paper 03-11 (National Poverty Center, 2003), which finds that families leaving welfare with child care subsidies had twice as many months of work as those who had not used care and nearly 15 percent more than those who used unsubsidized care; Fred Brooks and others, "Impacts of Child Care Subsidies on Family and Child Well-Being," *Early Childhood Research Quarterly* 17 (2002): 498–511, which compares subsidy recipients among the working poor with those on a waiting list, controlling for numerous factors, and finds an 18 percentage point difference in employment rates among the two groups just a few months after applying for subsidies; David Blau and Erdal Tekin, "The Determinants and Consequences of Child Care Subsidy Receipt by Low-Income Families," in *The Incentives of Government Programs and the Well-Being of Families*, edited by Bruce Meyer and Greg Duncan (Chicago and Evanston, Ill.: Joint Center for Poverty Research, January 2001), which calculates that among single mothers with a child under age thirteen, "subsidy recipients were about 2.5 percentage points more likely to be employed than nonrecipients, and about 5 percentage points more likely to be employed after controlling for a small set of family characteristics."

49. Rachel Schumacher and others, *All Together Now: State Experiences in Using Community-Based Child Care to Provide Prekindergarten* (Washington: Center for Law and Social Policy, 2005).

50. For an examination of the relationship between subsidy phase-outs and tax credit phase-ins based on the law and policies in effect at that time, see Thomas Gabe, Bob Lyke, and Karen Spar, *Child Care Subsidies: Federal Grants and Tax Benefits for Working Families,* Report for Congress RL30081 (Congresional Research Service, 1999).

A Health Plan to Reduce Poverty

Alan Weil

Summary
Noting that the failures of the U.S. health care system are compounding the problems faced by low-income Americans, Alan Weil argues that any strategy to reduce poverty must provide access to health care for all low-income families.

Although nearly all children in families with incomes under 200 percent of poverty are eligible for either Medicaid or the State Children's Health Insurance Program (SCHIP), the parents of poor children often lack health insurance. Parents who leave welfare normally get a year of coverage but then lose coverage unless their employer provides it, and many employers of low-wage workers do not offer health insurance. Similarly, parents who take low-paying jobs to avoid welfare usually have no coverage at all. This lack of coverage discourages adults from working and may also affect the health of children because adults without health insurance are less likely to take their children for preventive care.

Weil proposes creating a federal earned income health credit (EIHC) and redefining the federal floor of coverage through Medicaid and SCHIP. His aim is to make health insurance affordable for low-income families and to make sure enough options are available that individuals and families can get coverage using a combination of their own, their employer's, and public resources.

Weil would expand Medicaid eligibility to include all families whose income falls below the poverty line. The EIHC would be a refundable tax credit that would be available to parents during the year in advance of filing a tax return. The credit, which would be based on taxpayer earnings and family structure, would phase in as earnings increase, reach a plateau, and then phase out farther up the income scale. The credit would be larger for families with dependents. The EIHC would function seamlessly with the employee payroll withholding system. It would be available only to adults who demonstrate that they had health insurance coverage during the year and, for adults with children, only if their eligible dependent children were enrolled in either a private or public insurance program.

Weil's proposal would cover individuals who receive coverage from their employer and those who do not. The proposal smooths transitions from public to private coverage, and it anticipates a substantial role for states. Weil estimates that his policy would cost about $45 billion a year.

www.futureofchildren.org

Alan Weil is the executive director of the National Academy for State Health Policy.

Alan Weil

The many failures of the American health care system have badly exacerbated the financial and health-related hardship that low-income Americans face. Any comprehensive strategy to reduce poverty and improve the well-being of lower-income working families must include substantial changes in the way the nation pays for health care. Indeed one could argue that absent health care reform the United States is unlikely to undertake the many other important steps necessary to reduce poverty.

The Price of Health System Failures

Low-income Americans pay the price of health system failures in three ways. They pay through poor health and premature death, through personal financial hardship, and through lost opportunities for productive public investments that could improve their future prospects.

Health Consequences

The health of low-income Americans suffers because health insurance is not universally available. Of the more than 46 million nonelderly Americans without health insurance in 2005, 65 percent had family income at or below 200 percent of the federal poverty level ($39,942 for a family of four in 2005). An additional 16 percent of the uninsured had income between 200 and 300 percent of the federal poverty level.[1]

The importance of health insurance to good health has been well established. Although it is true that emergency care is available to all Americans, other types of care—preventive care, services that help people manage chronic conditions, diagnostic tests, and highly specialized care—are all hard to obtain without health insurance. Researchers

have found that people who lack health insurance are less likely to get preventive care and services for chronic and acute conditions, even after personal characteristics (such as health status and education) that affect use of care, are taken into account. Again, taking into account these measurable differences between the populations, analysts find that the uninsured are sicker, more likely to suffer from chronic conditions, and more likely to die younger than people with health insurance.[2] And the consequences of a lack of insurance extend beyond the individual to burden entire families and communities.[3]

In an effort to contain the rising cost of health insurance, many employers have increased the deductibles and copayments in the coverage they provide their employees. Although these cost-sharing strategies reduce the premiums employers must pay, a growing body of research shows that they cause lower-income employees and their dependents to forgo necessary care, yielding negative health consequences, particularly for those trying to manage chronic conditions.[4] Recent efforts to encourage people to purchase high-deductible insurance plans and to use health savings accounts to cover the deductibles also place lower-wage workers at risk. Fourteen percent of those with high-deductible plans have no funds in their health savings account, and another 16 percent have less than $200.[5] The combination of high deductibles and depleted health savings accounts will lead to even more care forgone than the incremental increases in cost sharing that face other Americans.

Financial Consequences

Good health—one's own and one's family's—is a precursor to adequate earnings. People in fair or poor health have average earnings far below those who report that their health is good or excellent.[6] Of course, poor health is both a cause and consequence of having low income, but good health care may offer a path to better health and higher earnings. The time required to care for a family member with a debilitating disease or a chronic condition makes it hard to work enough hours to earn one's way out of poverty. Having health insurance reduces the likelihood that a person leaving welfare will return to the rolls.[7]

Low-income Americans pay a heavy financial price for the nation's ailing health care system even when they are insured. Those who have insurance have a degree of financial protection, but the rising cost of coverage has made family budgets much tighter over recent decades. Between 2000 and 2005, median family income grew a total of 11 percent, from $50,732 to $56,194, with an annual growth rate of just over 2 percent.[8] During that same period, typical family insurance premiums rose almost 70 percent, from $6,200 to $10,400, with an annual growth rate of 11 percent.[9] Most economists believe that even though employers appear to subsidize their employees' health insurance, employees ultimately bear the cost through lower wages. If the money employers paid for more costly health insurance premiums had gone instead to workers' wages, median family income could have risen to as much as $60,400, an average annual growth rate of 3.5 percent—one and three-quarters times the 2 percent rate families experienced.

Even when Americans at the lower end of the income scale have insurance, they may find themselves "underinsured." Sixteen million people, or 9 percent, among those aged nineteen to sixty-four, have health insurance but are considered underinsured because they have inadequate financial protection

against high health costs.[10] Underinsurance is most prevalent among those with incomes below 200 percent of poverty.[11] People with inadequate insurance may gain access to services, but at the cost of substantial financial hardship in the event of an illness or injury.

The financial burdens associated with health care are greatest for those without insurance.

Low-income Americans pay a heavy financial price for the nation's ailing health care system even when they are insured.

When confronted with illness they often pay the highest prices for services because they do not benefit from the negotiated discounts available to group payers.[12] If they are unable to pay, collection agency reports will harm their credit ratings, forcing them to pay higher interest rates when borrowing for other purchases. Ultimately they may face bankruptcy.

Lost Opportunities
Rising costs for Medicaid and Medicare have limited federal and state options for spending on other public priorities. The share of state general fund spending consumed by Medicaid increased from 15.1 to 16.2 percent between 1999 and 2003.[13] The combined federal cost of Medicare and Medicaid rose from 18.6 to 20.1 percent of total federal outlays over the same period (from $317 billion to $435 billion).[14] Given policymakers' reluctance to increase taxes, these trends have tightened public spending in other areas.

Long-term projections of Medicaid and Medicare cost growth have contributed to the sense that Americans cannot afford additional investments in antipoverty programs because they seem unable to afford the programs they already have. Congressional Budget Office projections over the next few decades are particularly gloomy. In the absence of policy changes that control these costs it is almost impossible to imagine government making major new investments in anything else.[15]

Goals of an Antipoverty Health Plan

In this article I set forth a proposal to meet the health care needs of low-income families. In view of the dozens of health care reform proposals already in circulation, some readers may wonder what yet another proposal can contribute. My aim is to place health reforms in the context of broader antipoverty policies, thus raising a somewhat different set of questions and considerations than those typically at the center of health policy discussions.

When putting together a reform proposal, health policy analysts generally begin with the goal of extending health insurance coverage to new populations or making health insurance coverage universal. They then impose a set of values related to issues such as patient choice or the role of government, along with assumptions (drawing on the available data) about such matters as the effects of regulations or financial incentives on individual and organizational behavior. The result is a proposal that meets health care–related objectives while adhering to certain values.

My proposal begins with a purely financial goal: to ensure access to health care services and provide financial protection to low-income families so they can work and devote

their energies to the other tasks necessary for them to improve their financial and overall well-being. My proposal explicitly avoids (to the extent possible) some of the larger philosophical or ideological concerns that dominate health policy debates—taking as a given that Americans are closely divided on matters such as the appropriate role of government. Put differently, my proposal is by design politically incremental. It seeks to build on existing public and private coverage, not replace one with the other or fundamentally alter the nature of either.

What do low-income families need from health policy? At the most basic level they need affordable insurance that provides meaningful access to necessary health care services and financial protection against the burdens of illness and injury. But for health policy to meet a broader range of needs for low-income families, it must meet an additional challenge, one that generally receives less attention in policy discussions. Families need an effective range and ladder of options that meet changes in their circumstances without substantial disruption and without creating perverse financial incentives. For example, a young woman may be covered under her parents' insurance policy, lose that coverage on her nineteenth birthday, go to work for a small firm that does not offer coverage, become eligible for Medicaid when she becomes pregnant, and then lose coverage after the child is born. An effective health policy would bridge these gaps in coverage, providing continuity for the young woman without creating disincentives to work.

Current Policy Fails Working Families
High cost is the primary reason that health insurance is out of reach for so many working families. Yet many other aspects of the health

care system also make getting and keeping coverage difficult.

Most Americans get health insurance through the workplace. Although employer-sponsored insurance (ESI) is more widely available at higher income levels, it plays a major role throughout the income spectrum. Eighty-six percent of nonelderly people with incomes four times the poverty level or higher have ESI, but even 39 percent of people with incomes between 100 and 200 percent of poverty do also.[16]

Employers have complete discretion over whether to offer coverage, how much to subsidize the coverage, and the terms of that coverage.[17] Under federal law, states may not require employers to provide coverage.[18] Employer decisions vary by firm size, sector, average employee wage, and region of the country. Smaller firms are more likely to offer less generous policies that place a heavier financial burden on employees.

One-third of young adults aged eighteen to twenty-four are uninsured.[19] Among the next older group, adults aged twenty-five to thirty-four, 27 percent are uninsured.[20] Young families have relatively low incomes, which means they are less likely to have health insurance through their job. In the eighteen to twenty-four age group, only 47 percent have work-based insurance; the figure falls to 42 percent for those with only a high school diploma.[21]

Employer-sponsored insurance has become less prevalent over time. Employers gain tax advantages, as well as competitive advantages when hiring, if they provide health insurance coverage. But for many employers, especially smaller firms, these advantages are not enough to offset the cost of providing coverage. Data from 2005 show that although 98 percent of firms with 200 or more employees offer health insurance, only 59 percent of firms with 3 to 199 employees offer coverage—down from 68 percent in 2000.[22] The share of all workers in small firms who get insurance through their job fell from 57 percent to 50 percent between 2000 and 2005.[23] Thus any effort to fill in the gaps in employer-sponsored insurance must fight a strong tide.

Federal tax policy also works against low-income families. Workplace-based health insurance benefits are tax-exempt for the employer and the employee. The relatively low marginal tax rates for lower-wage workers mean that they receive smaller federal subsidies than higher-wage workers, even when their insurance benefits are identical. One study estimates that the tax benefits associated with employer-sponsored insurance, which totaled more than $188 billion in 2004, were heavily weighted toward the more affluent. Workers with family incomes greater than $100,000—14 percent of the population—received 26.7 percent of the benefit, while those with incomes less than $50,000—57.5 percent of the population—received only 28.4 percent.[24]

Although Medicaid and the State Children's Health Insurance Program (SCHIP) covered 46.5 million people in June of 2005, coverage varies substantially across states and by family structure.[25] Eligibility for public insurance is often on an individual basis—and extends much farther up the income scale for children than for adults. Through a combination of Medicaid and SCHIP, most states cover all children in families with income up to 200 percent of the federal poverty level; eight states do not extend eligibility that high and thirteen go higher. Eligibility for parents is quite variable, with many states capping eligibility at a small fraction of the poverty level, although some cover parents with incomes as high as two or three times the poverty level. States cannot cover adults without children (unless they are disabled) through Medicaid at all without a waiver; only a few states have gotten such waivers, and they rarely cover adults with incomes above the poverty line.

This complex, patchwork system . . . creates perverse incentives as families are forced to trade off decisions that might improve their earnings against decisions that will allow them to keep their insurance.

By contrast, private employer-sponsored health plans are sold to subscribers—that is, to employees. Subscribers can then choose to cover their dependents (a spouse and children), but the dependents cannot get coverage through the workplace without the subscriber. It is possible for the children in a family to be covered by Medicaid or SCHIP and the working adult to have a substantial employer-provided subsidy for coverage and therefore be able to buy insurance for one, but if family coverage is out of reach, the spouse may be uninsured. Many other combinations of public, private, and uninsured status within a family are possible.

This complex, patchwork system not only leaves many working families without health insurance, it also creates perverse incentives as families are forced to trade off decisions

that might improve their earnings against decisions that will allow them to keep their insurance. Medicaid offers the most dramatic example. Every state has a family income eligibility threshold for Medicaid. A person whose income exceeds that standard loses Medicaid coverage but is still likely to be in an income range where employer-sponsored insurance is only occasionally available. With a family insurance policy costing in excess of $10,000, the effective tax on the earnings that exceed the threshold is tremendous. The need to pay such a price for the increased earnings can serve as a strong work disincentive, or at best a severe penalty for advancing in a career.

State and federal policy reduce the size of the penalty in four ways. First, federal law provides for transitional Medicaid, which extends benefits for six or twelve months, depending upon the circumstances, when a person's income rises above the Medicaid eligibility threshold. But this benefit, which is underutilized, merely delays the penalty and does nothing to smooth the transition to private coverage. Second, federal law gives states the option of developing "medically needy" programs that allow people with incomes above the Medicaid threshold who incur substantial health costs to become eligible for assistance after they have "spent down" their excess resources. As of 2003, thirty-six states had elected this option. But although spend-down programs benefit those with substantial health costs, they do nothing to help low-income workers afford insurance coverage. Third, federal law and state choices have combined to increase the family income threshold for children's eligibility for public insurance beyond that for their parents. Thus, as a parent's income increases, the parent may lose coverage while the child retains it. Providing insurance for children reduces the effective marginal tax rate, but also means that families have some uninsured members and does little to facilitate a transition to private coverage.[26]

Finally, more than a dozen states have adopted "premium assistance" programs in their Medicaid or SCHIP programs, or both, to cover the employee's share of the cost of an employer-sponsored plan. Despite great effort on the part of many states, most of these programs are quite small, and a variety of barriers impede their success. The most difficult to overcome are the limited availability of employer-sponsored insurance among the lower-income population, the challenges of engaging the small-business community in delivering a public benefit, and the need to ensure that participants in the premium assistance program have adequate coverage through a combination of their employer-sponsored insurance and any available wraparound services the state may need to provide. Although premium assistance programs provide a valuable benefit to participants, families still face a large financial burden once they lose their Medicaid or SCHIP eligibility and must pay their share of premium costs on their own.

The Advantages of Universal Coverage

Health policy analysts gravitate toward universal coverage strategies when describing reforms to the health care system. Leading policy analysts on both the right and the left of the political spectrum have developed coherent, rational universal coverage proposals that essentially scrap the current patchwork of coverage and replace it with something universal that fits with their values and views of the appropriate roles of government and individuals.[27]

Universal coverage plans can readily meet the various needs of low-income families. They ensure coverage for all, rely on financing systems that are equitable, and eliminate eligibility threshold penalties and perverse incentives. Indeed, many universal coverage proposals achieve their goals at a substantially lower "per person newly covered" cost than incremental expansions can.

Despite the advantages of universal coverage, however, the current political environment is more hospitable to incremental coverage expansions. After all, the corollary to designing a rational system is the need to unravel the many irrational aspects of the current system which, despite its many flaws, meets the needs of many Americans and serves as an engine for economic growth and profits. Doing so would arouse substantial resistance from those who are happy with the current system. Although my proposal is not as ambitious as some would prefer, it is designed to meet the key objective of improving access to health care for low-income Americans.

Requirements for an Incremental Expansion

For an incremental program to meet the needs of low-income families it must address three core problems in the current system: transitions, disincentives to work, and the lack of horizontal equity—that is, similar treatment of all people who are similarly situated.

A reformed system must allow for smooth transitions, particularly from public to private coverage as a person's earnings and job quality improve. Public programs ensure comprehensive benefits with very limited cost sharing. When they charge premiums, these are the same regardless of the health status of enrollees. Public programs have public oversight and consumer protection to a degree not generally found in private health insurance. Private coverage provides a range of choices and opportunities for innovation. The higher provider payment rates that prevail in private insurance yield a broader range of networks and sites of care. The terms of coverage, however, are quite variable, and individuals or small firms may face high premiums because of age or poor health. The challenge for public policy is to bridge the gaps between these systems.

An effective policy must also minimize disincentives to work. Public subsidies for health insurance coverage, however, necessarily pose a substantial risk of such disincentives. In 2005 a typical health plan for a single employee cost $4,025, and family coverage ran $10,880.[28] If, for example, a reform proposal posits that a family should pay no more than 10 percent of its income for health insurance, then even a family earning $100,000 would require a subsidy to purchase family coverage. Subsidies reaching that income level are hard to imagine. A more realistic upper bound for receiving a subsidy is median family income, which was about $56,200 in 2005.[29]

Meanwhile, most health reform proposals start with the premise that people with income below poverty cannot afford to contribute at all to the cost of their coverage. If a benefit worth $10,000 is provided at no cost to a family with $20,000 annual income and is phased out completely at around $60,000 family income, the effective marginal tax rate associated with the phase-out is quite steep, at 25 percent ($10,000 ÷ [$60,000 – $20,000]). This high effective tax rate is particularly worrisome when viewed in conjunction with the effects of the phasing out of other benefits. In an effort to "make work pay," policymakers in 1996 combined welfare reform with a series of work supports that supplement wages when parents first go to work, but phase out slightly farther up the income scale.[30] If health benefits are phased out in the

same range as the work supports—income supplements, child care subsidies, and housing subsidies—are also phasing out, the financial benefit of additional work can become quite limited. Work disincentives cannot be eliminated in a targeted program, but they should be kept as small as possible.

Finally, an effective policy for low-income families must stress horizontal equity over target efficiency.[31] Although 33 percent of nonelderly people with family incomes below twice the poverty level are uninsured, 26 percent of people in that category have private coverage through their work.[32] A targeted program would deliver subsidies only to those who "need" them—the uninsured—while doing nothing for the 26 percent who are struggling to afford their share of the premium or who have taken lower-paying jobs to obtain a health benefit. Penalizing people who do the "right thing" violates fundamental notions of fairness. Indeed, the imposition of such penalties by the now-defunct Aid to Families with Dependent Children program led to the view that it was flawed and needed to be replaced through welfare reform. One recent analysis concluded that, ironically, steps designed to limit SCHIP coverage to those without access to employer-sponsored coverage block enrollment more among people without access to such coverage than among those with it.[33] Ensuring horizontal equity, however, would put a higher price tag on the proposal. Politics might dictate a less expensive program, in which case some horizontal equity may be lost. But although such a program might be easier to enact, it would be harder to sustain.

A Proposal for Improving Access to Health Care

Low-income families would benefit from a higher, federally defined floor of public coverage through Medicaid and SCHIP and a new federal earned income health credit that could be applied to the cost of coverage provided either by their state or by their employer. This combination of policies would help low-income families afford coverage while meeting the three goals of facilitating transitions across types of coverage, minimizing work disincentives, and providing equitable benefits to people who are similarly situated.

Proposal Overview

The proposal would first expand Medicaid eligibility to all people with family income below the federal poverty level and, through a combination of Medicaid and SCHIP, to all children with family income below twice the poverty level. The expansion for children would be modest—all but eight states already cover children up to or exceeding this level. The expansion for adults would be substantial. Only fourteen states and the District of Columbia cover parents living in poverty, and adults without children living with them are rarely eligible for Medicaid.[34] As is now the case with Medicaid, states would have the option of extending coverage farther up the income scale. The goal is not to make the Medicaid and SCHIP programs uniform across the country, but to create a clearly defined floor on which other sources of coverage can build.

The proposal would also create a new earned income health credit (EIHC) modeled on the well-regarded earned income tax credit (EITC).[35] The EIHC would be a refundable tax credit claimed each year on the federal tax return but, like the EITC, would be made available during the year in advance. The credit would be based on taxpayer earnings and family structure and would phase in as earnings increase, reach a plateau, and then

phase out farther up the income scale. The credit would be larger for families with dependents, reflecting the higher cost of family coverage.

The EIHC could be used in either of two distinct ways. When applied to a state-sponsored plan, it would reduce the premium that the state would otherwise bill the participant for

---

The proposal would also create a new earned income health credit (EIHC) modeled on the well-regarded earned income tax credit (EITC).

---

providing coverage. When applied to an employer-sponsored plan, it would reduce the contribution the employee would otherwise have to make to participate in the employer's plan. The amount of the credit and the mechanism for obtaining it would differ, depending on the source of the coverage. The EIHC would not be available to people who purchase insurance in the individual or nongroup market.

How the EIHC Would Work with the State Plan

All states would be required to design and implement a mechanism that enables anyone who receives the EIHC to purchase health insurance. States could meet this requirement in a variety of ways. They could open up their existing Medicaid or SCHIP programs, or both, to this new population. They could anchor the program to other groups, such as state employees. Or they could develop new entities, like the Massachusetts Connector, which was created as part of that state's recent health reforms to make subsidized insurance available to the low- and moderate-income population.[36] Whatever approach they choose, based on current practices, states are likely to contract with one or more private health insurance plans to provide the insurance. That is, the "state" insurance would generally be delivered through one or more private health plans.

Some states might develop an insurance product and make it available only to the target population of EIHC recipients. Other states might incorporate this effort into a larger initiative that markets products to small businesses or individuals whose incomes exceed the EIHC eligibility threshold. States could even consider supplementing the value of the federal EIHC with state funds to help targeted populations afford better coverage than they might otherwise be able to get.

The state insurance product would have to be community rated and guaranteed issue. That is, the price the enrollee is charged could vary by family size but not by age or health status, and no eligible applicant could be denied coverage. These requirements are essential to ensure that EIHC recipients get coverage, because the EIHC would not be any larger for older or sicker people than for those who are younger and healthy. Absent this requirement, people could find themselves with a subsidy that was too small to allow them to afford a suitable plan. In the extreme, some people with health conditions might not be able to find an insurance company that would sell them a plan at all.

The community-rating requirement adds a layer of complexity to the proposal. There is a significant risk that this new program would suffer from adverse selection—that is, it would attract those who could not get coverage elsewhere or who could get it elsewhere only at a high cost. Meanwhile, healthier, lower-cost populations would stay in the private market, where they could find lower prices. This risk has been discussed elsewhere in greater detail than is possible here.[37] In brief, the state plan is at greater risk if its rating rules differ from those in the market as a whole, if the subsidies are small, and if the program is less attractive in other respects than the broader market. These circumstances will vary from state to state. A few states already have tight rating rules similar to those that would exist for the new state product; most do not.

Ultimately, states would likely have five options to address concerns about adverse selection. First, they could examine their existing rules in the private market and bring them closer to community rating. Second, they could establish (or expand existing) high-risk pools or reinsurance mechanisms to try to segregate higher-risk populations from all markets into a separate, subsidized pool, thereby reducing the risk and burden in the state plan. Third, they could expand subsidies using state funds to reduce the potential for adverse selection. Fourth, they could open the state plan to a much larger share of the market, thereby diluting the effect of high-risk enrollees. Fifth, they could accept a certain amount of adverse selection and fund the excess risk from other resources.

How the EIHC Would Work with Employer Coverage

The EIHC would be designed to function seamlessly with the employee payroll withholding system. Employees would determine their expected credit by completing the appropriate forms. Employers would subtract the amount of the credit from the amount they withhold from each employee's paycheck and remit to the federal government as taxes. The employer would bundle the credit with employer and employee contributions in a single payment to the health plan that provides insurance to the firm's employees. This process is described more fully in two reports that have examined the implementation of a tax credit that supports employer-sponsored insurance.[38]

Beneficiaries of the federal earned income tax credit can receive the credit in advance during the year through a similar payroll credit, though less than 1 percent of those eligible take advantage of this option.[39] Ensuring that EIHC beneficiaries use the advance option will require full integration of the EIHC with not only the employer's withholding system but also the employer's open enrollment and plan selection processes. The idea is to make applying for the EIHC, calculating the credit, and participating in an employer-sponsored plan a single event.

As with the EITC, the ultimate value of the EIHC will have to be calculated on the year-end tax return. If applicants claim a larger credit during the year than they are actually owed, they will have to pay the excess back to the Internal Revenue Service when they file their tax returns. Some proponents of health insurance tax credits have suggested dropping the reconciliation aspect entirely, so as not to discourage participation. Such a step, however, might undermine the integrity of the overall approach. It would be preferable to make it very unlikely that people who accurately report their income will owe money. One option would be to calculate the credit based on monthly income and health insurance participation. If employees were able easily and quickly to report status changes, such as family size or composition, the value

of the credit could be adjusted automatically and immediately to reflect the change.

How the Value of the EIHC Would Be Established

Each tax filing unit would have two EIHC values: the maximum credit available and the credit it actually receives.[40] The maximum available credit would be calculated individually for each member of the tax filing unit and then summed to create a total value for the family. The EIHC would be available only to taxpayers who paid out of their own resources for a health insurance policy. All members of the tax filing unit would have to have coverage before the unit could claim the credit for anyone. A family whose children were eligible for and covered by Medicaid or SCHIP could claim the credit for the parents, but parents who did not secure coverage for their children would not be eligible for the credit at all. The EIHC value would be prorated on a monthly basis for those who had health insurance for a portion of the year.

The design and computation of the credit would be different for state-sponsored and employer-sponsored coverage. For state plans, the maximum and actual credits would be the same. The credit would be based on family income, with a design similar to that of the EITC. That is, the credit would phase in at 50 cents for each dollar of earned income, hit a plateau that would be sustained through the poverty level for adults and twice the poverty level for children, and then phase out to zero at three times the poverty level. The plateau would be set at 90 percent of the cost of a typical health plan, or roughly $3,600 for an adult.

The EIHC would reduce the price an enrollee pays for the public plan from its market value to a lower, subsidized level. The

Figure 1. Proposed Earned Income Health Credit

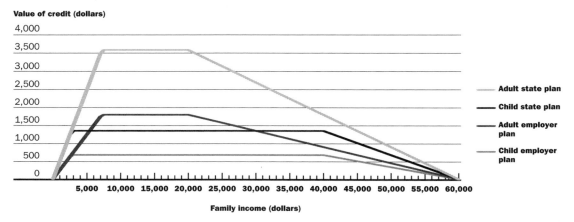

Note: Based on a federal poverty level of $20,000 for a family of four and a cost of coverage of $4,000 per adult and $1,500 per child.

plan would have a very low net price for those who receive the maximum EIHC, gradually rising to the unsubsidized amount as family income increased.

For employer-sponsored coverage, the maximum credit should be lower because most employees already receive a subsidy from their employer. Subsidies of less than 50 percent for employee-only coverage are extremely rare (only 4 percent of workers in small firms have subsidy rates this low).[41] Only 12 percent of all workers have family coverage subsidy rates lower than 50 percent, although the rate is 24 percent among workers in small firms.[42] It seems reasonable to use 50 percent as the starting point for the public subsidy as it will capture the large majority of people, whether they need individual or family coverage. Thus the maximum credit for the EIHC in employer-provided coverage would plateau at 45 percent of the cost of coverage, to reflect a 90 percent public subsidy when the employee contribution is 50 percent.

The maximum EIHC value is shown in figure 1. Many employees receive subsidies from

their employer of more than 50 percent, and almost one-quarter of workers contribute nothing toward the cost of employee-only insurance coverage.[43] The maximum credit would thus exceed what these workers have to pay out of their own pocket for coverage. For reasons I discuss in more detail below, their EIHC would be calculated as follows. First, workers would receive the amount they contribute toward their coverage. In addition, one-sixth of the difference between their contribution and their maximum EIHC would be deposited on their behalf into a flexible spending account that could be applied toward the out-of-pocket costs the employee incurred during the year. The same amount would go to the employer as a credit against the cost of providing health insurance. Thus, the government would pay out a total of one-third of the amount by which the maximum credit exceeds the amount the worker has to pay.

How the Proposal Addresses the Challenges Facing Low-Income Families

My plan is designed to overcome the challenges facing low-income families by facilitating transitions across sources of coverage, minimizing work disincentives, and pursuing the goal of horizontal equity. It is also designed to minimize incentives for employers and employees to replace their current payments with public support.

The plan facilitates transitions by providing realistic options for new sources of coverage when another source ends. As the parent (or parents) in a family goes to work and income rises, the family will at some point exceed the income thresholds for the fully subsidized Medicaid program. If the parent works at a firm that offers health insurance coverage, the EIHC will be there to subsidize the share the employee is expected to pay, and in some circumstances subsidize part of the employer's cost as well. If there is no employer-sponsored coverage, the state plan is available, also on a subsidized basis. Movement across these forms of coverage will still involve some changes, but will avoid the penalties and discontinuities in today's health care system.

The plan minimizes work disincentives by trying to keep as low as possible the effective marginal tax rates families face as their earnings increase. Because the plan must meet the needs both of people without access to employer-sponsored coverage and of those who do have access and have widely varying rates of employer subsidy, achieving that goal is complicated. The design is best explained by considering three families, each with one worker, a nonworking spouse, and two children. In each family the worker earns $40,000 a year. In one family, the employer does not offer health insurance; in the second family, employer-provided coverage is available if the employee contributes 40 percent of the $10,000 cost of the plan; in the third family, workplace coverage is available with an employee contribution of 20 percent, or $2,000.

Although all three families have the same income, their ability to obtain health insurance is quite different. If a family with income of $40,000 can afford to contribute 2.5 percent of its income, or $1,000, toward the cost of coverage, the first family faces a shortfall of $9,000, the second a shortfall of $3,000, and the third a shortfall of $1,000.

The plan is designed to overcome the challenges facing low-income families by facilitating transitions across sources of coverage, minimizing work disincentives, and pursuing the goal of horizontal equity.

A tax credit that treats all three families the same will be either inadequate or inefficient. If the credit is much less than $9,000, the first family will have inadequate coverage. If the credit is high enough to meet the first family's needs, the second and third families will receive much more than they need to get coverage.

A tax credit that exactly meets each family's needs would be adequate and appears to be efficient, but creates a different problem. If the second family receives a credit of $3,000 and the third family a credit of $1,000, the third family's employer has no incentive to continue providing such a generous subsidy toward coverage. The third employer could reduce its subsidy by $2,000 and the employee would be no worse off. In the extreme, both the second and third employers might choose to drop coverage entirely, knowing the families would get a $9,000 credit, which would come close to meeting the family's financial needs for obtaining good coverage.

In fact, substantial barriers keep employers from making such radical changes.[44] But even having to replace some private dollars with public dollars would be expensive and could make the cost of the program, relative to the number of people who newly gain insurance coverage, unacceptably high.

Two features of the plan are designed to address these problems while still striving for equity. First, the large credit available to those without employer coverage can be used only to purchase a public plan, and the credit falls short of the value of a typical private plan. An employer who drops coverage entirely would leave the firm's employees substantially worse off with respect to insurance choices. Some employers might take this step nonetheless, but the plan is designed to minimize the likelihood that they will.

Second, the plan rebates a portion of the gap between each family's out-of-pocket premium costs and its EIHC maximum credit. An employer who offers generous subsidies would receive a modest rebate for the employees of the firm who are eligible for the EIHC. The employees also receive a modest rebate, which provides them with additional value associated with the employer contribution toward coverage even if they lose some of the value of the credit. Together these features should help discourage employers from reducing their contribution levels.

The plan also supports workers who are increasing their earnings. Consider two possible scenarios for the second worker. In the first, the worker gets a raise in cash salary from $40,000 to $42,000. In the second, the worker moves to a new job that gives the same salary but an increase in the employer subsidy for health insurance from $6,000 to $8,000, so that the worker's situation is now identical to that of the third worker. Both scenarios represent a $2,000 increase in the worker's total compensation, which public policy should support. As workers' earnings go up, their need for assistance falls, so some decline in support is appropriate. But the design of the credit should not "tax" away all of the increase or it will impede career advancement.

The first scenario moves the worker farther along the phase-out schedule of the EIHC (see table 1). The credit will decline at the rate of the phase-out, but the worker will be much better off after the raise. In the second scenario the employee will lose $1,150 in EIHC, because the value is capped at the actual amount the employee must pay. The employee and employer will each get a rebate of $192, which represents one-sixth of the amount by which the maximum EIHC exceeds the employee contribution to coverage. The employee in the second scenario faces a steeper marginal tax rate. However, the extra salary in scenario one is subject to payroll and income taxes that reduce the difference between the net effect of the two scenarios.

Although the policy goal is to keep marginal tax rates from becoming too large, a family may consider the situation somewhat differently. In its original circumstances, with a $40,000 salary and a $4,000 contribution toward coverage, the family must come up with $850 to purchase coverage. With a cash raise, the family now has substantially more resources available to make a slightly larger contribution. If the worker takes a job with a higher employer subsidy, he no longer needs to make a contribution out of his own pocket,

Table 1. Change in Family Well-Being from Increase in Salary or Decrease in Employee Health Insurance Contribution

Dollars except when otherwise noted

Item	Starting point	Scenario 1	Scenario 2
Annual salary/employee health insurance contribution	$40,000/$4,000	$42,000/$4,000	$40,000/$2,000
Maximum EIHC	3,150	2,835	3,150
Actual EIHC	3,150	2,835	2,000
Net contribution to coverage (rebate)	850	1,165	(192)
Family resources after contribution	39,150	40,835	40,192
Increase in resources relative to starting point		1,685	1,042
Effective marginal tax rate		15.8%	47.9%

Note: Based on federal poverty level of $20,000 for a family of four and structure of EIHC as described in text.

and he gains a small rebate to deposit into a flexible spending account. Either change is positive for the family, regardless of the precise marginal tax calculation.

Proposal Costs

The price tag of this proposal is sure to be quite high. A recent analysis placed the cost of expanding Medicaid to all adults with incomes below the poverty line at $24 billion in 2006, with the federal government bearing $14 billion of that cost and the states, $10 billion.[45] Most tax credit proposals have been on a much smaller scale than the one proposed here, and the cost estimates are quite sensitive to their structure. One tax credit proposal that was capped at 30 percent of the cost of insurance coverage was estimated to cost about $15 billion in 2005.[46] The Congressional Budget Office estimated the cost of a maximum credit of $2,750 for a family with a phase-out point of 300 percent of the federal poverty level to be $3.1 billion in 2008.[47] A far more ambitious and generous proposal that includes sliding-scale subsidies for people with incomes up to 400 percent of the federal poverty level to purchase employer-sponsored insurance was estimated to cost $27.1 billion in 2007.[48] This proposal included subsidies for purchasing nonemployer

plans, at an estimated cost of $31.4 billion. Based on these figures, I estimate that my proposal will cost about $45 billion a year, with the federal government paying about $35 billion and the states, about $10 billion.

This cost estimate is very rough. A more precise estimate would require a much more sophisticated modeling approach. The dynamics of the health care system are such that small changes in policy variables can ripple through the system with large and unexpected effects. Models cannot perfectly anticipate those effects, but they provide important information that can be used to either prepare for the effects or modify the plan. In this proposal, small changes to the structure of the EIHC could yield large unexpected changes in employer and employee behavior and in overall cost. The proposal was designed with the intention of keeping those changes modest, but if modeling results suggested changes on a large scale, it would be worth considering modifying the proposal.

The cost could be brought down in many ways. The obvious options are to reduce the maximum value of the EIHC, make the phase-out steeper, or scale back the public program expansion. Each would limit what the plan could achieve. Another option would be to put an age limit on eligibility for this new program. If the primary goal is to reduce poverty for low-income families, the policy could target younger adults and families. Such an approach would focus resources on the share of the uninsured that has, on aver-

---

In fact, it is reasonable to expect the proposal to raise overall health care spending because people without health insurance use about 60 percent as many services as those with insurance.

---

age, lower costs, because health costs tend to increase with age.

Variations on the Proposal

The proposal provides a credit of uniform value in a nation where health care and health insurance costs vary.[49] It will be relatively easy for people who live in low-cost regions to get good coverage, whereas those in regions with higher costs may find the credit inadequate to purchase a good policy. Some reform proposals vary the credit by the underlying cost of insurance. This adds a substantial layer of complexity and creates some troubling incentives for the health system as a whole (the more expensive you are, the more you get paid).

Similarly, the credit value could vary by the age or health status of the applicant. This would avoid the risk-selection problems already noted, but would be extremely difficult

to administer. Alternatively, the proposal could mandate that states adopt community rating policies for health insurance. This would solve the risk-selection problems, but create other disruptions within the current health insurance market. It would also fundamentally alter the balance between state and federal power in health insurance regulation—a change to which the states would be sure to object.

Finally, the proposal could have provided an option for people to receive the EIHC if they purchase coverage in the individual insurance market. Such a structure provides less of an assurance that the insurance policies will be adequate, is far more prone to the substitution of private dollars with public dollars, and requires the creation of an entirely new administrative structure to enable the credit to flow to families.

Conclusion

My proposal is designed to make health insurance a viable option for all Americans with low or moderate income. It builds on existing public programs and private sector coverage.

The proposal is designed with an implicit affordability calculation in mind. That is, it begins with the notion that it is reasonable to expect individuals and families at a certain income level to pay a modest share of their income toward health insurance coverage. The EIHC provides the subsidy that brings the net cost for the family down from the market price to the affordable price. The implicit affordability calculation is rough—some people will still view coverage as unaffordable at these subsidized prices; others would have purchased coverage anyway, even if it had cost them more. Those who still find insurance unaffordable even after the subsidies are applied and those who value other priorities more than they value having insurance coverage will remain uninsured. A more generous EIHC could be offered that would help more people at a greater cost to taxpayers. The EIHC could also be calibrated more closely to other factors that might influence a family's ability to afford coverage. Public programs routinely do this through income disregards—for example, by deducting child care or transportation costs from family income when determining program eligibility. However, the information collected on the tax return does not lend itself to such calibration.

While seeking to build a solid floor of public coverage, the proposal does not smooth out the major differences in how states regulate the health insurance market. In states with limited regulation, individuals and firms with employees with certain health conditions may find that they cannot obtain coverage at anything near the average prices used to develop the EIHC. Rather than seeking to standardize state insurance regulation, the plan requires every state to operate a plan that is available to everyone. Such a plan will cost states with limited regulation more than it will cost states with tighter regulation because the state program is more likely to attract sicker people when the private market charges higher rates to sicker people.

Ultimately, this proposal is not designed to reduce or control the rate of growth of health care or health insurance costs, nor is it designed to improve the quality of health care. In fact, it is reasonable to expect the proposal to raise overall health care spending because people without health insurance use about 60 percent as many services as those with insurance. Cost containment and quality improvement are critical issues for the health care system as a whole and they warrant far more attention than can be given in a brief paper focused on insurance coverage.

The proposal made here would not solve all that ails the American health care system. It would, however, make coverage more nearly affordable and accessible to all, especially poor families. It would ease the concerns of lower-income families about health insurance and access to health care services. It would enable these families to focus on advancing their careers and taking care of their children, rather than on trying to navigate a system that falls short in so many ways. And finally, it would reduce the disincentives for poor families to work and thereby increase the odds that they could earn their way out of poverty.

Alan Weil

Notes

1. Kaiser Commission on Medicaid and the Uninsured, *Health Insurance Coverage in America 2005 Data Update* (Washington, November 2006), p. 14.

2. Committee on the Consequences of Uninsurance, Institute of Medicine, *Coverage Matters* (Washington: National Academies Press, 2001).

3. Committee on the Consequences of Uninsurance, Institute of Medicine, *A Shared Destiny: Community Effects of Uninsurance* (Washington: National Academies Press, 2003).

4. Amy Davidoff and Genevieve Kenney, *Uninsured Americans with Chronic Health Conditions: Key Findings from the National Health Interview Survey* (Washington: Urban Institute, May 2005), p. 4.

5. Paul Fronstin and Sara R. Collins, *The 2nd Annual EBRI/Commonwealth Fund Consumerism in Health Care Survey, 2006: Early Experience with High-Deductible and Consumer-Driven Health Plans*, Issue Brief 300 (Washington: Employee Benefit Research Institute, December 2006), p. 27.

6. Jack Hadley, "Sicker and Poorer—The Consequences of Being Uninsured: A Review of the Research on the Relationship between Health Insurance, Medical Care Use, Health, Work, and Income," *Medical Care Research and Review* 60, no. 2 (June 2003): 3S–75S.

7. Pamela Loprest, "Who Returns to Welfare?" Assessing the New Federalism, no. B-49 (Washington: Urban Institute, September 2002), p. 5.

8. U.S. Census Bureau, "Historical Income Tables—Families," www.census.gov/hhes/www/income/histinc/f08ar.html (accessed March 20, 2007).

9. Kaiser Family Foundation and Health Research Educational Trust, *Employer Health Benefits 2005 Annual Survey* (Menlo Park, Calif., September 2005), p. 61.

10. Cathy Schoen and others, "Insured but Not Protected: How Many Adults Are Underinsured?" *Health Affairs* web exclusive (June 14, 2005) http://content.healthaffairs.org/cgi/content/abstract/hlthaff.w5.289v1 (accessed February 28, 2007). The authors define underinsurance to include one or more of the following: (1) medical expenses of 10 percent or more of income; (2) among low-income adults (those with incomes below 200 percent of the federal poverty level), medical expenses of 5 percent or more of income; (3) health plan deductibles equal to or exceeding 5 percent of income.

11. Ibid.

12. Committee on the Consequences of Uninsurance, *Coverage Matters* (see note 2).

13. Based on National Association of State Budget Officers, *State Health Expenditure Report 1998–1999* and *2002–2003*, www.nasbo.org/publications.php (accessed February 22, 2007).

14. Based on Congressional Budget Office, *Historical Budget Data*, www.cbo.gov/budget/historical.shtml (accessed February 22, 2007).

15. Joseph R. Antos and Alice M. Rivlin, "Rising Health Care Spending—Federal and National," in *Restoring Fiscal Sanity 2007: The Health Spending Challenge*, edited by Antos and Rivlin (Brookings, 2007).

16. Kaiser Commission, *Health Insurance Coverage in America* (see note 1), p. 1.

17. States can and do regulate the types of products insurance companies can sell. When an employer purchases coverage from an insurance company it is subject to these regulations. Larger firms generally self-

insure (bear their own financial risk). Since they are not purchasing a regulated product, they are not subject to the terms a state may establish for insurance policies.

18. Since 1975, Hawaii has had in place an "employer mandate" that all firms provide coverage to their employees (but not the employees' dependents). Congress provided Hawaii with explicit permission to adopt this policy, but it is not available to any other state.

19. U.S. Census Bureau, *Current Population Survey, Annual Social and Economic Supplement, 2006*, www.census.gov/hhes/www/cpstc/cps_table_creator.html (accessed February 22, 2007).

20. Ibid.

21. Ibid.

22. Kaiser and HRET, *Employer Health Benefits 2005 Annual Survey* (see note 9), p. 35.

23. Ibid., exhibit 3.1.

24. John Sheils and Randall Haught, "The Cost of Tax-Exempt Health Benefits in 2004," *Health Affairs* web exclusive (February 25, 2004), http://content.healthaffairs.org/cgi/content/abstract/hlthaff.w4.106v1 (accessed March 2, 2007).

25. Kaiser Family Foundation, Statehealthfacts.org, www.statehealthfacts.org (accessed March 20, 2007). Note that this point-in-time measure differs from a count of people who were ever enrolled in a program in a year.

26. In some instances a family may face three or more different eligibility levels. Children's eligibility levels often vary by age, so that two children may be in separate programs (one in Medicaid, one in SCHIP) or one may be covered and the other uninsured, while the parents face yet another eligibility threshold.

27. For one compilation of ten such proposals, see Jack A. Meyer and Elliot K. Wicks, eds., *Covering America: Real Remedies for the Uninsured* (Washington: Economic and Social Research Institute, June 2001).

28. Kaiser and HRET, *Employer Health Benefits 2005 Annual Survey* (see note 9).

29. Census Bureau, "Historical Income Tables–Families" (see note 8).

30. Gregory Acs and others, "Does Work Pay? An Analysis of the Work Incentives under TANF," Assessing the New Federalism, Occasional Paper 9 (Washington: Urban Institute, 1998).

31. A discussion of this trade-off appears in Linda J. Blumberg, "Balancing Efficiency and Equity in the Design of Coverage Expansions for Children," *Future of Children* 13, no. 1 (Spring 2003).

32. Derived from Kaiser Commission on Medicaid and the Uninsured, *The Uninsured: A Primer* (Washington: Kaiser Commission, October 2006), table 4, 31.

33. Jonathan Gruber and Kosali Simon, "Crowd-Out Ten Years Later: Have Recent Public Insurance Expansions Crowded Out Private Health Insurance?" Working Paper 12858 (Cambridge, Mass.: National Bureau of Economic Research, January 2007).

34. Kaiser Family Foundation, "Income Eligibility for Parents Applying for Medicaid by Annual Income as a Percent of Federal Poverty Level (FPL), 2006," www.statehealthfacts.org.

35. Steve Holt, "The Earned Income Tax Credit at 30: What We Know," Research Brief (Metropolitan Policy Program, Brookings, February 2006).

36. For a good description of the Massachusetts reform, see John E. McDonough, "The Third Wave of Massachusetts Health Care Access Reform," *Health Affairs* web exclusive 25, no. 6 (September 14, 2006) http://content.healthaffairs.org/cgi/content/abstract/hlthaff.25.w420.

37. Rick Curtis and Ed Neuschler, "Insurance Markets: What Health Insurance Pools Can and Can't Do," Issue Brief (Oakland, Calif.: California HealthCare Foundation, November 2005).

38. Alan Weil, "Implementing Tax Credits for Affordable Health Insurance Coverage" (Boston: Blue Cross/Blue Shield of Massachusetts Foundation, October 2005); and Lynn Etheredge and others, "Administering a Medicaid + Tax Credits Initiative" (Washington: Health Insurance Reform Project, February 2007).

39. U.S. General Accounting Office, "Earned Income Tax Credit: Advance Payment Option Is not Widely Known or Understood by the Public," GAO/GGD-92-26 (February 1992); U.S. Department of the Treasury, "Taxpayers Were Assessed Additional Tax for Advance Earned Income Credit Payments not Received," Memorandum for Commissioner, Wage and Investment Division, 2003-40-126 (June 2003).

40. Tax filing units, insurance units, coverage categories for public programs, and families all take different forms that are sometimes aligned but often not. How to handle the differences between these concepts requires more attention than it is given in this paper. Some discussion of this topic appears in Weil, "Implementing Tax Credits for Affordable Health Insurance Coverage" (see note 38). For the sake of simplicity, this paper uses the term *family* for all of these categories.

41. Kaiser and HRET, *Employer Health Benefits 2005 Annual Survey* (see note 9).

42. Ibid.

43. Ibid.

44. Most firms have a heterogeneous mix of salaries and family circumstances among their employees. IRS rules prohibit discrimination across employees on benefits, so a change in employer contributions could not be focused exclusively on the subset of employees who would obtain a tax credit. In addition, compensation provided in the form of benefits receives certain advantages in the tax code. Still, if the financial incentives are strong, some nontrivial number of firms can be expected to change their behavior.

45. John Holahan and Alan Weil, "Toward Real Medicaid Reform," *Health Affairs* web exclusive 26, no. 2 (February 23, 2007), http://content.healthaffairs.org/cgi/content/abstract/hlthaff.26.2.w254.

46. John Sheils, Paul Hogan, and Randall Haught, "Health Insurance and Taxes: The Impact of Proposed Changes in Current Federal Policy" (Washington: Lewin Group, October 18, 1999), www.lewin.com/NR/rdonlyres/BD11A6A0-1A58-4E87-94F5-C66A3CAFE50F/0/NCHC_Tax_Credit_Paper.pdf.

47. Congressional Budget Office, *Budget Options* (February 2007), p. 158.

48. Federation of American Hospitals, "Health Coverage Passport," www.fahs.com/passport/HCP%20PPT%20Designed%202-16-07.pdf (accessed March 20, 2007).

49. The average annual health insurance premium for family coverage varied by a factor of 1.22 between the highest and lowest among the ten largest states in 2004. However, most states were clustered quite close to the national mean. James M. Branscome, "State Differences in the Cost of Job-Related Health Insurance, 2004," Statistical Brief 135 (Agency for Healthcare Research and Quality, Medical Expenditure Panel Survey, July 2006).

Decreasing Nonmarital Births and Strengthening Marriage to Reduce Poverty

Paul R. Amato and Rebecca A. Maynard

Summary

Since the 1970s, the share of U.S. children growing up in single-parent families has doubled, a trend that has disproportionately affected disadvantaged families. Paul Amato and Rebecca Maynard argue that reversing that trend would reduce poverty in the short term and, perhaps more important, improve children's growth and development over the long term, thus reducing the likelihood that they would be poor when they grew up. The authors propose school and community programs to help prevent nonmarital births. They also propose to lower divorce rates by offering more educational programs to couples before and during marriage.

Amato and Maynard recommend that all school systems offer health and sex education whose primary message is that parenthood is highly problematic for unmarried youth. They also recommend educating young people about methods to prevent unintended pregnancies. Ideally, the federal government would provide tested curriculum models that emphasize both abstinence and use of contraception. All youth should understand that unintended pregnancies are preventable and have enormous costs for the mother, the father, the child, and society.

Strengthening marriage, argue the authors, is also potentially an effective strategy for fighting poverty. Researchers consistently find that premarital education improves marital quality and lowers the risk of divorce. About 40 percent of couples about to marry now participate in premarital education. Amato and Maynard recommend doubling that figure to 80 percent and making similar programs available for married couples. Increasing the number of couples receiving services could mean roughly 72,000 fewer divorces each year, or around 65,000 fewer children entering a single-parent family every year because of marital dissolution. After seven or eight years, half a million fewer children would have entered single-parent families through divorce. Efforts to decrease the share of children in single-parent households, say the authors, would almost certainly be cost effective in the long run and could reduce child poverty by 20 to 29 percent.

www.futureofchildren.org

Paul R. Amato is a Distinguished Professor of Sociology and Demography at the Pennsylvania State University. Rebecca A. Maynard is University Trustee Chair Professor of Education and Social Policy at the University of Pennsylvania. The authors thank Robin Dion, Howard Markman, Theodora Ooms, Scott Stanley, the editors of this volume, and the participants in the authors' conference at Princeton University on October 12–13, 2006, for helpful comments and suggestions.

Paul R. Amato and Rebecca A. Maynard

One key strategy for U.S. policymakers seeking to reduce childhood poverty would be to increase the share of children who grow up with continuously married parents. Married couples with children enjoy, on average, a higher standard of living and greater economic security than do single-parent families with children. In 2003 the median annual income of families with children was almost three times that of single-parent households—$67,670 compared with $24,408.[1] Correspondingly, the child poverty rate was more than four times higher in single-parent households than in married-couple households—34 percent compared with 8 percent. Moreover, the economic advantages of married couples are apparent across virtually all racial and ethnic groups. But over the past half-century those economic advantages have been denied to a growing share of America's children.

In 2004, nearly 36 percent of U.S. children were born to unmarried mothers. Even when children are born to married couples, many will spend part of their childhood living with a single parent because of parental divorce.[2] Between 1960 and 2005, increases in nonmarital births, low marriage rates for women who have children out of wedlock, and rising divorce rates pushed the share of children living with a single parent (mostly the mother) from 8 percent to 28 percent.[3] And these sobering figures underestimate the share of children who will ever live with a single parent, because they refer to a single year. Overall, demographers project that only half of all children in the United States will grow up with two continuously married parents.[4] The clear correlation between family structure and economic resources has led researchers to conclude that a major cause of the rise in child poverty in the United States

during the second half of the twentieth century is the decline in married-couple households.[5] Effective public policies to boost the share of children living in two-parent families could thus help to reduce child poverty.

How Marriage Promotes the Economic Well-being of Children

Both theory and logic support the view that marriage contributes to the economic well-being of children and families—and a great deal of empirical research backs that view as well. Studies by Robert Lerman, for example, show that the economic benefits of marriage are evident across all socioeconomic groups—especially among black families.[6]

One obvious reason for these benefits is economies of scale. Married couples can share expenses, such as rent and utilities, and use the savings to support a higher standard of living or to invest for the future. In 2005 a mother who earned $13,461 and had one child would live exactly at the poverty threshold. A single man who earned $10,160 also would live exactly at the poverty threshold. But if the two were to marry and live together, their combined earnings would place them 50 percent above the poverty threshold.[7]

Marriage also gives a household two potential workers rather than one. In 2004, 59 percent of married mothers with children under the age of six and 76 percent of married mothers with children between the ages of six and seventeen were in the labor force.[8] Clearly, it has become normative for married mothers to contribute to household income, and having two earners substantially increases a family's standard of living. In 2000, for example, the median family income among married couples in which both spouses were aged fifty-five or younger was $55,000 if the husband only was employed, $62,500 if the wife worked part time (thirty-four or less hours a week), and $70,000 if she worked full time (thirty-five or more hours a week).[9] Having two earners also buffers the household economy if one earner should become jobless or temporarily disabled.

Two-parent families have more flexibility in how they divide their time between home and market production. Two parents can decide that one should specialize in home production, while the other maximizes earnings by devoting more time to work-related activities (including commuting)—an arrangement that also makes it easier for the working spouse to cope with job-related stress.[10]

People who are married—wives as well as husbands—also enjoy better physical and mental health than do single people.[11] The health advantages appear to be due partly to the social support provided by a spouse. Married people also tend to take better care of themselves. Following marriage, men in particular tend to decrease their use of alcohol and drugs. Good mental and physical health, in turn, promotes productivity at work and economic security.

Married couples also receive more assistance from their extended family, on average, than do single parents or cohabiting couples. The assistance might take the form of gifts, such as wedding presents; help with a down payment for a home; or care for children, which reduces child care expenses for the couple.[12]

Marriage appears to provide especially important benefits for single mothers, many of whom are young and poor. A study based on the National Longitudinal Study of Family Growth found that single mothers who married tended to benefit economically, regardless of family background, education, or race.

Moreover, single mothers who married were substantially less likely to experience poverty than those who remained unmarried. Marriage, the study shows, provides an escape from poverty for many young mothers.[13]

In principle, cohabiting couples could enjoy the same economic well-being as married couples. In practice, however, they are less likely to share income than are married cou-

---

Two-parent families have more flexibility in how they divide their time between home and market production.

---

ples and, because most cohabiting relationships are short-lived, the couples have less time to accumulate wealth. Nor do cohabiting couples get as much economic assistance from their families.

Some of the differences in the well-being of married-couple and single-parent or cohabiting-couple families may be attributable to "selection." That is, some of the personal qualities that contribute to labor market success and wealth accumulation—a good education, a strong work ethic, good physical health, and positive psychological adjustment—may also make certain people more likely to find and keep a marriage partner. Indeed, research shows that people with high levels of human capital, occupational status, and earnings are more likely to marry—a trend that holds for women as well as for men.[14]

But although selection contributes to the advantages of married-couple families, the best available evidence suggests that marriage enhances economic well-being above and be-yond the characteristics that spouses may bring to the union. That is, even for people whose employment history, education, health, and family background are compara-ble, married couples still tend to earn more income and accumulate more wealth than do single or cohabiting people.[15]

Just as marriage confers economic advantage, divorce carries with it economic disadvan-tage. Although studies show that low income and perceived economic stress increase ten-sion in marriage and increase the risk of di-vorce, divorce usually erodes the economic well-being of custodial mothers and their children.[16] Using the Panel Study of Income Dynamics, Sara McLanahan and Gary Sande-fur found that median household income for custodial-parent households declined 40 per-cent, on average, during the five years follow-ing divorce. Moreover, the decline in eco-nomic well-being held for poorly educated and highly educated couples alike.[17] Other research has estimated that divorce increases by 46 percent the likelihood that families with children will be poor.[18] The economic well-being of divorced families is further eroded by the division of property between former spouses, which lowers accumulated assets.[19] Replacing lost assets is difficult, if not impossible, with only a single parent and wage earner in the household.

Fighting Poverty through Policies That Promote Child Rearing within Healthy Marriages

We propose two strategies to increase the like-lihood that children grow up with two continu-ously married parents. The first is to expand educational programs and social marketing campaigns to prevent nonmarital births. The second is to expand support for marriage edu-cation and relationship skills programs.

The aim of the first strategy is to promote abstinence among unmarried teenagers and improve contraception use among sexually ac-tive young women who do not intend to be-come pregnant. This strategy focuses on un-married teens and young adults, who together account for 62 percent of all nonmarital births. It seems well aligned with the goals of young women, as two-thirds of the births to women under the age of twenty and almost all of those to unmarried teens are reported to be unintended, as are one-third of all births to women aged twenty to twenty-four.[20]

The aim of the second strategy is to improve the quality of marital relationships and lower divorce rates by teaching couples communi-cation, conflict resolution, and social support skills within marriage. Educational programs to prevent divorce should not only improve the economic well-being of children and their families, but also strengthen marital relation-ships and improve the quality of parenting.

Together, the two strategies could reduce the number of children born to unmarried moth-ers, increase the share of children growing up with two continuously married parents, and improve the economic well-being of the fam-ilies in which children are reared.[21] In both strategies, the central pathway for reducing poverty is to raise the share of children reared by married couples.

Abstinence and Pregnancy Prevention for Young Adults

One potentially powerful strategy to reduce poverty among families with children is to promote both abstinence among unmarried teenagers and effective contraception use among teens and young adults who are sexu-ally active but do not intend to become preg-nant. The number of potentially affected indi-viduals is large, and the risk of poverty is great

Table 1. Total and Nonmarital Births by Age of the Mother, 2004

Mother's age	Total number of births	Nonmarital births	
		Number of births	Percent of all births
Under age 15	6,779	6,603	97.4
15-17	134,008	120,948	90.3
18-19	281,204	221,240	78.7
20-24	1,033,542	566,381	54.8
25 or older	2,651,140	555,017	20.9
Total	4,106,673	1,470,189	35.8

Source: *National Vital Statistics Report 55*, no.1, table 18, p. 57; www.cdc.gov/nchs/data/nvsr/nvsr55/nvsr55_01.pdf.

when young women have nonmarital births. In 2004, nearly 1.5 million infants—more than one in three newborns—in the United States were born to unmarried women. Most of these women were aged twenty-five or younger; one-quarter were teens (table 1). Most of these births were first births, and few children were born to unmarried women who had previously given birth within marriage.[22] Only a small share (12.5 percent in the early 1990s) of unmarried women who become pregnant marry before they give birth.[23]

The Fragile Families Study indicates that roughly half of unmarried mothers and fathers are living together when their child is born; roughly another one-third are in some type of romantic (or visiting) relationship.[24] Most of these couples view marriage favorably, and most believe that they are likely to marry. For many, however, maintaining a relationship requires overcoming a variety of obstacles, such as poverty, unemployment, physical and mental health problems, substance abuse, high male incarceration rates, and a lack of trust between partners. Not surprisingly, these nonmarital unions tend to be unstable.[25] Within one year of the child's birth, 15 percent of cohabiting couples had married and 21 percent were no longer in a romantic relationship. Among romantically

involved couples who were not living together, only 5 percent had married and 49 percent had split up. Five years after the child's birth, 29 percent of cohabiting couples had married and 42 percent had separated. Correspondingly, 7 percent of visiting couples had married and 74 percent had split up.[26] Other studies also find that the marriage prospects for women who give birth out of wedlock are dim. By one set of estimates, just under half marry within the next ten years and just over one-third will be married when they have their second child.[27]

The good news is that childbearing among teenagers has declined since 1990.[28] To the extent that the policy environment of the past fifteen years has contributed to that decline, it seems prudent to build on rather than replace existing policies. Favorable trends in teen birth rates appear to be due to the combined effects of delayed sexual debut and more effective use of contraception.[29] It would thus be useful to maintain a balance between promoting abstinence among teens and encouraging wise contraceptive practices among sexually active young adults who do not wish to become pregnant.

Using the 2004 cohort size of fifteen- to nineteen-year-old females and data on sexual ex-

Figure 1. Effect of Proposed Policies on Sexual Activity and Contraception on Number of Teen Births, by Marital Status, 2004

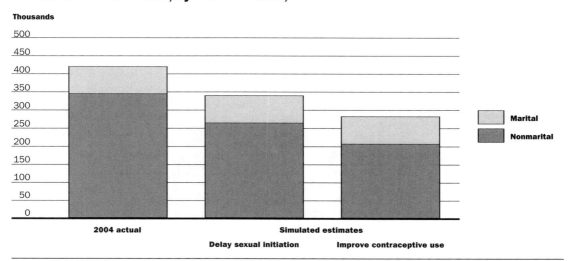

Source: 2004 data are from Joyce A. Martin and others, "Births: Final Data for 2004," *National Vital Statistics Reports* 55, no. 1 (2006): table 18, p. 57; simulated estimates under assumptions of behavioral change (sexual initiation delayed by one year and half of teens not using contraception begin to do so) computed by the authors.

perience rates, contraceptive use, and birth rates, we explored how policies that delay sexual activity and improve contraception use would play out in terms of teen and nonmarital births. Other things being equal, delaying first intercourse for one year would lower the share of twelve- to nineteen-year-olds at risk for pregnancy and birth by about 9 percentage points. The delay would reduce the number of teen births, at present rates, by about 81,000 a year—a proportional decline of 24 percent (figure 1). Because almost all of these births would have been to unmarried teens, the share of all teen births to single mothers would fall from 82 percent to 78 percent.

Combining policies that delay sexual activity for one year with policies that stress abstinence and increase the likelihood that sexually active young adults who do not intend to become pregnant use effective methods of contraception could substantially increase these benefits. For example, if half of those not now using contraception were to become consistent users

of condoms, the pill, an injectable form of contraception, or an implant, the number of unintended births would fall roughly another 60,000 a year, or 14 percent. And the estimated share of all teen births to single mothers would fall another 5 percentage points, to about 73 percent of all teen births.

Influencing the nonmarital childbearing of young adults, though, is a challenge because only half of all women in this country marry by age twenty-five, whereas most become sexually active during their teen years. The gap between the average age of first intercourse (seventeen) and the age at first marriage (twenty-five) is seven years.[30] Still, it should be possible to improve the ability of young adult women to avoid many of the 40 percent of births (439,000 births) that are unintended and occur predominantly to unmarried women.[31] These unintended births constitute more than one-third of all nonmarital births.[32] Even if they achieve half the success rate in preventing unintended births assumed in the above projections for teens, policy initiatives that enable sexually active young adults to avoid unintended pregnancies could mean about 40,000 fewer nonmarital births each year.

How might delayed childbearing affect poverty, particularly among children? One study estimated that delaying childbearing among teens would increase median family income by a factor of 1.5 to 2.2 and reduce poverty rates by even more.[33] It could also substantially reduce the number of abortions, which are especially common among never-married women and teens. In 1994, for example, 34 percent of pregnancies to women under age twenty-five were estimated to have ended in abortion, as did 31 percent of the more than 2 million pregnancies of unmarried women.[34]

The task confronting policymakers is to fashion programs that will alter current behavior of teens and young adults. Evidence on the effectiveness of programs to delay sexual debut of particular groups of youth is limited and not overly encouraging.[35] Yet recent trends in teen sexual activity, contraceptive use, and births suggest that something in the public policy arena or the larger culture, or both, produced favorable change beginning in the 1990s.

Our recommendation, therefore, is to continue full-bore with efforts by parents, schools, and community groups to encourage abstinence among teenagers, support the use of effective contraception among sexually active young adults, and emphasize the message that pregnancies are 99 percent preventable. In particular, we recommend that all school systems offer health and sex education, beginning no later than middle school, whose primary message is that unintended

pregnancies are not only highly preventable, but also have substantial costs for the pregnant woman, the father, the child, and society in general.[36] We also recommend that school systems (as well as parents and community groups) educate young people about methods to prevent unintended pregnancies, as well as life-threatening sexually transmitted diseases.

Simply knowing about and having access to contraception does not guarantee a high compliance rate among sexually active teens and young adults. It is thus important to challenge the social norms and cultural views that nonmarital childbearing is an expected stage in the life course, especially among low-income populations, where these beliefs have taken hold most strongly.[37] School-based programs, as well as public education campaigns, should emphasize the importance of bearing children within the security provided by a marital relationship. A child-focused message may be particularly effective. That is, children's economic, social, and psychological well-being is greatly enhanced when they have married parents.

Because almost all youth in this country already receive some form of education about sexual behavior and health as part of their schooling, enacting this recommendation would, in most cases, require refining the course content and extending the time devoted to this goal.[38] Consistent with the overwhelming desire of parents that their teenage children remain abstinent, most programs now promote abstinence as the healthiest and most socially appropriate behavior.[39] Then, with varying emphases, these programs teach young people strategies for developing healthy relationships with peers, resisting negative peer pressure, communicating with parents and other important adults in their lives, and setting and pursuing realistic life goals.[40] Supplementing this course content with relationship skills training for couples is likely to make the programs more effective. For example, young women with good negotiating skills may be better able to say no to unwanted sexual advances or to insist that their male partners use contra-

> *For example, young women with good negotiating skills may be better able to say no to unwanted sexual advances or to insist that their male partners use contraception.*

ception. And teenage boys need to hear the message that if they father a child, they will be responsible for paying child support for many years. Boys, like girls, also need to be aware of the negative consequences for children reared in single-parent homes.

The major policy challenge is to learn which information in these courses is helpful, and which is not helpful, in supporting teens to remain abstinent or to return to an abstinent lifestyle. A key goal is to identify a menu of "best practices" from the current array of courses. Ideally, the federal government could provide school districts with tested curriculum models, though it could probably not do so in the near future. There are several sources of guidance about programs and practices judged to be effective in reducing pregnancy risk. The evidence supporting the effectiveness of various programs is far from conclusive, though.[41] Before dismissing the findings, however, it is useful to consider that virtually no program has been tested in a

truly experimental setting, where the comparison group is "treatment free." Moreover, because the programs tend to be low in cost, even small effects that are hard to detect with the small samples typical of research in this area are likely to be cost effective. The estimated costs of such a policy would be quite modest and well below the expected savings to taxpayers. For example, in a steady state, taxpayers incur yearly net costs of over $20,000 per teenage parent, whereas the annual estimated cost of a biweekly health and sex education class would be less than $200 per student.[42] If such a universal program initiative succeeded in cutting the teenage birth rate in half, the estimated return on the investment would be about 20 percent.[43]

We are reluctant to promote comprehensive interventions, such as the community centered Carrera program for at-risk youth. In addition to sex education (which includes information about abstinence and contraception), the Carrera program focuses on career exploration, employment assistance, academic tutoring, art workshops, sports activities, and comprehensive health care.[44] Such programs, though useful, are costly and have myriad goals other than preventing teen pregnancy and childbearing. Moreover, their success in preventing teen pregnancies and births has been mixed.[45] Clearly, more research on program and curriculum effectiveness is needed. In the meantime, communities and school districts will need to sort through the many home-grown and commercial curricula now in use and tailor programs to perceived local needs.

Increase the Share of Couples Receiving Marriage and Relationship Education Services

Marriage education and relationship programs are designed to improve couple communication, teach conflict resolution skills, increase mutual social support between partners, strengthen commitment, help troubled couples avoid divorce, and generally improve the quality and stability of marriages. Numerous reviews of evidence indicate that the programs are effective for many couples.[46] A recent meta-analysis examined eleven studies that randomly assigned participants to treatment and control groups, and two quasi-experimental studies of the effects of marital education programs on problem-solving skills, marital conflict, and marital satisfaction.[47] Twelve of the thirteen studies found significant differences favoring couples who received the treatment. The mean effect size across all experimental and quasi-experimental studies was 0.80 of a standard deviation—a large effect size that is equivalent to a 12 point difference on an IQ test. Across all marital outcomes, the typical couple who received marital education scored higher than 79 percent of couples who did not. With respect to relationship stability, a German study found that after three years, 9 percent of intervention couples had broken up compared with 22 percent of control couples.[48] Similarly, a U.S. study found that after five years, only 4 percent of intervention couples had broken up, compared with 25 percent of non-intervention couples.[49] Although some studies do not show benefits in relationship stability, most show benefits in relationship quality.[50]

Increasing the share of couples who receive marital and relationship education is likely to improve marital quality, decrease the frequency of divorce and, correspondingly, decrease the share of children shifted into poverty. Among the limits of the studies cited earlier is that most focused on middle-class, white couples, and few followed couples for more than a few years. These limits were partly overcome by a recent large, representative survey of currently and formerly married people in four states: Oklahoma, Texas, Kansas, and Arizona.[51] The survey found that couples who participated in any type of marital education program before marriage were 18 percent less likely than other couples to be divorced after twenty years. And among couples who did not divorce, premarital education was associated with higher marital satisfaction and less marital conflict. Moreover, the estimated effects of premarital education held for low-income as well as high-income couples.[52]

Not surprisingly, in view of such evidence policymakers are paying increasing attention to marriage. Since launching the Healthy Marriage Initiative in 2002, the Administration for Children and Families (ACF) has backed programs to provide marital education and relationship skills training on a voluntary basis to interested individuals and couples, as well as public education efforts that emphasize the value of marriage education programs, and research to evaluate these services.[53] Some of these initiatives have focused particularly on African American, Latino, and Native American populations.

In February 2006, President Bush signed the Deficit Reduction Act of 2005, which reauthorized the Temporary Assistance to Needy Families (TANF) program. Over a period of five years, the law allocates $100 million a year to promote healthy marriage and another $50 million a year to promote responsible fatherhood. In May 2006, the ACF announced the availability of Healthy Marriage Demonstration Grants, which may be used for public advertising campaigns about the value of marriage and the skills needed to increase marital quality and stability; high school courses on the value of marriage, relationship skills, and budgeting; premarital education programs for engaged couples and those interested in marriage; and marriage enhancement and relationship skills programs for married couples.[54] By October 2006, the ACF had funded more than 300 individual programs to promote healthy marriage and responsible fatherhood.

We support expanding marriage and relationship education. Statistics on the share of couples who receive such education before marriage are hard to locate, but the four-state survey already noted put the figure at about 40 percent of recently married couples, and an estimate from a national telephone survey conducted in 1996 was nearly identical.[55] We propose doubling that share to 80 percent.

About 2.3 million couples married in 2004, according to the National Center on Health Statistics.[56] If 40 percent received marital and relationship education, that would come to 0.92 million couples. Doubling the share to 80 percent would mean that another 0.92 million couples would participate in these programs each year. We recommend that states go beyond this goal, however. Marital and relationship education programs appear to be beneficial for married couples as well. Indeed, one study found that they were most beneficial for couples who had been married for between five and ten years.[57] They may also be useful for cohabiting couples, as well as single people with an interest in marriage. We recommend providing these services to roughly a million married couples as well, bringing the total number of additional couples receiving the services to approximately 2 million a year.

Raising the share of people who take these courses will require increasing the number of people qualified to teach them. The Okla-

homa Marriage Initiative (OMI) serves as an example of one way to increase the supply of teachers.[58] The OMI has trained many people to provide the Prevention and Relationship Enhancement Program (PREP), a commonly used program developed by Howard Markman, Scott Stanley, and their colleagues.[59] Trained providers in Oklahoma include state employees from the Department of Human Services, the Health Department, and the State University Extension Service. Oklahoma also provides free training for volunteers from the community, including mental health practitioners, marriage and family therapists, social workers, and ministers. In exchange for free training, the volunteers agree to deliver a minimum of four workshops to the public at no cost.

In recent years, the PREP program has been given to more than 100,000 people throughout Oklahoma. Although marriage education traditionally has been provided through churches, the availability of secular sources makes it possible to serve couples who are not religious or planning a church wedding. And though PREP was developed for middle-class couples planning to marry, Oklahoma has developed a more intensive program for poor, unmarried couples who are expecting a child.[60] Other special versions have been adapted for prisoners, Hispanic couples, couples who are adopting a high-risk child, and high school students.

A typical workshop involves about twelve couples. To meet our target of 2 million couples, this would mean adding 167,000 workshops every year. (A typical workshop involves ten to twelve hours of participation, although programs that focus on unmarried couples with children generally involve more time.) Most trained providers hold jobs that limit the number of workshops that they can offer every year. If each provider were to offer three or four workshops over the course of a year, then about 48,000 new providers across the United States would need to be recruited and trained. One major cost that states will face, therefore, involves training marriage education providers.

States must also increase public demand for these services. Public education campaigns are one way to promote the benefits and availability of marriage education programs in the community. Partnering with other organizations in the community, such as churches and civic groups, is another. Low-income couples, in particular, can be recruited when they apply for public assistance. Getting people to attend the programs, though, is another matter. One way to increase attendance would be to reduce the cost of a marriage license for couples who complete a premarital education workshop taught by a certified provider. Today the cost of a marriage license varies from $10 to more than $100, depending on the state. If a state charges, say, $30 for a marriage license, it could increase the charge to $150 for couples without premarital education and provide the license without charge to those with premarital education. If the state achieves its goal of 80 percent participation by couples about to marry, its net revenue would remain the same. That is, for every 100 couples, 80 would pay nothing and 20 would pay $150. The total would be $3,000 for every 100 couples—the same amount collected as if every couple paid $30. Several states, such as Florida and Oklahoma, already have adopted similar policies.

What would be the implications of providing relationship skills training to an additional 0.92 million couples before they marry, each year? In 2004 the United States recorded some 1 million divorces.[61] Assuming, based on the findings of the four-state study already noted, that marriage education lowers the risk of divorce by 18 percent, then expanding premarital education services from 40 percent to 80 percent of couples would eventually result in a decline of about 72,000 divorces annually (or 7.2 percent). Each

---

One way to increase attendance would be to reduce the cost of a marriage license for couples who complete a premarital education workshop taught by a certified provider.

---

divorce involves an average of 0.9 children.[62] Thus 65,000 fewer children would be entering a single-parent family every year because of marital dissolution. This number seems small compared with the 24 million children now living in single-parent families.[63] But the number of children spared the experience of divorce would accumulate annually. After seven or eight years, half a million fewer children would have entered single-parent families through divorce. And these estimates are conservative because they exclude the married couples, cohabiting couples, and single individuals who also would be eligible for these services. Indeed, if states were to provide services to 2 million couples every year, then the estimated reduction in divorce could be 144,000—twice the number indicated above. In addition, because marital education programs not only lower the risk of divorce but also improve the quality of marriage, focusing on declines in divorce alone ignores the benefits for couples who remain married, and hence underestimates the total value of these programs for children.

The economic costs of implementing the proposal would include recruiting and training providers, running public education campaigns to increase the demand for services, and hiring staff to administer the programs. Monitoring and periodically evaluating these interventions will be essential to ensure that quality remains high and that programs do not drift into ineffectiveness. Based on the experiences of many local and state efforts, we estimate that total program costs to provide a basic ten- to twelve-hour marriage and relationship education course would be about $100 per person, or $200 per couple.[64] If services are provided to an additional 2 million couples per year, then the total cost to the federal government would be about $400 million. The estimated cost also would be higher if the government paid for additional services, such as expanded counseling services for couples who are contemplating divorce, or longer and more intensive programs focused specifically on poor, unmarried couples with children.

We assume that the states would administer these programs, with the federal government providing the funding either directly or indirectly, if states divert unused TANF funds for this purpose. We believe that it would be most effective for states to administer these services, because marriage and divorce laws are formed at the state level, states have the administrative infrastructure to facilitate large-scale service delivery, and states can ensure program consistency across multiple sites. At the same time, state-based programs can adapt services to meet local state needs and engage in experimentation and innovation that may ultimately improve program quality.

Estimating the Benefits of Marriage for Reducing Child Poverty

Promoting healthy and stable marriages will not be easy, especially among poor couples and unmarried parents with children. Moreover, it is not clear how much of an economic boost marriage provides, given the uncertainty over the effects of selection noted earlier. Nevertheless, it is useful to consider the range of effects on child poverty that might result.

One straightforward method (referred to as a shift-share analysis) estimates how the child poverty rate would change if a certain share of children were "shifted" from single-parent to two-parent households. For example, in 2000, 15.6 percent of all children were poor.[65] The poverty rate was substantially lower (8.2 percent) for children living with married parents than for all other children (31.2 percent). In that year, 67.8 percent of children lived with two married parents. If the share of children with married parents in 2000 were the same as it was in 1990 (72.5 percent), then the overall share of children in poverty in 2000 would decline to 14.5 percent (see table 2). The 1.1 percentage point decrease from 15.6 percent to 14.5 percent would represent a 7 percent decline in child poverty. If the share of children living with married parents in 2000 were the same as it was in 1980 (76.7 percent), the overall share of children in poverty would decline to 13.6 percent—a 2 percentage point decline that corresponds to a 13 percent decline in child poverty. Finally, if the share of children with married parents in 2000 were the same as it was in 1970 (85.2 percent), then the overall share of children in poverty would decline to 11.6 percent—a 4 percentage point decline that corresponds to a 26 percent decline in child poverty.[66]

Table 2. Estimates of the Percentage of Children in Poverty, Assuming the Share of Children with Married Parents Remained as in Selected Earlier Decades

Percent

Method	Poor in 2000	Poor in 2000 if family structure were the same as in		
		1990	1980	1970
Shift-share analysis	15.6	14.5	13.6	11.6
Matching analysis	16.9	15.9	14.7	13.5
Regression analysis	15.6	14.4	13.3	11.1

Sources: Shift-share analysis and regression analysis estimates are authors' calculations based on data from the U.S. Census Bureau. Matching analysis estimates are from Adam Thomas and Isabel Sawhill, "For Love and Money? The Impact of Family Structure on Family Income," *Future of Children* 15, no. 2 (2005): 57–74.

Note: The matching analysis uses 1998 rather than 2000 as the base year and, unlike the other estimates, adjusts for federal tax liabilities, food stamp benefits, child-care expenses, and family size. The respective percentages of children living in two-parent households in each decade were 67.8 (2000), 72.5 (1990), 76.6 (1980), and 85.2 (1970).

A more sophisticated approach is to simulate marriages by hypothetically matching single women and men in the population on the basis of factors such as age, education, and race. This approach makes it possible to estimate how these "marriages" would affect family income and child poverty. This approach is particularly useful because it takes into account the earnings of men, thus decreasing the influence of selection. It also acknowledges that appropriate matches will not exist for everyone. When Adam Thomas and Isabel Sawhill applied this method to Current Population Survey data from 1970 and 1998, they found that if single mothers married eligible men at the same rate as they did in 1970, overall child poverty would fall from 16.9 percent to 13.5 percent.[67] Their study is notable because it adjusted the findings for a wide range of benefits and taxes, such as food stamps, the earned income tax credit, and child care expenses.

We use the Thomas and Sawhill findings to estimate the effects of smaller increases in marriage (using interpolation based on the assumption of a linear relationship). If the share of children living with married parents were the same in 1998 as it was in 1990, then child poverty would decline 6 percent. If the share were the same as it was in 1980, child poverty would decline 13 percent. Finally, as noted, if the share were the same as it was in 1970, child poverty would decline 20 percent. Note that the findings from this method differ somewhat from the shift-share analysis, at least in part because Thomas and Sawhill adjusted for a variety of benefits and taxes and in part because the matching procedure adjusts for some sources of selection.

To provide a range of estimates, we used a third method: time-series regression based on the years 1970–2004. The shares of children living in poverty and living without two parents increased in tandem from 1970 through the early 1990s. During the second half of the 1990s, the share of children living in poverty declined, while the share of children living without both parents remained stable. This decline in poverty (without a corresponding change in single-parent households) may have been due to the passage of welfare reform legislation in 1996, as well as to general improvements in the economy during these years. After 2000, however, child poverty and the share of children living without two parents both began to increase again. The regression analysis suggested that increasing the share of children living with two parents to 15.6 percent—the same share as in 1970—would result in a 29 percent decline in the share of children living in poverty—a decline larger than that found by Thomas and Sawhill.[68]

To put these figures in perspective, it is useful to think in terms of the absolute number of children who might be affected. In 2000, 11 million children lived in poverty.[69] It is estimated that increasing the share of children living with two married parents to the same share as in 1970 would lift between 2.2 million and 3.2 million children above the poverty threshold, depending on the estimation method used. (Given that child poverty rates have increased since 2000, these figures underestimate the total number of children who would benefit. Moreover, the figures ignore benefits to the mothers of these children, who also would be lifted out of poverty.) These estimates lead to a straightforward conclusion. Although marriage programs will not eliminate all child poverty, or even most of child poverty, increasing the number of stable marriages will improve the economic well-being of many children and their mothers. Even if we conservatively assume that half of the estimated effect of marriage is due to selection, the decline in child poverty would be substantial.[70]

Can the policies we recommend bring about increases in the share of children living with two parents comparable to the changes shown in table 2? We believe the answer is yes, but it will take time. Based on our estimates of reductions in nonmarital births and the number of children whose parents divorce every year, our policy recommendations, if fully implemented, would take about ten years to make two-parent families as common as they were

in 1990 and about twenty years to make them as common as they were in 1980. The slow rate of change reflects a process that social scientists call cohort replacement. That is, the current high rates of nonmarital fertility and marital instability originated in an era when childrearing outside marriage was seen as socially acceptable and divorce, even when a couple had children, was widely viewed as a reasonable solution to a less-than-satisfying marriage. As new cohorts enter their childbearing years with different attitudes about nonmarital births, the ability and commitment to use contraception more effectively, better relationship skills, and a stronger commitment to the norm of lifelong marriage, they will gradually represent a larger share of the population. But because cohort replacement is a slow process, most social change occurs gradually. Policymakers will need to be patient, and the leadership of different political parties must agree that these are worthwhile long-term goals.

Of course, other developments may intervene to speed up the process of change. For example, pro-marriage policies, even when directed at specific populations (such as couples about to marry or in the early years of marriage), may gradually generalize and permeate the larger culture. Similarly, other antipoverty proposals described in this volume, if implemented and successful, would reinforce the marriage-focused policies that we recommend. Poverty and family disorganization mutually reinforce one another. Although our goal has been to suggest how poverty might be lowered through family interventions, policies that improve people's economic resources and decrease economic hardship also help to strengthen marriages and families. In this sense, any policy that lowers the rate of poverty in the United States is a pro-marriage policy.

Criticisms

Some observers will object to these proposals by arguing that government should not intervene in arrangements as private as childbearing and marriage. But the high rates of nonmarital births and divorce impose substantial costs on the American public. Teen childbearing alone cost U.S. taxpayers an estimated $7.3 billion in 2004.[71] One scholar has estimated that each divorce costs U.S. society about $30,000, which represents $30 billion every year.[72] The cost includes heavy caseloads in family courts, the hiring of court personnel (such as counselors and mediators), the use of public assistance by many recently divorced mothers and their children, the loss of work productivity because of divorce-related stress, declining academic success among children, and higher rates of teen delinquency. The cost is even higher when one considers how marital conflict itself affects work productivity. One study estimated that the days of work lost because of marital distress translate into nearly $7 billion a year.[73] Programs to reduce nonmarital births and strengthen marriage could reduce these costs substantially. Under our proposal, participation in government-subsidized marriage and relationship education programs will be voluntary. Thus, the programs will not infringe on individual liberties. Moreover, most couples who participate in these programs find them to be useful and worthwhile.[74]

Although marriage promotion programs may benefit many couples, they may produce unintended negative consequences, particularly of an economic nature, for some couples—especially poor couples with children. For example, if a poor single mother marries her partner, and if her partner is employed, her family income will increase. This rise in income, however, means that the mother and her children are likely to lose some means-tested government benefits. The overall effect of marriage on a family's standard of living is complex, and it depends on the amount of the husband's earnings, as well as the specific benefits that mothers and children were receiving before marriage. Single mothers who received a wide range of benefits, and whose new husbands earn low to moderate income, may be worse off economically fol-

---

Although marriage promotion programs may benefit many couples, they may produce unintended negative consequences, particularly of an economic nature, for some couples—especially poor couples with children.

---

lowing marriage.[75] Nevertheless, most cohabiting couples with children who marry will enjoy improved economic well-being because of planned increases in the earned income tax credit and the child tax credit.[76] Despite these changes in tax laws, policymakers should consider policies that allow mothers and their children to continue to receive government assistance for a period of time following marriage.

The long-term benefits of marriage also depend on whether mothers stay married. One study found that marriage offsets the economic disadvantage of becoming a single mother, provided that the couple remains together.[77] The marriages of previously single mothers, however, are less stable than other marriages. The same study found that single mothers who married but then divorced were worse off economically in the long run than were single mothers who did not marry—a finding that may largely reflect selection effects. Other research shows that multiple family transitions are associated with higher risks of behavioral and emotional problems among children.[78] These findings reinforce the importance of developing marriage and relationship education programs that attend to special needs of low-income couples.

One difficulty encountered in marriage education programs is that sometimes only one partner shows up for training—usually the woman. This problem may be especially pronounced among low-income couples. But a single partner may still benefit from learning communication and conflict-resolution skills and then modeling them in her relationship. In this manner, the relationship may still benefit even if only one partner attends—though not as much as if both do so. It is important to think creatively about how to get reluctant low-income men to participate in marriage education programs, perhaps by moving training sessions to more "masculine" settings, such as the workplace, or to familiar community settings, such as churches. Another possibility is to link marriage programs with job training programs for unemployed men. It may also be useful to stress that premarital education differs from therapy, on the assumption that men (and some women) are more likely to respond positively to educational than to therapeutic interventions. Men also may be more likely to attend when workshops are run by men rather than women, which suggests the importance of recruiting and training providers of both genders. The same principle applies to recruiting and training providers from diverse racial, ethnic, and cultural backgrounds. We suspect that increasing the motivation of men to partici-

pate would at least partly offset the tendency of some low-income couples to attend sessions sporadically. An alternative would be to provide a modest cash incentive (or its equivalent in gifts) to low-income couples who complete the program successfully.

One problem that typical marriage programs may not address is that a single mother is likely to marry a man who is not the father of her child (or at least not the father of some of her children). Many children of single mothers who marry (or remarry) thus live in stepfamilies. Although marriage increases the economic resources in the household, research consistently shows that children fare no better in stepfamilies than in single-parent families in terms of psychological and behavioral adjustment.[79] Tension between stepfathers and stepchildren is not uncommon, and family discord can offset the potential benefits of a higher standard of living. These research findings suggest that the needs of stepfamilies may differ sufficiently from those of natural parent couples to warrant specially designed programs.

Some observers have expressed concern that public policies supporting marriage may inadvertently lead some women to become trapped in abusive relationships. Although the concern is valid, research indicates that most instances of relationship aggression involve "situational couple violence."[80] Situational violence reflects everyday arguments that escalate out of control, rather than the intent of one partner (usually the male) to dominate and control the other. Such violence usually does not result in serious injury (although it can) and is as likely to be initiated by wives as by husbands. Consequently, couples who have experienced a few episodes of aggression, especially when it is not severe, should not necessarily be screened out of marriage education programs. Nevertheless, the risk of serious violence remains a possibility for some mothers and their children, particularly low-income women.[81] For this reason, program administrators must work closely with domestic violence experts to ensure that adequate safeguards are in place for vulnerable mothers and children. Indeed, all federal government programs are required to take this step and to develop domestic violence protocols to protect mothers and children at risk of domestic violence.[82]

The risk of domestic violence can be reduced by helping single young women (and men) make healthy choices about relationships. Within My Reach, a program being deployed in numerous settings, including classes for welfare recipients, in Oklahoma, is an example of an initiative for individuals (rather than couples).[83] It includes strong messages about feeling safe in relationships, as well as strategies for exiting or avoiding potentially dangerous relationships or marriages. The curriculum places explicit emphasis on the value of moving slowly and deliberately toward major relationship transitions, such as having a child, cohabiting, or marriage.

Finally, some observers may argue that the money spent on these programs would be better spent by being transferred directly to single parents with children. As noted, however, the costs per person are not large. Diverting these funds directly to single parents and their children would have only a minimal and short-term effect on a single-parent family's standard of living. The opportunity cost is the potential for long-term gains through more and stronger two-parent families.

Conclusions

Researchers do not yet know whether programs to promote healthy marriage will be effective when delivered on a large scale, especially to low-income couples. Some observers might argue that such uncertainty is a good reason not to expand these services. The next several years, however, should begin to provide some answers. The Administration for Children and Families has funded three large-scale marriage demonstration projects, complete with rigorous evaluations. One, Supporting Healthy Marriage, involves marriage education and relationship skills training for couples who already are married or are planning to marry.[84] The second, the Community Healthy Marriage Initiative, involves communitywide interventions, including public education campaigns to raise marital quality and improve parenting skills.[85] The third, Building Strong Families, focuses on low-income, unmarried couples around the time of the birth of their child. It provides long-term marriage and relationship skills education, along with a variety of linked family support services, such as assistance with parenting, employment, or health problems.[86]

The evaluations of these programs, based on random assignment of couples to intervention and control groups, represent a good investment of government funding. Of the hundreds of programs for couples that exist today, surprisingly few have been rigorously evaluated. These ongoing evaluations will provide substantial information on what works and what does not. The findings will allow practitioners and policymakers to focus on programs that have the greatest chance of increasing the number of children growing up in stable and healthy two-parent families.

Much remains to be learned about how to foster healthy and stable marriages, especially among low-income couples. Still, evidence suggests that programs to reduce nonmarital childbearing and strengthen marriage can be useful tools in fighting poverty. Such programs, on their own, will never be a panacea for eradicating economic disadvantage in American society. Wendy Sigle-Rushton and Sara McLanahan, using data from the Fragile Families Study, found that if the unmarried parents in the sample were to marry, nearly half of the poor single mothers and their children would rise above the poverty line. But about half of the mothers and their children would remain in poverty.[87] That finding is a sobering reminder that poverty has many causes and that there is no simple strategy for improving the well-being of all the poor. Nevertheless, programs to reduce nonmarital childbearing and increase the number of healthy and stable marriages, when combined with a variety of other antipoverty policies, can play a useful role in easing economic hardship in the United States.

Notes

1. Adam Thomas and Isabel Sawhill, "For Love and Money? The Impact of Family Structure on Family Income," *Future of Children* 15, no. 2 (2005): 57–74.

2. U.S. Census Bureau, *Statistical Abstract of the United States 2006* (2007), table 586; R. Kelly Raley and Larry Bumpass, "The Topography of the Divorce Plateau: Levels and Trends in Union Stability in the United States after 1980," *Demographic Research* 8 (2003): 246–59; Rose Kreider, "Number, Timing, and Duration of Marriages and Divorces: 2001," *Current Population Reports* (U.S. Census Bureau, 2005); S. C. Clarke, "Advance Report of Final Divorce Statistics, 1989 and 1990," *Monthly Vital Statistics Report* 43, no. 8 (Hyattsville, Md.: National Center for Health Statistics, 1995).

3. Joyce Martin and others, *National Vital Statistics Report* 55, no. 1 (U.S. Department of Health and Human Services, National Center for Health Statistics, 2006).

4. Andrew J. Cherlin, "Should the Government Promote Marriage?" *Contexts* 2 (2003): 22–30.

5. David Eggebeen and Daniel Lichter, "Race, Family Structure, and Changing Poverty among American Children," *American Sociological Review* 56 (1991): 801–17; Robert I. Lerman, "The Impact of the Changing U.S. Family Structure on Poverty and Income Inequality," *Economica* 63 (1996): S119–39; John Iceland, "Why Poverty Remains High: The Role of Income Growth, Economic Inequality, and Changes in Family Structure, 1949–1999," *Demography* 40 (2003): 499–519.

6. Robert I. Lerman. *Impact of Marital Status and Parental Presence on the Material Hardship of Families with Children* (Washington: Urban Institute, 2002); Robert I. Lerman. *How Do Marriage, Cohabitation, and Single Parenthood Affect the Material Hardships of Families with Children?* (Washington: Urban Institute, 2002).

7. U.S. Census Bureau, *Poverty Thresholds* (2005), www.census.gov/hhes/www/poverty/threshld/thresh05 .html (November 21, 2006).

8. *Statistical Abstract of the United States 2006*, table 586 (see note 2).

9. Paul R. Amato and others, *Alone Together: How Marriage in America Is Changing* (Harvard University Press, 2007).

10. Steven L. Nock, *Marriage in Men's Lives* (Oxford University Press, 1998).

11. Charlotte Schoenborn, *Marital Status and Health: United States, 1999–2002. Advance Data from Vital and Health Statistics* (Hyattsville, Md.: National Center for Health Statistics, 2004); Linda Waite, "Does Marriage Matter?" *Demography* 32 (1995): 483–507.

12. L. Hao, "Family Structure, Private Transfers, and the Economic Well-Being of Families with Children," *Social Forces* 75 (1996): 269–92; David Eggebeen, "Cohabitation and Exchanges of Support," *Social Forces* 83 (2005): 1097–110; Anne E. Winkler, "Economic Decision-Making by Cohabitors: Findings Regarding Income Pooling," *Applied Economics* 29 (1997): 1079–90.

13. Dan Lichter, Deborah R. Graefe, and J. Brian Brown, "Is Marriage a Panacea? Union Formation among Economically-Disadvantaged Unwed Mothers," *Social Problems* 50 (2003): 60–86.

14. Lynn K. White and Stacy J. Rogers, "Economic Circumstances and Family Outcomes: A Review of the 1990s," *Journal of Marriage and Family* 62 (2000): 1035–51; Jay Teachman, Lucky M. Tedrow, and Kyle D.

Crowder, "The Changing Demography of America's Families," *Journal of Marriage and Family* 62 (2000): 1234–46.

15. Gregory Acs and Sandi Nelson, *What Do "I Do's" Do? Potential Benefits of Marriage for Cohabiting Couples with Children* (Washington: Urban Institute, 2004); Robert I. Lerman, *Married and Unmarried Parenthood and Economic Well-Being: A Dynamic Analysis of a Recent Cohort* (Washington: Urban Institute, 2002); Nock, *Marriage in Men's Lives* (see note 10); Paula Roberts, "I Can't Give You Anything but Love: Would Poor Couples with Children Be Better Off Economically if They Married?" *Couples and Marriage Series Brief* 5 (Washington: Center for Law and Social Policy, 2004); Waite, "Does Marriage Matter?" (see note 11).

16. Juliana M. Sobolweski and Paul R. Amato, "Economic Hardship in the Family of Origin and Children's Psychological Well-Being in Adulthood," *Journal of Marriage and Family* 67 (2005): 141–57; Rand D. Conger and Glenn H. Elder, *Families in Troubled Times: Adapting to Change in Rural America* (Aldine de Gruyter, 1994); Matthew Bramlett and William Mosher, "Cohabitation, Marriage, Divorce, and Remarriage in the United States," *Vital and Health Statistics,* Series 23, no. 22 (Hyattsville, Md.: National Center for Health Statistics, 2002).

17. Sara McLanahan and Gary Sandefur, *Growing Up with a Single Parent: What Hurts, What Helps* (Harvard University Press, 1994). Also see Pamela Smock, Wendy Manning, and Sanjiv Gupta, "The Effect of Marriage and Divorce on Women's Economic Well-Being," *American Sociological Review* 64 (1999): 794–812.

18. Jay D. Teachman and Kathleen M. Paasch, "Financial Impact of Divorce on Children and Their Families," *Future of Children* 4, no 1 (1994): 63–83.

19. Jay L. Zagorsky, "Marriage and Divorce's Impact on Wealth," *Journal of Sociology* 41 (2005): 406–24.

20. *National Vital Statistics Report* 54, no. 2 (U.S. Department of Health and Human Services, National Center for Health Statistics, 2005), table 2, p. 30, and table 17, p. 52.

21. It also would be useful to design programs geared toward helping unwed couples with children (or expecting a child) to solidify their relationships and learn effective methods of co-parenting (whether in marriage or not). We do not focus specifically on this policy initiative in this article, however, for two reasons. First, the size and character of the target population for such interventions will be determined by the success of our main proposals. Second, major demonstration projects are under way that eventually will inform the design of such efforts. The major evaluation effort focused on this population refers to Building Strong Families programs (www.buildingstrongfamilies.info [November 21, 2006]).

22. Susan Brown, "Child Well-Being in Cohabiting Families," in *Just Living Together: Implications of Cohabitation on Families, Children and Social Policy,* edited by Alan Booth and Ann C. Crouter (Mahwah, N.J.: Lawrence Erlbaum, 2002), pp. 173–87; Larry L. Wu, Larry L. Bumpass, and Kelly Musick. "Historical and Life Course Trajectories of Nonmarital Childbearing," CDE Working Paper 99-23 (University of Wisconsin-Madison: Center for Demography and Ecology, 1999).

23. A. Bachu, "Trends in Marital Status of U.S. Women at First Birth: 1930 to 1994," *Population Division Working Papers* 35 (U.S. Bureau of the Census, 1998), table 1.

24. Sara McLanahan and others, *The Fragile Families and Child Wellbeing Study: Baseline National Report* (Princeton University: Bendheim-Thoman Center for Research on Child Well-Being, 2003).

25. Cynthia Osborn, *Maternal Stress and Mothering Behaviors in Stable and Unstable Families* (Princeton University: Bendheim-Thoman Center for Research on Child Well-Being, 2003); Cynthia Osborne and Sara McLanahan, *The Effects of Partnership Instability on Parenting and Young Children's Health and Behavior* (Princeton University: Center for Research on Child Well-Being, 2004).

26. We thank Sara McLanahan and Kevin Bradway for providing these statistics from their five-year follow-up of the Fragile Families sample.

27. Wu, Bumpass, and Musick, "Historical and Life Course Trajectories of Nonmarital Childbearing" (see note 22).

28. *Statistical Abstract of the United States 2006,* table 82 (see note 2).

29. See John S. Santelli and others, "Can Changes in Sexual Behaviors among High School Students Explain the Decline in Teen Pregnancy Rates in the 1990s?" *Journal of Adolescent Health* 35, no. 2 (2004); Jacqueline E. Darroch and S. Singh, "Why Is Teenage Pregnancy Declining? The Roles of Abstinence, Sexual Activity, and Contraceptive Use," Occasional Report 1 (New York: Alan Guttmacher Institute, 1999).

30. U.S. Bureau of the Census, www.infoplease.com/ipa/A0005061.html (February 7, 2007).

31. Stanley K. Henshaw, "Unintended Pregnancy in the United States," *Family Planning Perspectives* 30, no. 1 (1998): 24–29 and 46, table 1.

32. U.S. House of Representatives, Committee on Ways and Means, *Green Book: Background Material and Data on Programs within the Jurisdiction of the House Committee on Ways and Means,* appendix M (2004), www.gpoaccess.gov/wmprints/green/2004.html (February 8, 2007).

33. Saul D. Hoffman and E. M. Foster, "Economic Correlates of Nonmarital Childbearing among Adult Women," *Family Planning Perspectives* 29, no. 3 (1997): 137–40.

34. Henshaw, "Unintended Pregnancy in the United States" (see note 31).

35. For example, see Lauren Scher, Rebecca Maynard, and Matthew Stagner, *Interventions Intended to Reduce Pregnancy-Related Outcomes among Adolescents* (Campbell Collaboration, 2006), www.campbellcollaboration.org/doc-pdf/scherteenpregnancyprot.pdf (February 7, 2007); Douglas Kirby, *No Easy Answers: Research Findings on Programs to Reduce Teen Pregnancy* (Washington: National Campaign to Prevent Teen Pregnancy, 1997); J. Manlove and others, "Preventing Teenage Pregnancy, Childbearing, and Sexually Transmitted Diseases: What the Research Shows," Child Trends Research Brief (Washington: Child Trends, 2002); and A. DiCenso and others, "Interventions to Reduce Unintended Pregnancies among Adolescents: Systematic Review of Randomized Controlled Trials," *BMJ* 324 (2002): 1426–30.

36. Saul D. Hoffman and Rebecca A. Maynard, eds., *Kids Having Kids: The Economic and Social Consequences of Teenage Childbearing,* 2nd ed. (Washington: Urban Institute Press, forthcoming).

37. Kathryn Edin and Maria Kefalas report that even when children are not strictly intended, many poor women are happy to discover that they are pregnant. Because educational and occupational routes to satisfaction are limited, these young women see parenthood as a way to enhance their self-esteem and sense of purpose in life. Kathryn Edin and Maria Kefalas, *Promises I Can Keep: Why Poor Women Put Motherhood before Marriage* (University of California Press, 2005).

38. Tabulations of the National Survey of Adolescent Health and the Youth Risk Behavior Surveillance Survey data for 1995 indicate that more than 90 percent of school districts provide some form of health and sex education and that nearly the same proportion of youth report having been taught about HIV/AIDS infections.

39. See, for example, Centers for Disease Control and Prevention, *School Health Policies and Programs Study* (2000); Laura Kann, Nancy D. Brener, and Diane D. Allensworth, "Health Education: Results from the School Health Policies and Programs Study 2000," *Journal of School Health* 71, no. 7 (2001); Cynthia Dillard, "Sex Education: Politicians, Parents, Teachers, and Teens," *Guttmacher Report on Public Policy* 4, no. 1 (2001).

40. See, for example, the descriptions of a sampling of abstinence education programs funded under Title V, Section 510, of the Social Security Act, as reported in Rebecca Maynard and others, *First-Year Impacts of Four Title V, Section 510, Abstinence Education Programs* (Princeton, N.J.: Mathematica Policy Research, Inc., 2005), compared with the descriptions of the predominantly comprehensive sex education programs in a synthesis of research by Douglas Kirby, *Emerging Answers* (Washington: National Campaign to Prevent Teen Pregnancy, 2001).

41. For example, see National Campaign to Prevent Teen Pregnancy, "Curriculum Based Programs That Prevent Teen Pregnancy," www.teenpregnancy.org/resources/reading/pdf/What_Works.pdf (February 7, 2007). The inconclusive nature of the evidence on program effectiveness is illustrated in the systematic reviews of evidence reported by Scher, Maynard, and Stagner, *Interventions Intended to Reduce Pregnancy-Related Outcomes among Adolescents* (note 35); and Kirby, *No Easy Answers* (see note 35). Also see Douglas Kirby, *Abstinence Programs Delay the Initiation of Sex among Young People and Reduce Teen Pregnancy* (2002), www.teenpregnancy.org/resources/data/pdf/abstinence_eval.pdf (February 7, 2007).

42. See Rebecca Maynard and Saul Hoffman, "The Costs of Adolescent Childbearing," in *Kids Having Kids*, edited by Hoffman and Maynard (see note 36). The estimated program costs assume an average of 630 students per educator, salary and benefits for the educators of $100,000 a year, and material costs per student of $30 a year.

43. Total program costs would be about $2.7 billion, and the projected savings associated with halving the rate of teen childbearing would be about $3.6 billion annually.

44. See www.advocatesforyouth.org/programsthatwork/13carrera.htm (February 8, 2007).

45. Scher, Maynard, and Stagner, *Interventions Intended to Reduce Pregnancy-Related Outcomes among Adolescents* (see note 35).

46. W. K. Halford and others, "Best Practice in Couple Relationship Education," *Journal of Marital and Family Therapy* 29 (2003): 385–406; Theodora Ooms, "The New Kid on the Block: What Is Marriage Education and Does It Work?" Brief 7 (Washington: Center for Law and Social Policy Research, July 2005); Jane Reardon-Anderson and others, *Systematic Review of the Impact of Marriage and Relationship Programs* (U.S. Department of Health and Human Services, Administration for Children and Families, 2005).

47. J. S. Carroll and William J. Doherty, "Evaluating the Effectiveness of Premarital Prevention Programs: A Meta-Analytic Review of Outcome Research," *Family Relations* 52 (2003): 105–18.

48. Kurt Hahlweg and others, "Prevention of Marital Distress: Results of a German Prospective Longitudinal Study," *Journal of Family Psychology* 12 (1998): 543–56.

49. Howard Markman and others, "Preventing Marital Distress through Communication and Conflict Management Training: A 4- and 5-Year Follow-Up," *Journal of Consulting and Clinical Psychology* 61 (1993): 70–77.

50. W. Kim Halford and others, "Benefits of a Flexible Delivery Relationship Education: An Evaluation of the Couple CARE Program," *Family Relations* 53 (2004): 469–76; W. Kim Halford and others, "Do Couples at High Risk of Relationship Problems Attend Premarriage Education?" *Journal of Family Psychology* 20 (2006): 160–63.

51. Scott Stanley and others, "Premarital Education, Marital Quality, and Marital Stability," *Journal of Family Psychology* 20 (2006):117–26.

52. Because this study is based on survey data, selection may account for some of the estimated effect of premarital education on divorce. Nevertheless, the study included a large number of controls, including whether couples were married in a religious setting. Given that most premarital education services traditionally have been offered by religious organizations, this variable represents a strong control for selection. The researchers also used biprobit regression with correlated errors and found no evidence that omitted variables upwardly biased the estimated program effect.

53. Administration for Children and Families, *Healthy Marriage Initiative Activities and Accomplishments 2002–2004* (U.S. Department of Health and Human Services, 2005).

54. Elisa Minoff, Theodora Ooms, and Paula Roberts, "Healthy Marriage and Responsible Fatherhood Grants: Announcement Overview" (Center for Law and Social Policy, May 30, 2006), www.clasp.org/publications/marriage_fatherhood_rfp.pdf (January 28, 2007).

55. National telephone survey conducted by Scott Stanley and Howard Markman, 1996.

56. See www.cdc.gov/nchs/fastats/divorce.htm (February 6, 2007).

57. Elizabeth B. Fawcett, Alan J. Hawkins, and Victoria L. Blanchard, "Does Marriage Education Work? A Comprehensive Review of the Effectiveness of Marriage Education," paper presented at the annual meeting of the National Council on Family Relations, Minneapolis, November 8, 2006.

58. See www.okmarriage.org (February 7, 2007).

59. The basic principles of PREP are described in Howard J. Markman, Scott Stanley, and Susan L. Blumberg, *Fighting for Your Marriage: Positive Steps for Preventing Divorce and Having a Lasting Love* (San Francisco: Jossey-Bass, 2005). For recent evaluations of PREP, see Philippe-Jean Laurenceau and others, "Community-Based Prevention of Marital Dysfunction: Multilevel Modeling of a Randomized Effectiveness Study," *Journal of Consulting and Clinical Psychology* 72 (2004): 933–43; Scott Stanley and others, "Dissemination and Evaluation of Marriage Education in the Army," *Family Process* 44 (2005): 187–201.

60. Oklahoma uses a version of Pam Jordan and colleagues' Becoming Parents Program (BPP), which is based on the PREP model but also addresses changes in the couple relationship pre- and postbirth. See M. Robin Dion and others, *Implementing Healthy Marriage Programs for Unmarried Couples with Children: Early Lessons from the Building Strong Families Project* (Mathematica Policy Research, 2006).

61. In the late 1990s, the federal government stopped publishing national counts of divorce, mainly because several states habitually failed to provide data on divorce. The current estimate is based on the authors' cal-

culations from states that provided data in 2004 and assumes that the frequency of divorce is, overall, comparable in states that comply and those that do not.

62. U.S. Census Bureau, *Statistical Abstract of the United States 1999*, table 159.

63. *Statistical Abstract of the United States 2006*, table 60 (see note 2).

64. This estimate is based on conversations between the authors and organizations that currently administer various marriage programs.

65. *Statistical Abstract of the United States 2006*, table 694 (see note 2).

66. For examples of shift-share analyses, see Eggebeen and Lichter, "Race, Family Structure, and Changing Poverty" (see note 5); Lerman, "The Impact of the Changing U.S. Family Structure on Poverty" (see note 5); Wendy Sigle-Rushton and Sara McLanahan, "For Richer or Poorer? Marriage as an Anti-Poverty Strategy in the United States," Working Paper 01-17-FF (Princeton University, Bendheim-Thoman Center for Research on Child Wellbeing, 2003).

67. Thomas and Sawhill, "For Love and Money?" (see note 1).

68. The time-series analysis controlled for variables that may be correlated with single-parent family formation and poverty, including the unemployment rate, the value of the minimum wage in constant dollars, the percentage of female high school graduates, and the introduction of TANF legislation in 1996.

69. *Statistical Abstract of the United States 2006*, table 694 (see note 2).

70. Although we present a range of estimates, our most optimistic projections are not unreasonable. In recent years, some communities have adopted pro-marriage programs that include premarital education, annual enrichment retreats for married couples, interventions for couples at risk of divorce, and the introduction of support groups for stepfamilies. Most of these interventions are based in religious organizations. A recent study estimated the effect of community marriage support policies on divorce rates. In general, the divorce rate declined modestly during the evaluation period. But communities that adopted these policies experienced a decline in the rate of divorce that was about twice as large as the decline in other communities. This study suggests that interventions to strengthen marriage, even when limited to religious organizations, can have a significant effect on the rate of divorce. Paul James Birch, Stan E. Weed, and Joseph Olsen, "Assessing the Impact of Community Marriage Policies on County Divorce Rates," *Family Relations* 53 (2004): 495–503.

71. Hoffman and Maynard, eds., *Kids Having Kids* (see note 36).

72. David G. Schramm, "Individual and Social Costs of Divorce in Utah," *Journal of Family and Economic Issues* 27 (2006): 133–51.

73. Melinda S. Forthofer and others, "Associations between Marital Distress and Work Loss in a National Sample," *Journal of Marriage and the Family* 58 (1996): 597–605.

74. Reardon-Anderson and others, *Systematic Review of the Impact of Marriage and Relationship Programs* (see note 46); Fawcett, Hawkins, and Blanchard, "Does Marriage Education Work?" (note 57).

75. Adam Carasso and C. Eugene Steuerle, "The Hefty Penalty on Marriage Facing Many Households with Children," *Future of Children* 15, no. 2 (2005): 157–75.

76. Gregory Acs and Elaine Maag. "Irreconcilable Differences? The Conflict between Marriage Promotion Initiatives for Cohabiting Couples with Children and Marriage Penalties in Tax and Transfer Programs," Report B-66 (Washington: Urban Institute: 2005).

77. Lichter, Graefe, and Brown, "Is Marriage a Panacea?" (note 13).

78. Jan Pryor and Bryan Rogers, *Children in Changing Families: Life after Parental Separation* (London: Blackwell, 2001).

79. Paul R. Amato, "The Implications of Research on Children in Stepfamilies," in *Stepfamilies: Who Benefits? Who Does Not*, edited by Alan Booth and Judy Dunn (Hillsdale, N.J.: Lawrence Erlbaum, 2004).

80. Michael P. Johnson and Kathleen Farraro, "Research on Family Violence in the 1990s: Making Distinctions," *Journal of Marriage and Family* 62 (2000): 948–63; Michael P. Johnson and Janel M. Leone, "The Differential Effects of Intimate Terrorism and Situational Couple Violence: Findings from the National Violence against Women Survey," *Journal of Family Issues* 26 (2005): 322–49.

81. Janel M. Leone and others, "Consequences of Male Partner Violence for Low-Income Minority Women," *Journal of Marriage and Family* 66 (2004): 472–90; Edin and Kefalas, *Promises I Can Keep* (note 37).

82. Paula Roberts, "Building Bridges between the Healthy Marriage, Responsible Fatherhood, and Domestic Violence Movements: Issues, Concerns, and Recommendations," Couples and Marriage Series Brief 7 (Washington: Center for Law and Social Policy, September, 2006).

83. Scott Stanley, Marline Pearson, and Galena H. Kline, "The Development of Relationship Education for Low-Income Individuals: Lessons from Research and Experience," paper presented at the meeting of the Association for Public Policy Analysis and Management, Washington, 2005.

84. See www.supportinghealthymarriage.org (February 7, 2007).

85. See www.acf.hhs.gov/programs/opre/strengthen/eval_com/index.html (February 7, 2007).

86. See www.buildingstrongfamilies.info (February 7, 2007).

87. Sigle-Rushton and McLanahan, "For Richer or Poorer?" (note 66).

Reducing Poverty through Preschool Interventions

Greg J. Duncan, Jens Ludwig, and Katherine A. Magnuson

Summary

Greg Duncan, Jens Ludwig, and Katherine Magnuson explain how providing high-quality care to disadvantaged preschool children can help reduce poverty. In early childhood, they note, children's cognitive and socioemotional skills develop rapidly and are sensitive to "inputs" from parents, home learning environments, child care settings, and the health care system.

The authors propose an intensive two-year, education-focused intervention for economically disadvantaged three- and four-year-olds. Classrooms would be staffed by college-trained teachers and have no more than six children per teacher. Instruction would be based on proven preschool academic and behavioral curricula and would be provided to children for three hours a day, with wraparound child care available to working parents.

The authors estimate that the annual cost of the instructional portion of the program would be about $8,000, with child care adding up to another $4,000. The program would fully subsidize low-income children's participation; high-income parents would pay the full cost. The total cost of the proposal, net of current spending, would be $20 billion a year.

Researchers have estimated that a few very intensive early childhood programs have generated benefits of as much as $8 to $14 for every $1 in cost. The authors think it unrealistic that a nationwide early education program could be equally socially profitable, but they estimate that their proposal would likely have benefits amounting to several times its cost. Some of the benefits would appear quickly in the form of less school retention and fewer special education classifications; others would show up later in the form of less crime and greater economic productivity. The authors estimate that their program would reduce the future poverty rates of participants by between 5 percent and 15 percent.

www.futureofchildren.org

Greg J. Duncan is the Edwina S. Tarry Professor of Human Development and Social Policy at Northwestern University. Jens Ludwig is professor of social services administration, law, and public policy at the University of Chicago and a faculty research fellow at the National Bureau of Economic Research. Katherine A. Magnuson is an assistant professor of social work at the University of Wisconsin, Madison. The authors are grateful for support provided by the Buffett Early Childhood Fund and the McCormick Tribune Foundation to the National Forum on Early Childhood Program Evaluation. They thank Amy Claessens, Dorothy Duncan, Irv Garfinkel, Ron Haskins, James Heckman, Craig Ramey, Arthur Reynolds, Larry Schweinhart, Belle Sawhill, and seminar participants at the Brookings Institution and Princeton University for helpful comments on an earlier version of this paper. They also thank Clive Belfield for additional results for the Perry Preschool program, and Katie Clabby for excellent research assistance. All opinions and any errors are their own.

Can public policy reduce poverty in the future by investing more in today's children, particularly young children? Research suggests that increased investments in prenatal and infant health and in high-quality preschool education programs will improve children's life chances and generate benefits to society that can easily cover the costs of these government programs. Based on this evidence, we propose a national program providing high-quality preschool education for three- and four-year-olds.

Increased policy attention to early childhood is warranted by new evidence regarding the lifelong implications of brain development during the early years, as well as the efficacy of early education programs.[1] Neuroscience research has documented how complex cognitive capacities are built on earlier foundational skills and that many cognitive skills are sensitive to early life experiences.[2] Preschool interventions may improve lifetime outcomes in part through the possibility that "learning begets learning"—that mastery by young children of a range of cognitive and social competencies may improve their ability to learn when they are older.[3]

Children's early learning environments differ profoundly across lines of both race and class. For example, compared with kindergarteners from families in the bottom fifth of the socioeconomic distribution, children from the most advantaged fifth are four times as likely to have a computer at home, have three times as many books, are read to more often, watch far less television, and are more likely to visit museums or libraries.[4] One study found that three-year-olds in families of low socioeconomic status had half the vocabulary of their more affluent peers, which in turn could be ex-

plained by the lower quality and quantity of parental speech.[5]

Differences in children's learning environments contribute to large gaps in test scores, even among preschoolers. Numerous studies have compared the skills of preschool children from different socioeconomic backgrounds and racial or ethnic groups and found large differences in language and cognitive skills at school entry, age three, and perhaps even as early as age one.[6]

The early years also appear to be a sensitive period for the development of socioemotional skills, such as self-regulation.[7] Such skills are connected, too, with brain development, as early emotional experiences literally become embedded in the architecture of infants' brains.[8] Research has documented a number of differences in the socioemotional skills of poor and nonpoor children—as young as seventeen months in the case of physical aggression.[9] Among behavioral skills, a child's ability to regulate his attention appears to contribute the most to success in elementary school.[10] The attributes that make children eager learners in school may also influence the willingness of parents to engage them in learning activities at home.

Researchers have learned that rudimentary reading and, especially, mathematics skills at kindergarten entry are highly predictive of later school achievement, a finding that supports our emphasis on building these skills in our proposed preschool program.[11] Although the correspondence is far from perfect, children who score poorly on academic assessments before entering kindergarten are more likely to become teen parents, engage in crime, and be unemployed as adults.[12] Moreover, preschool problem behaviors like physical aggression are predictive of criminal behavior later in life.[13]

Preschool gaps in cognitive and socioemotional skills tend to persist through the school years and into later life. By the end of high school, the gap in achievement test scores between white and black children is at least as large as the preschool gap.[14]

The influence of the preschool years on children's later achievement and success is not well reflected in current federal government budget priorities, which allocate nearly seven times as much money per capita for K–12 schooling as for prekindergarten (pre-K) early education and child care subsidies for three- to five-year-olds.[15] Given the opportunities for profitable preschool investments in children's cognitive and socioemotional development, current U.S. spending is not well targeted. Most social policies are devoted to playing catch-up against children's early disadvantages, but disparities are already apparent among young children, and many disadvantaged children never catch up. Efforts to improve young children's school readiness with proven, high-quality programs should play a much more prominent role in America's antipoverty strategy than they do today.

Our Proposal in Brief

We propose an intensive two-year, education-focused intervention for disadvantaged three- and four-year-olds. In a program modeled loosely after Perry Preschool and several state pre-K programs, college-trained teachers would staff the classrooms and administer the curriculum for three hours each day and spend some of their remaining work time engaging parents in outreach activities. Child-to-staff ratios would average 6:1. Wraparound child care would also be available to

working parents. A national curriculum for the program would be developed from preschool reading, mathematics, and behavioral interventions with proven ability to foster children's academic and attention skills in engaging ways.

We estimate that the annual per child cost of the early education component of our program would amount to $8,000, or $16,000 over the entire two-year enrollment period. Child care costs would add $4,000 annually to this total, for a total two-year cost of $24,000. Children from families with incomes below 1.5 times the poverty line would be able to participate in the educational component free of charge, and partial subsidies would be available for children from families with incomes up to three times the poverty line. Higher-income families could also participate, but would not receive a subsidy. The total gross cost of our proposal to the government is on the order of $30 billion a year. Because our proposed intervention overlaps with some existing services, we estimate that about $20 billion of additional government spending is required.

Social benefits generated from our program are difficult to estimate, but we argue that the benefit-cost ratio is almost certainly going to exceed unity and is likely to be between 4:1 and 7:1, making it one of the nation's most profitable social investments. The intervention we propose, once fully scaled up, will reduce poverty in both the short and the long runs. Short-run effects are likely to follow from increased employment and work effort among families receiving subsidized education and care. Program effects on children's future earnings and behavior might plausibly reduce future poverty rates in the United States by around 5 to 15 percent of current levels (or 1 to 2 percentage points).

In what follows we first show why a proposal such as ours is needed, and then explain some of its details.

The Promise of Early Childhood Education

A rigorous body of research demonstrates that very intensive early childhood programs can produce lasting improvements in the life chances of poor children. Recent research also suggests that even less expensive Head Start and pre-K programs may boost early achievement significantly, and in the case of Head Start, improve children's long-term outcomes as well. By contrast, more typical day care or preschool settings have smaller effects on achievement and behavior. One important lesson is that not all early childhood education programs produce similar effects.

For policy purposes, the goal is not to find the program that produces the biggest benefits but rather to find programs that generate the largest benefits relative to their costs. Programs that generate large benefits but even larger costs are unwise public expenditures. Our proposed program is modeled after early childhood interventions that, according to the best available evidence, appear to generate the largest surplus of benefits relative to costs.

The ability of intensive model programs to improve the life chances of disadvantaged children is illustrated by the well-known Perry Preschool intervention. Perry provided one or two years of part-day educational services and home visits to a sample of low-income, low-IQ African American children aged three and four in Ypsilanti, Michigan, during the 1960s. Perry Preschool hired highly educated teachers (with at least a B.A.) and was implemented as a randomized experiment. Some mothers and their children were randomly assigned to the Perry program while others were assigned to a control group that did not receive the Perry intervention. The great advantage of randomized assignment is that parents and children in the program of interest can be expected, on average, to be similar at baseline to those randomly assigned to the control group, so differences in outcomes for treatments and controls can be attributed to the effects of the program with a high degree of confidence.

When the children entered school, those who had participated in the Perry program scored higher on IQ tests than those who had not—an impressive nine-tenths of a standard deviation higher.[16] These IQ effects, however, disappeared by third grade. Nevertheless, the program produced lasting effects through age forty on employment rates (76 percent compared with 62 percent) and earnings (median annual earnings of $20,800 compared with $15,300 in 2000 dollars) and substantially reduced the chances that participants had ever been arrested (29 percent of the participating children reached age 40 without an arrest as compared with 17 percent of the control group).[17]

The Abecedarian program, which began in 1972 and served a sample of low-income, mostly African American women from Chapel Hill, North Carolina, was even more intensive than Perry. Mothers and children assigned to the Abecedarian "treatment" received year-round, full-time care for five years, starting with the child's first year of life. The Abecedarian preschool program included transportation, individualized educational activities that changed as the children aged, and low child-teacher ratios (3:1 for the youngest children and up to 6:1 for older children). Abecedarian teachers followed a curriculum that focused on language development and explained to them the importance of each task as well as how to teach it. High-quality health care, additional social services, and nutritional supplements were also provided to participating families.[18] A full-time family nurse practitioner and a part-time pediatrician worked on staff and in the same building as the children. They provided immediate treatment for ear infections, which could have had an effect on the children's language development.

Abecedarian was a high-cost, high-quality program run by researchers rather than by a government agency. It cost about $18,000 a year for each of a child's first five years and produced dramatic effects on the future life outcomes of its participants.[19] At the start, Abecedarian and control group children had IQ scores that averaged about 1 standard deviation below the mean, as would be expected for children from economically disadvantaged backgrounds. By the time the Abecedarian children reached age five, however, their IQ scores were close to the national average and higher than the scores of children who did not participate. Similarly large effects were observed for achievement on verbal and quantitative tests.[20] Nearly fifteen years later, the program's effect on IQ scores at age twenty-one was smaller than at age five (around 0.38 standard deviation) but still impressive. This problem of partial "fade-out" of the effects of early education, which has been widely documented for a variety of different programs, suggests that sustaining the effects of early interventions on the child's ability to learn may require high-quality follow-up learning environments. We return to this point below.

Although IQ effects faded somewhat over time with Abecedarian, other long-term ef-

fects were dramatic and arguably just as important for reducing poverty. For example, children who received the Abecedarian program entered college at 2.5 times the rate of the control group. The Abecedarian intervention also reduced rates of teen parenthood and marijuana use by nearly half. Smoking rates of Abecedarian participants were about 30 percent lower than those of the control

---

A rigorous body of research demonstrates that very intensive early childhood programs can produce lasting improvements in the life chances of poor children.

---

group.[21] Although employment rates were not statistically different between the Abecedarian and control groups (64 percent compared with 50 percent), children who had participated in the program were about two-thirds more likely to be working in a skilled job (67 percent compared with 41 percent).[22] Even with its $18,000 cost and the need to discount benefits accrued in the distant future, the total economic value of Abecedarian's benefits far exceeded the costs of participating in the program.[23]

Evidence on the existing publicly funded early education programs, which illustrate what can be achieved for large numbers of children in programs of more variable quality than the one we advocate, is also encouraging. A recent random-assignment experimental evaluation of Head Start found positive short-term effects of program participation on elementary prereading and prewriting for three- and four-year olds equal to about 0.3 and 0.2 of a standard deviation, respectively, but not on advanced skills in these two outcome domains.[24] Head Start participation also increased parent-reported literacy skills of children by around 0.45 of a standard deviation. Statistically significant effects on other outcome domains were typically concentrated among three-year-olds, with effect sizes of 0.15 for vocabulary and 0.20 for problem behaviors. Effects on math skills were positive but not statistically significant.[25] If one calculates Head Start effects pooling together the three- and four-year-olds in the experiment, however, rather than showing results separately for each age group, the increased statistical power leads to statistically significant program effects on math and almost all of the other main cognitive skill outcomes in the report.[26]

For policy purposes, the crucial question is whether Head Start effects persist over time; if so, program benefits may be likely to outweigh program costs. Nonexperimental studies of children who participated in Head Start several decades ago suggest lasting effects on school attainment and perhaps criminal activity, although test score effects appear to fade out over time.[27] As in the Abecedarian and Perry programs, these effects were large enough that the benefits to society likely outweighed the program costs.

Studies of previous cohorts of children, however, may not provide a good indication of how today's children will fare. Both center-based care and early education alternatives to Head Start have proliferated, and many provide enriching environments. In addition, better maternal education and parenting education programs have likely improved the developmental environments of poor children. For this reason we suspect that the benefits of Head Start compared with the most likely alternative for poor children may have declined.

Numerous recent studies have examined the short-term effects of state-initiated pre-K programs on children's test scores. These studies typically find short-run effects on achievement test scores that are slightly larger than those estimated for Head Start and, importantly, find that participation in the programs improves both language and math skills.[28] A study by Steven Barnett, Cynthia Lamy, and Kwanghee Jung of pre-K in five states found effects on receptive vocabulary and math of just over one-quarter of a standard deviation and effects on print awareness of nearly two-thirds of a standard deviation.[29] Studies of the Tulsa pre-K program find effects on prereading skills (letter-word identification) of around 0.8 of a standard deviation and on early math scores (applied problems) of around 0.38 of a standard deviation.[30]

How can we explain why the effects estimated for recent state pre-K programs are slightly larger than those for Head Start? One possible explanation is that pre-K programs hire more qualified teachers, pay them more, and offer a more academically oriented curriculum than do Head Start programs. For example, only about one-third of Head Start teachers have completed a bachelor's degree, whereas all the pre-K programs evaluated by Barnett, Lamy, and Jung had college-educated teachers.[31] Another explanation is that the Head Start comparison group received more center-based care than did children in the pre-K comparison group.[32]

A third possible explanation is that the recent Head Start study relies on a rigorous randomized experimental design. Although the recent state pre-K studies are big improvements over past efforts to examine such programs, all are nonetheless derived from a research design that may be susceptible to bias overstating the benefits of pre-K participation.[33]

Our Proposed Early Childhood Intervention

Our proposed educational intervention builds on these encouraging research findings. It combines what we believe are likely to be the "active ingredients" behind the success of previous interventions, including college-educated teachers, small class sizes, academically oriented curricula, and parent outreach. Because resources are scarce, we propose the lowest-cost combination of these program features that is likely to improve the lifetime outcomes of poor children.

Specifically, we propose that all low-income children in the United States (from families with incomes below 1.5 times the poverty line) be eligible to participate at no cost in two years of intensive, high-quality early childhood education at three and four years of age. Classes would meet for one-half day for the duration of the regular academic year and be led by a college-educated teacher. Class sizes would be small, limited to six students per teacher, with no more than twelve students in a classroom. Teachers would devote the remaining half of their workday to parent outreach efforts, both to involve parents as partners in their children's learning and to help them access available support and social services.[34] In addition, our proposed program would include the same health services as are now incorporated into Head Start.

Instruction would be organized around a new national curriculum that would be developed for the program from previous preschool reading, mathematics, and behavioral interventions that have proven to foster children's academic and attention skills in developmentally appropriate ways.[35] We recognize that the idea of a fairly prescriptive national curriculum will be controversial and not without drawbacks, such as imposing some constraints on the ability of local teachers and schools to tailor instruction to the particular needs of their children. But we are impressed by evidence from programs like Perry Preschool and Abecedarian that rely on prescriptive curricula. Moreover, evidence suggests that the Success for All program for slightly older, elementary school children achieved gains across a wide variety of program settings using the same reading-focused curriculum.[36]

Participation in our program would not be limited to poor families, although the subsidy given to participating children would decline as family income increased. Families with incomes of 1.5 to two times the poverty threshold would be required to pay one-third of the program cost, while families with incomes two to three times the poverty threshold would pay two-thirds of the program's costs. Families with incomes equal to more than three times the poverty threshold could participate in the program but would not receive a subsidy from the government. Mixing children from low- and higher-income families would help to mitigate program stigma and may even generate beneficial peer effects.

To support parents' employment, our proposed program would also offer wraparound child care. The child care component would not require a college-educated teacher or the same very small class sizes as the education component, thereby helping to contain overall program costs. Participation in child care would be voluntary; parents would have the

Table 1. Subsidy and Expected Participation Rates for the Proposed Early Childhood Intervention

Percent

Ratio of family income to the poverty line	Early childhood education		Child care	
	Subsidy	Participation rate	Subsidy	Participation rate
Less than 1.25	100	80	100	60
1.25–1.5	100	80	75	50
1.5–1.75	67	80	50	40
1.75–2.0	67	80	25	30
2.0–2.5	33	50	0	20
2.5–3.0	33	50	0	10
More than 3.0	0	25	0	10

option of participating only in the education program.

Given that our child care component is likely much less important for promoting child development than our proposed early education classes, our subsidy for child care is considerably less generous to lower-income families. Families with incomes up to 1.25 times the poverty line would not be required to contribute anything toward the cost of care, while families with incomes between 1.25 and two times the poverty line would contribute a share of the half-day child care costs ranging from 25 percent to 75 percent, depending on their income (table 1). As with the education component, families with incomes too high to qualify them for a government subsidy would still be eligible to participate.

We remain agnostic about whether the program should be operated by local public schools and overseen by the states (subject to federal requirements for program quality and performance) or instead involve direct grant making between the federal government and local service providers, as with the current Head Start program. The former arrangement would have the advantage of helping public schools align their elementary school

curricula with the skills children learn in our proposed program. As with state prekindergartens, however, local public schools might choose to contract with existing providers to deliver the program rather than create new programs within the confines of the public school system. If the program followed the Head Start model of directly funding local service providers, it would be important that the federal government create incentives for local public schools to align their curricula with the new program we propose, perhaps by using existing Title I funding as leverage.

We estimate the annual cost per child for the early childhood education component of our program to be on the order of $8,000 a year. That figure is somewhat higher than the estimated per child expenditures of Head Start (around $7,000 a year), even though the Head Start figure is an average cost of both half-day and full-day programs and ours is half-day only. Our estimated costs are also roughly in line with existing pre-K programs. Michigan's half-day pre-K program, at $3,300 per child, costs considerably less than our program, but it has a higher teacher-child ratio than we propose (8:1 rather than 6:1) and does not include the health and parent outreach services. New Jersey's Abbott intervention has a per child cost of $10,000, but it is a full-day program.

We estimate the cost of the half-day wrap-around child care component of our proposal to be on the order of $4,000 per child per academic year. The figure is higher than most families now pay for center-based care. David Blau and Janet Currie report that the average family using center-based care pays about $2,000 in 2005 dollars for forty weeks of half-time care.[37] The quality of the program we envision is probably higher than the average for center-based child care among families nationwide.

The expected gross cost to the government of our program would be on the order of $30 billion a year. That figure comes from combining the subsidy rates by family income with our best estimates of the rates at which families will sign up to participate in the early childhood and child care components (both shown in table 1), and then multiplying by the total number of children aged three to four in each of these family income categories as estimated from the March 2005 Current Population Survey.

The net cost of the program would be less than $30 billion, because some of the families who sign up for our program will have received other early childhood education or child care subsidies from existing programs, although the exact amount of these offsets is difficult to predict.[38] Taking these offsets together, the total amount of new spending by government at any level required to implement our program would be on the order of $20 billion.

It is possible that our assumed participation rates are too high for low-income children who are already enrolled in either Head Start

or state pre-K programs. One could argue that our proposed pre-K program ought to replace Head Start, since its likely impacts are larger. But it might make sense to preserve the Head Start program at least for the medium term, so as to add to the choices available to low-income families. In this case, the total offsets would be lower than we project, but the total gross cost of our proposed program would be lower as well.

Expected Benefits of Our Proposal

Because our proposed early childhood education intervention is not an exact replica of existing programs, much less of an existing large-scale program, determining its long-term benefits necessarily requires some assumptions and guesswork. Our assumptions about take-up rates, as noted, imply that about 30 percent of children receiving subsidies under our program (that is, from families with incomes below three times the poverty line) would otherwise be in Head Start, about another 20 percent or so would be in state pre-K programs, just over 10 percent would be in other forms of center-based care, and the rest would be in some form of parental or other informal care arrangement.

The net impact of our proposed program will be based on the difference in effects between our early childhood education intervention and the effects of the other early childhood and child care programs that participants would have experienced in the absence of our program. Based on our reading of the evaluation literature, our program's effects on early childhood test scores would range from about one-third to one-half of a standard deviation.[39]

Our proposed intervention may have other long-term benefits for society as well. One study of the Perry Preschool program estimated that taxpayer benefits were four times as large as benefits to participants. For example, the study found that Perry Preschool reduced criminal activity: 83 percent of the control group had been arrested by age forty, as against 71 percent of the treatment group.[40]

With the most recent estimates suggesting a benefit-cost ratio for Perry Preschool on the order of 13:1, if our assumption about program effects is even close to being correct, then the early childhood program that we propose would easily pass a benefit-cost test.[41] If our program's net lifetime benefits are one-quarter to one-half as large as those for Perry, and our net program costs to the government (after expected offsets) are about the same as Perry's, then the expected ratio of benefits to costs would be between 4:1 and 7:1.[42] The benefits of our proposal would likely rival or exceed any of the social investments now available.

How to go from effects on short-term test scores to effects on what is ultimately of interest for this volume of *The Future of Children*—adult poverty status? We assume that our program's long-term effects on adult poverty will be proportional to its effects on short-term test scores relative to those of Perry Preschool. In unpublished calculations that he generously shared with us, Clive Belfield found that Perry reduced adult poverty rates by about one-fifth at age twenty-seven and one-quarter at age forty. If our program's long-term effects are about one-third to two-thirds as great as those observed for Perry Preschool, then our intervention would reduce the chances of adult poverty for program participants by between 7 and 17 percent. If we assume that our program would reduce the risk of future poverty for children only from families with incomes below three times the poverty line, then

under our assumption that about 80 percent of children from these family backgrounds would participate in our program, our proposed intervention would reduce future poverty by roughly 5–15 percent. (Put differently, the net effects of our program might be around one-quarter to one-half as great as those from Perry Preschool.)

Finally, we note that our proposal will reduce both future and current poverty. The provision of subsidized care may result in increased parental employment and work effort, and thus, in turn, higher earnings for participating families. Moreover, poor families with three- and four-year-olds who participate in the early childhood education component of the program receive $8,000 worth of services, while those in afternoon child care receive an additional $4,000 of services a year. A good portion of this spending amounts to "near cash" income for the poor families and should figure into a poverty status calculation based on an expansive definition of family income.

Potential Criticisms of the Proposal

It is only natural that taxpayers who are being asked to contribute $20 billion in new funding for our proposal would want to be sure that the program will accomplish its stated goals. We address here several of the more obvious doubts.

Is the program too expensive? Do we really need to require—and pay—college-educated teachers and insist on such small classes? The evidence on the effects of particular early childhood programs tells more about the net effect of these programs than about which program elements matter most for their success. Many—though clearly not all—successful programs involve highly educated teachers and small classes. These findings are consistent both with social science research that finds, for example, better life outcomes for children of highly educated mothers than for those whose mothers have less schooling or lower cognitive test scores and with research from class-size experiments studying slightly older children, in kindergarten through third grade.[43] Even with the expense of highly educated teachers and small class sizes, this intensive intervention is still likely to pass a benefit-cost test quite easily.

Is program intensity too low? How do we know that half a day of educational instruction is enough? We have no direct evidence on whether a full-day early education program will yield larger or more lasting effects than a part-day program. Indirect evidence on the effects of full-day and part-day kindergarten may be informative, however. Studies have found that although students in full-day kindergarten programs learn more during the kindergarten year than students in part-day programs, the differential gains are relatively small and do not persist much beyond that year.[44] Researchers have pointed out that additional time in the classroom does not necessarily translate into greater exposure to enriching opportunities, and thus it is important to know how programs structure children's "extra" time.[45] With these considerations in mind, we propose a part-day preschool program.

Why wait until age three to provide educational services, given that disparities in cognitive and noncognitive skills are apparent in even younger children? We certainly agree that the period between conception and age three is vital for children's healthy development.[46] We choose to concentrate on ages three and four for several reasons. First, model programs such as Perry Preschool have generated lasting effects for poor children by waiting until ages three and four to provide services. Second, although Abecedarian started even earlier than age three and achieved more pronounced and longer-lasting effects on outcomes such as IQ scores, it cost twice or three times as much as our proposed program (in part because class sizes for very young children in Abecedarian were about half of what we propose for our intervention). Yet we are far from certain that if the proposed program spent that extra money by starting earlier, effects would be commensurately greater. Third, many low-income families seem wary of sending very young children to center-based care, so starting our early childhood education services at age three is likely to enhance take-up rates and fit better with the preferences of our target population. For example data from the Department of Health and Human Services show that around 43 percent of eligible low-income children from birth to age two received federal child care subsidies, compared with 56 percent for poor children aged three to five.[47] Nevertheless, we agree that targeted health care and child maltreatment interventions are clearly warranted at an early age, although more work is needed to better understand what types of health and parent services are beneficial for particular populations.

Wouldn't spending $20 billion more a year on income transfer programs do more to reduce poverty in the United States? The reason for devoting scarce resources to preschool education rather than to income transfer programs rests with cost-benefit analysis. It is true that income transfer programs will do more to reduce poverty than preschool interventions, in part because prevention programs such as those we propose here are imperfectly targeted. Although poor children are disproportionately likely to become poor adults, many of tomorrow's poor adults come from families that are not poor today.[48]

In contrast, income transfer programs are by definition directly targeted toward those people who wind up poor during adulthood, and provide cash assistance precisely during the periods when people need it. However, income transfer programs are usually a zero-sum game in a benefit-cost analysis, since they merely transfer resources from one group in society (taxpayers) to another (poor families). Consequently, the extent to which they are cost-effective depends on the benefits that accumulate to children from their parents' enhanced income. Although recent research has found that work-conditioned income transfers do improve children's achievement, the effects are relatively small.[49] In contrast, the sort of preschool education program that we propose here reduces poverty by making children more productive when they grow up, as well as more likely to engage in pro-social activities, such as work, and less likely to engage in antisocial behaviors, such as crime, that impose substantial costs on society. And in fact, as noted, we believe that the benefits to society generated by our proposed program are likely to be as much as four times the program costs.

Finally, is this a targeted or a universal program? Although our program is available to all three- and four-year-olds, we recommend publicly subsidizing its cost only for families with incomes less than three times the federal poverty threshold. Thus, access may be universal, but we are targeting public support to relatively economically disadvantaged children. Some researchers are concerned that targeted programs are both less efficient and less popular than universal programs.[50] But the "target" of our public funding is much broader than that of most targeted programs. More than 60 percent of all three- and four-year-olds would be eligible to receive some public support to attend our proposed early education program. Moreover, all children would be able to attend, even if they do not receive subsidies. One other concern about targeted benefits is that they create a disincentive for parents who qualify to increase their earnings. For this reason, we have recommended a sliding scale for subsidies to avoid penalizing a family with the loss of a valuable benefit when its earnings exceed the benefit eligibility level by just a little. But we also note that because a child would be attending the program for at most two years, any labor disincentives would be short lived.

Concluding Thoughts

Basic science and social program evaluations often conflict. Not so with the emerging neuroscience of early childhood development and the growing evaluation literature examining existing early education programs. As neuroscience documents the process by which increasingly sophisticated skills are wired into the brain, evaluations of high-quality early education programs show that early skill building can generate a host of long-term benefits both for children in these programs and for society as a whole. Because there are good reasons to believe that program quality is a key ingredient for success, we propose a preschool education program with, among other features, small classes and well-qualified teachers. At $20 billion in annual cost, our proposed program is not cheap. But even if early education programs generate only a fraction of the social benefits demonstrated by model programs, they are one of the most profitable social investments for fighting future poverty.

Notes

1. Charles A. Nelson, "Neural Plasticity and Human Development: The Role of Early Experience in Sculpting Memory Systems," *Developmental Science* 3, no. 2 (2000): 115–36; Jack P. Shonkoff and Deborah A. Phillips, eds., *From Neurons to Neighborhoods: The Science of Early Childhood Development* (Washington: National Academy Press, 2000); Lynn Karoly, "Investing in the Future: Reducing Poverty through Human Capital Programs," in *Understanding Poverty in America: Progress and Problems*, edited by Sheldon H. Danziger and Robert H. Haveman (Harvard University Press, 2002).

2. Eric I. Knudsen and others, "Economic, Neurobiological and Behavioral Perspectives on Building America's Future Workforce," *Proceedings of the National Academy of Sciences of the United States of America* 103, no. 27 (July 2006): 10155–62.

3. Pedro Carneiro and James J. Heckman, "Human Capital Policy," in *Inequality in America: What Role for Human Capital Policies?* edited by Heckman and Alan B. Krueger (MIT Press, 2004), 77–240; Flavio Cunha and others, "Interpreting the Evidence on Life Cycle Skill Formation," Working Paper 11311 (Cambridge, Mass.: National Bureau of Economic Research, 2005).

4. Valerie E. Lee and David T. Burkham, *Inequality at the Starting Gate* (Washington: Economic Policy Institute, 2002), pp. 25–28.

5. Betty Hart and Todd Risley, *Meaningful Differences in the Everyday Experiences of Young American Children* (Baltimore: Brookes, 1995).

6. Christopher Jencks and Meredith Phillips, eds., *The Black-White Test Score Gap* (Brookings, 1998); Roland Fryer and Steven D. Levitt, "Understanding the Black-White Test Score Gap in the First Two Years of School," *Review of Economics and Statistics* 86, no. 2 (2004): 447–64; Lee and Burkham, *Inequality at the Starting Gate* (see note 4); Cecilia Rouse, Jeanne Brooks-Gunn, and Sara McLanahan, "Introducing the Issue," *Future of Children* 15, no. 1 (2005): 5–14; Donald A. Rock and A. Jackson Stenner, "Assessment Issues in the Testing of Children at School Entry," *Future of Children* 15, no. 1 (2005): 15–34; J. Brooks-Gunn and L. B. Markman, "The Contribution of Parenting to Ethnic and Racial Gaps in School Readiness," *Future of Children* 15, no. 1 (2005).

7. Nelson, "Neural Plasticity and Human Development" (see note 1); National Scientific Council on the Developing Child, "Excessive Stress Disrupts the Architecture of the Developing Brain," Working Paper 3 (2005), www.developingchild.net/pubs/wp/excessive_stress.pdf (February 2007).

8. J. LeDoux, "Emotion Circuits in the Brain," *Annual Review of Neuroscience* 23 (2000): 155–84.

9. Richard Tremblay and others, "Physical Aggression during Early Childhood: Trajectories and Predictors," *Pediatrics* 114, no. 1 (2004): e43–50; Cunha and others, "Interpreting the Evidence on Life Cycle Skill Formation" (see note 3).

10. Greg Duncan and others, "School Readiness and Later Achievement," *Developmental Psychology* (forthcoming); Cybele C. Raver and others, "Self-Regulation across Differing Risk and Sociocultural Contexts: Preliminary Findings from the Chicago School Readiness Project," paper presented at the biennial meeting of the Society for Research in Child Development, Atlanta, April 2005.

11. Duncan and others, "School Readiness and Later Achievement" (see note 10).

12. Rouse and others, "Introducing the Issue" (see note 6).

13. Albert J. Reiss and Jeffrey A. Roth, *Understanding and Preventing Violence* (Washington: National Academies Press, 2003).

14. Meredith Phillips, James Crouse, and John Ralph, "Does the Black-White Test Score Gap Widen after Children Enter School?" in *The Black-White Test Score Gap*, edited by Jencks and Phillips (see note 6), pp. 229–72. For a discussion of measurement issues, see Jens Ludwig, "Educational Achievement and Black-White Inequality: The Great Unknown," *Education Next* 3, no. 3 (2003): 79–82.

15. According to U.S. Budget, Fiscal Year 2005, the United States now spends more than $530 billion a year on elementary and secondary schooling for children aged five and older, including $13 billion in extra federal funding through the Title I program for schools serving poor children. In contrast, the federal government spends only about $18 billion on the Head Start program and child care subsidies, most of which go to preschoolers; see testimony of Douglas J. Besharov before the Subcommittee on 21st Century Competitiveness of the Committee on Education and the Workforce, February 27, 2002, www.welfareacademy.org/pubs/testimony-022702.pdf (February 2007).

16. Standard deviation units are a common way of expressing effect sizes. For comparison, the standard deviation for a typical IQ test is 15–16 points, and for the SAT, 100 points.

17. Lawrence Schweinhart and others, *Lifetime Effects: The High/Scope Perry Preschool Study through Age 40* (Ypsilanti, Mich.: High/Scope Press, 2005).

18. Frances A. Campbell and others, "Early Childhood Education: Young Adult Outcomes from the Abecedarian Project," *Applied Developmental Science* 6, no. 1 (2002): 42–57; Steven Barnett and Leonard Masse, "Comparative Benefit-Cost Analysis of the Abecedarian Program and Its Policy Implications," *Economics of Education Review* (2007, forthcoming); Craig Ramey and Frances Campbell, "Compensatory Education for Disadvantaged Children," *School Review* 87, no. 2 (1979): 171–89.

19. The cost estimate is in 2005 dollars. See Janet Currie, "Early Childhood Education Programs," *Journal of Economic Perspectives* 15, no. 2 (2001): 213–38.

20. Craig T. Ramey and Frances A. Campbell, "Preventive Education for High-Risk Children: Cognitive Consequences of the Carolina Abecedarian Project," *American Journal of Mental Deficiency* 88, no. 5 (1984): 515–23.

21. Campbell and others, "Early Childhood Education: Young Adult Outcomes from the Abecedarian Project" (see note 18).

22. In addition, criminal involvement was less common for treatments than controls (14 percent versus 18 percent for misdemeanor convictions, and 8 percent versus 12 percent for felony convictions), although the absolute numbers of those arrested in the two Abecedarian groups were small enough that it is impossible to prove statistically that this particular difference did not result from chance.

23. Barnett and Masse, "Comparative Benefit-Cost Analysis of the Abecedarian Program and Its Policy Implications" (see note 18).

24. Michael Puma and others, *Head Start Impact Study: First Year Findings* (U.S. Department of Health and Human Services, Administration for Children and Families, 2005). Note that the point estimates we report

in the text are larger than those in this report. The Head Start report presents the difference between average outcomes for all children assigned to the treatment group and all children assigned to the control group, known in the program evaluation literature as the "intent to treat" (ITT) effect. But not all children assigned to the experimental group participated in Head Start (the figure is around 84 percent), while some children (18 percent) assigned to the control group enrolled in the program. If we divide the ITT effect by the difference between the treatment and control groups in Head Start participation (66 percent), the implied effect of Head Start participation on participants is around 1.5 times as large as the ITT effects presented in Puma and others' report. For a discussion of this methodology, see H. S. Bloom, "Accounting for No-Shows in Experimental Evaluation Designs," *Evaluation Review* 8 (1984): 225–46. If we define the "treatment" more broadly, as participation in any center-based care, the effects of Head Start participation may be up to 2.5 times as large as the ITT impacts reported by Puma and others, since more than 96 percent of the treatment group receives some sort of center-based care in the experiment but so does around 53–60 percent of the control group (see exhibits 3.2 and 3.3 in Puma and others' report). For more on our calculations, see Jens Ludwig and Deborah Phillips, "The Benefits and Costs of Head Start," Working Paper 12973 (Cambridge, Mass.: National Bureau of Economic Research, 2007).

25. The Early Head Start initiative serves children under age three in a mix of home and center-based programs. A rigorous evaluation of the Early Head Start program found some evidence that the program had positive effects on some aspects of children's development and of parenting practices, but in general the effects were smaller than those produced by the Head Start program. See John M. Love and others, *Making a Difference in the Lives of Infants and Toddlers and Their Families: The Impacts of Early Head Start* (U.S. Department of Health and Human Services, Administration for Children and Families, 2002).

26. Ludwig and Phillips, "The Benefits and Costs of Head Start" (see note 24).

27. Janet Currie and Duncan Thomas, "Does Head Start Make a Difference?" *American Economic Review* 85, no. 3 (1995): 341–64; Eliana Garces, Duncan Thomas, and Janet Currie, "Longer-Term Effects of Head Start," *American Economic Review* 92, no. 4 (2002): 999–1012; Jens Ludwig and Douglas L. Miller, "Does Head Start Improve Children's Life Chances? Evidence from a Regression-Discontinuity Design," *Quarterly Journal of Economics* 122, no. 1 (2007): 159–208.

28. W. Steven Barnett, Cynthia Lamy, and Kwanghee Jung, "The Effects of State Prekindergarten Program on Young Children's School Readiness in Five States" (Rutgers University, National Institute for Early Education Research, 2005); William T. Gormley and Ted Gayer, "Promoting School Readiness in Oklahoma: An Evaluation of Tulsa's Pre-K Program," *Journal of Human Resources* 40, no. 3 (2005): 533–58; William T. Gormley Jr. and others, "The Effects of Universal Pre-K on Cognitive Development," *Developmental Psychology* 41, no. 6 (2005): 872–84.

29. Barnett, Lamy, and Jung, "The Effects of State Prekindergarten Program on Young Children's School Readiness in Five States" (see note 28).

30. Gormley and others, "The Effects of Universal Pre-K" (see note 28).

31. Barnett, Lamy, and Jung, "The Effects of State Prekindergarten Program on Young Children's School Readiness in Five States" (see note 28); Katie Hamm and Danielle Ewen, "Still Going Strong: Head Start Children, Families, Staff, and Programs in 2004," Head Start Series Policy Brief 6 (Center for Law and Policy, November 2005), www.clasp.org/publications/headstart_brief_6.pdf (February 2007); Gormley and others, "The Effects of Universal Pre-K" (see note 28).

32. Thomas Cook, Northwestern University, PowerPoint presentation, www.northwestern.edu/ipr/events/briefingdec06-cook/slide16.html.

33. Specifically, these recent studies all use a regression discontinuity design that compares fall semester tests for kindergarten children who participated in pre-K the previous year and have birthdates close to the previous year's enrollment cutoff with fall tests of children who are currently starting pre-K because their birthdates just barely excluded them from participating the previous year. The key assumption behind these studies is that the selection of children into pre-K does not change dramatically by child age around the birthday enrollment cutoff (that is, it changes "smoothly" with child age). But this need not be the case, because there is a discrete change at the birthday threshold in terms of the choice set that families face in making the decision to select pre-K. Suppose, for instance, that among the children whose birthdays just barely excluded them from enrolling in pre-K during the previous year, those with the most motivated parents were instead sent to private programs that are analogous to the public pre-K program that year and are then enrolled in private kindergarten programs in the fall semester when the pre-K study outcome measures are collected. This type of selection would reduce the share of more motivated parents among the control group in the pre-K studies and lead them to overstate the benefits of pre-K participation.

34. Evaluations do not produce definitive evidence on the importance of the parental outreach component of early childhood education programs. The outreach we propose is more modest than Perry's, which involved home visits, although it does build the connections between classroom teachers and parents.

35. A variety of developmental and academic curricula have been developed for preschool programs, but since few have been evaluated rigorously it is hard to compare the relative effectiveness of these programs. The Institute for Educational Sciences is currently sponsoring a number of evaluations, the findings of which should help guide the selection of the national curriculum for our proposed program.

36. Geoffrey D. Borman and others, "The National Randomized Field Trial of Success for All: Second-Year Outcomes," *American Educational Research Journal* 42, no. 4 (2005): 673–96.

37. David M. Blau and Janet Currie, "Preschool, Daycare and Afterschool Care: Who's Minding the Kids?" Working Paper W10670 (Cambridge, Mass.: National Bureau of Economic Research, August 2004).

38. State and federal governments spend about $9 billion a year on child care subsidies through the Child Care and Development Fund (CCDF), and about 25 percent of these subsidies go to children of ages three and four, about 70 percent of whom attend center-based care; see www.acf.hhs.gov/programs/ccb/data/index.htm (February 8, 2007). Our take-up rates assume that every child whose family income is below three times the poverty line and who is currently in center-based child care will participate in our program. In this case, CCDBG expenditures would decline by (0.25 x 0.7 x $9 billion) = $1.6 billion. Similarly, TANF programs currently spend about $2.5 billion in funding each year for child care subsidies, and under our assumed take-up rates for low-income children a portion of these expenditures would no longer be necessary; see www.clasp.org/publications/childcareassistance2004.pdf. Current Head Start program expenditures are on the order of $7 billion a year; if our take-up rate assumptions are correct, then more than four-fifths of Head Start participants would switch over to the program we propose, either because their current Head Start providers would take over operation of the program or because these participants would move to another provider, who was providing our program. In either case, spending on Head Start in its current form would decline by around $5.8 billion. Similarly, states are now spending more than $2 billion on pre-K programs, and under our assumed take-up rates about three-quarters of these children would switch over to the new program we propose, saving $1.5 billion in government spending.

39. Specifically, we assume that Head Start's impact on children's cognitive achievement test scores will be on the order of 0.2 of a standard deviation, effects of pre-K programs will be around 0.3 of a standard deviation, and effects of center-based care will be about 0.1 of a standard deviation. The "intent to treat" effects in the recent national randomized experimental impact of Head Start are on the order of 0.1 to 0.25, where the effects are statistically significant (Puma and others, *Head Start Impact Study*; see note 24); the implied effect of treatment on the treated will be more on the order of 0.15 to 0.35 standard deviation, and so averaging across relevant outcome domains (including those where standard errors did not allow for detectable impacts) suggests that 0.2 is a reasonable assumption for this program. Our assumption of 0.3 for state pre-K programs is the average across five states found by Barnett, Lamy, and Jung, "The Effects of State Prekindergarten Program on Young Children's School Readiness in Five States" (see note 28), for the PPVT vocabulary and Woodcock-Johnson early math tests. Because our program entails the same level of spending per child on early childhood intervention as Perry Preschool (about $16,000 in current dollars for two years of half-day high-quality early education), if "scale-up" of our program does not reduce the intervention's effectiveness by more than half compared with the Perry model demonstration result, then our program's effect would be around 0.4 of a standard deviation. School-based research suggests that the benefits of two years of instruction are roughly twice those of a single year; D. Card, "The Causal Effect of Education on Earnings," in *Handbook of Labor Economics: Volume 3A*, edited by. O. Ashenfelter and D. E. Card (New York: Elsevier, 1999), pp. 1801–63. Because our intervention is about equal to twice the early childhood instruction provided by current high-quality, one-year, state pre-K programs, our proposed program could generate impacts of about 0.6 of a standard deviation (twice the single-year pre-K impact). We also note that the average impact per participant of our program would be higher if more children than we have assumed stick with Head Start and pre-K. The reason is that both of these programs have larger impacts on children's cognitive skills compared with either "regular" center-based or other types of child care. If there is an increase in the fraction of children who switch into our program from center-based, parental, or informal care and a decline in the fraction who switch over from Head Start or pre-K, then the average effect of participating in our program rather than the alternative care arrangements they would have experienced will increase as well.

40. Schweinhart and others, *Lifetime Effects* (see note 17).

41. Clive R. Belfield and others, "The High/Scope Perry Preschool Program: Cost-Benefit Analysis Using Data from the Age 40 Follow-up," *Journal of Human Resources* 41, no.1 (2006): 162–90.

42. The standard cost estimate for two years of Perry Preschool is around $16,000, less than the $24,000 figure for our proposed program. The difference in costs is due in part to the wraparound child care that we propose. However, as discussed in the text, we think that offsets from reduced spending on other programs will reduce the costs of our proposal by up to one-third, which would make our per-child costs about the same as Perry Preschool.

43. Robert Haveman and Barbara Wolfe, "The Determinants of Children's Attainments: A Review of Methods and Findings," *Journal of Economic Literature* 23 (December 1995): 1829–78; Alan B. Krueger, "Economic Considerations and Class Size," *Economic Journal* 113 (2003): 34–63.

44. Jill S. Cannon, Allison Jacknowitz, and Gary Painter, "Is Full Better than Half? Examining the Longitudinal Effects of Full-Day Kindergarten Attendance," *Journal of Policy Analysis and Management* 25, no 2. (2006): 299–321; John R. Cryan and others, "Success Outcomes of Full-Day Kindergarten: More Positive Behavior and Increased Achievement in the Years After," *Early Childhood Research Quarterly* 7, no. 2

(1992): 187–203; Amy Rathburn, Jerry West, and Elvira Germino Hauskens, *From Kindergarten through Third Grade: Children's Beginning School Experiences* (U.S. Department of Education, National Center for Educational Statistics, 2004).

45. James Elicker and Sangeeta Mathur, "What Do They Do All Day? Comprehensive Evaluation of a Full-School-Day Kindergarten," *Early Childhood Research Quarterly* 12 (1997): 459–80; Nancy Karweit, "The Kindergarten Experience," *Educational Leadership* 49 (1992): 82–86.

46. "The Science of Early Childhood Development: Closing the Gap between What We Know and What We Do," National Scientific Council on the Developing Child, January 2007, www.developingchild.net/pubs/persp/pdf/science_of_development.pdf.

47. "Child Care Eligibility and Enrollment Estimates for Fiscal Year 2003," Policy Issue Brief (Department of Health and Human Services, Office of the Assistant Secretary for Planning and Evaluation, April 2005), http://aspe.hhs.gov/hsp/05/cc-elig-est03/index.htm (February 2007).

48. Jens Ludwig and Susan E. Mayer, " 'Culture' and the Intergenerational Transmission of Poverty: The Prevention Paradox," *Future of Children* 16, no. 2 (2006): 175–96..

49. Gordon Dahl and Lance Lochner, "The Effects of Family Income on Child Achievement," Working Paper 1305-05 (University of Wisconsin Institute for Research on Poverty, 2005); Pamela Morris, Greg Duncan, and Christopher Rodrigues, "Does Money Really Matter? Estimating Impacts of Family Income on Children's Achievement with Data from Random-Assignment Experiments," paper presented at the Chicago Workshop on Black-White Inequality, University of Chicago, 2006.

50. W. Steven Barnett, Kristy Brown, and Rima Shore, "The Universal versus Targeted Debate: Should the United States Have Preschool for All?" (Rutgers University, National Institute for Early Education Research, 2004).

Improving the Education of Children Living in Poverty

Richard J. Murnane

Summary

Richard Murnane observes that the American ideal of equality of educational opportunity has for years been more the rhetoric than the reality of the nation's political life. Children living in poverty, he notes, tend to be concentrated in low-performing schools staffed by ill-equipped teachers. They are likely to leave school without the skills needed to earn a decent living in a rapidly changing economy. Murnane describes three initiatives that the federal government could take to improve the education of these children and increase their chances of escaping poverty. All would strengthen the standards-based reforms at the heart of the No Child Left Behind Act of 2001 (NCLB) by bracing the three legs on which the reforms rest: accountability, incentives, and capacity.

Congress, says Murnane, should improve accountability by amending NCLB to make performance goals more attainable. The goals should emphasize growth in children's skills rather than whether children meet specific test score targets. Congress should also amend NCLB to develop meaningful goals for high school graduation rates.

Congress should strengthen states' incentives to improve the education of low-income students. It should also encourage states to develop effective voluntary school choice programs to enable students who attend failing public schools to move to more successful schools in other districts.

Finally, Congress should use competitive matching grants to build the capacity of schools to educate low-income children and the capacity of state departments of education to boost the performance of failing schools and districts. The grants would help develop effective programs to improve teaching and to serve students who do not fare well in conventional high school programs.

Murnane estimates the annual cost of these three initiatives to be approximately $2.5 billion.

www.futureofchildren.org

Richard J. Murnane is the Thompson Professor of Education and Society at the Harvard Graduate School of Education. He thanks David Cohen, Michael Cohen, Richard Elmore, Nora Gordon, Harry Holzer, Julia Isaacs, Brian Jacob, Jack Jennings, Susan Johnson, James Kemple, Daniel Koretz, Robert Linn, Lawrence Mead, Jal Mehta, Jerome Murphy, Thomas Payzant, Edward Pauly, Paul Reville, Robert Schwartz, Adria Steinberg, David Stern, and William Taylor for valuable conversations about the topic of this paper. He also thanks Jesse Rothstein and the editors of this issue for valuable comments on earlier drafts. Finally, he thanks Trent Kaufman and John Papay for helpful research assistance.

Equality of educational opportunity has been part of the rhetoric of American political life for many years. Reality, however, does not match the rhetoric. Children living in poverty, disproportionately children of color, tend to be concentrated in schools with inadequate resources and poorly skilled teachers. Many of these children are likely to leave school before earning a high school diploma. Even if they graduate, many leave school without the skills needed to earn a decent living.

Equal access to a good education has become especially crucial over the past twenty-five years, as a rapidly changing economy has made skills and education ever more important determinants of labor market outcomes. Figure 1 shows trends in the average hourly wages of Americans with different educational attainments. In 1979 graduates of a four-year college earned 46 percent more than high school graduates earned on average. By 2005 that gap had widened to 74 percent. During that same period the average inflation-adjusted earnings of high school dropouts fell 16 percent.[1]

Not surprisingly, the cognitive skills of students, even young students, predict accurately how likely they are to graduate from high school, enroll in college, and get a four-year degree.[2] Inequality in mathematics and reading skills results in inequality in educational attainment and inequality in labor market earnings. The best evidence on the reading and math skills of American children comes from the National Assessment of Educational Progress (NAEP), often called the nation's report card. Math skills are particularly important predictors of subsequent labor market outcomes.[3] On the 2005 assessment of the math skills of eighth graders,

only 13 percent of children living in poverty achieved a score of proficient compared with 40 percent of children who were not poor. Almost half—49 percent—of children living in poverty had scores below the threshold for basic competency, compared with just 21 percent of nonpoor children.[4]

The differences in the mathematics and reading skills of eighth graders of different groups translate into striking differences in high school graduation rates. Although about three-quarters of white youth earn high school diplomas on schedule, the corresponding figure for black and Hispanic youth—who are especially likely to be living in poverty—is roughly half.[5] These numbers provide striking evidence both that the United States is far from providing equality of educational opportunity and that improving the education of children living in poverty is critical to improving their life outcomes. In this article I propose and defend a set of actions that the federal government could take to improve the education of children living in poverty.

Recommendations

The federal government could improve the education of poor children and increase their chances to escape poverty by taking three steps. First, it could strengthen educational accountability by amending the No Child Left Behind Act of 2001 (NCLB) to make test score goals attainable and to develop meaningful goals for increasing the share of students who graduate from high school. Second, it could address the problems of low-income students by encouraging states to strengthen high school graduation requirements so that they better reflect the skills needed for success after graduation and by also encouraging states to develop voluntary interdistrict school choice programs. Third, it

Figure 1. Real Hourly Wage for U.S. Workers, by Educational Attainment, 1973–2005

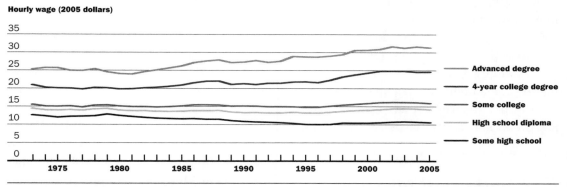

Source: Based on Current Population Survey data from the Economic Policy Institute Data Zone (www.epi.org/datazone/05/wagebyed_a.xls).

could build the instructional capacity of schools to educate low-income children.

To readers familiar with the structure of American education, it may seem odd to suggest that actions by the federal government would improve the education of disadvantaged children. After all, this country has historically left the governance of public education to the states, which in turn have delegated a great deal of responsibility and power to local school districts. Washington has traditionally been relatively powerless to affect what happens in American public school classrooms. In recent years, however, things have begun to change. In the next section I describe these changes and explain why federal actions can now influence the quality of education provided to children living in poverty. I then turn to the recommendations.

The Federal Role

From one perspective, improving the education of children living in poverty is straightforward. Policymakers should define clearly the skills and knowledge students should master at each grade level. Schools should be run by school principals who know how to recruit and support effective teachers and provide them the tools to do this work. Schools

should attract and support experienced, skilled teachers committed to working together over an extended period to continuously improve instruction. School staff should monitor the learning of every student, intervene rapidly at the first sign that a student is not making good progress toward mastering critical skills, and provide alternatives when conventional pedagogies are not effective. And the school day and school year should be long enough that students can have extra time to acquire critical skills if they need it.

But few children living in poverty attend such schools. Instead, they typically attend schools where leadership is weak, many teachers lack critical skills, instruction is inconsistent, and learning problems are left unattended. A great many disadvantaged children thus leave school without the skills they need to earn a decent living and to provide for their own children.

The reasons why disadvantaged children typically receive a poor education are numerous and interrelated. Housing patterns leave poor children, who have especially great learning needs, concentrated in particular schools and school districts.[6] Precarious and uncertain city budgets prevent urban districts from hiring skilled teachers in a timely manner. Difficult working conditions, combined with seniority provisions of collectively bargained labor agreements, leave low-performing schools with the least teaching talent.

During the past fifteen years virtually every state in the country has adopted standards-based educational reforms, often called test-

---

During the past fifteen years virtually every state in the country has adopted standards-based educational reforms as its primary strategy for improving public education.

---

based accountability, as its primary strategy for improving public education. Although details vary greatly from state to state, all standards-based educational reforms include three components. The first is the standards themselves: content standards that specify what students should know and be able to do, performance standards that describe how students should demonstrate their knowledge and skills, and assessments that measure the extent to which students meet performance standards. The second component is incentives to encourage educators and students to devote the time and energy needed to meet the performance standards.[7] The final component is teachers who have the knowledge, skills, and resources to prepare all students to meet the performance standards.

The third component—building capacity to deliver consistently high-quality instruction

to all children—has been the most neglected part of standards-based reforms in most states. By themselves, the first two components—standards and incentives—will not improve student performance. Teachers must know how to achieve the mandated outcomes. But in most schools serving high concentrations of poor children teachers lack the requisite skills and knowledge and have few opportunities to acquire them. Building teaching capacity is thus as critical to improving student outcomes as appropriate standards and incentives are.

Since the passage of the Elementary and Secondary Education Act of 1965 (ESEA), the federal government has provided funding to improve the education of economically disadvantaged children. Title I of this law has been the nation's primary compensatory education program, distributing funds to school districts on the basis of a formula that weights heavily the number of children living in poverty.[8] The most recent reauthorization of ESEA, the No Child Left Behind Act of 2001, marked a significant change in the federal role in public K–12 education. The new law requires states to test annually the reading and mathematics skills of all public school students in grades three through eight. It also specifies that all schools are expected to make adequate yearly progress (AYP) toward ensuring that all groups of students, including groups defined by race or ethnicity and poverty, reach proficiency within twelve years (by 2014). School districts and schools that fail to demonstrate adequate yearly progress for all groups of students are subject to corrective actions that can ultimately include the replacement of staff and school reconstitution.

One strength of NCLB is that it draws attention to the academic skills of children from low-income families, children of color, children whose first language is not English, and children with disabilities—groups that historically have not been well served by American schools. The importance of creating incentives for schools to pay attention to these often forgotten groups cannot be overestimated. It is the primary reason that some civil rights groups have supported NCLB.

At the same time, several provisions of the new law create perverse incentives for states and for educators. One source of perverse incentives is the fact that the adequate yearly progress requirements are well beyond the reach of even the states that have made the most progress in improving students' reading and math skills. North Carolina, for example, made the greatest gain between 1990 and 2000 in the share of students who score proficient or above on the eighth-grade NAEP mathematics test. If North Carolina were able to sustain this top-ranking rate of progress, almost 60 percent of its eighth graders would earn scores of proficient or above by 2014—a remarkable accomplishment, but well short of the required 100 percent.[9]

A related problem is that the accountability system has only two categories: schools that make adequate yearly progress and those that do not. Thus a school in which a few students in one ethnic group in a single grade fail to make adequate yearly progress is not distinguished from a school in which all ethnic groups at every grade level fail to do so.

It makes sense to have ambitious performance goals. But an accountability system with unrealistically high goals will not improve public education. As educators become increasingly aware that even consistently good teaching will not allow their schools to satisfy adequate yearly progress requirements, their

behavior will become increasingly dysfunctional and contrary to the interests of children. Skilled teachers, for example, will be likely to leave schools serving high concentrations of poor children. And some teachers will focus instruction unduly on test preparation.[10] In addition, in a system in which a great many schools, even those that have made real progress, are labeled "underperforming," it may be difficult to identify the schools most in need of intervention.

A second source of perverse incentives in NCLB is the fact that states are allowed to choose their own tests and their own minimum scores for achieving proficiency. This latitude, combined with the pressure of having to meet adequate yearly progress requirements, encourages states to make their tests relatively undemanding and to set low minimum scores. A look at how students perform on state-mandated tests and on the National Assessment of Educational Progress highlights this problem. In 2003, 77 percent of fourth graders in Alabama scored "proficient" on the state Reading-Language Arts exam, but only 22 percent scored "proficient" on the NAEP fourth-grade examination.[11]

A third weakness of NCLB concerns high school graduation rates. Although the law requires states to include graduation rates in setting adequate yearly progress goals for high schools, it does not specify how they must do this. In interpreting the law, the U.S. Department of Education has allowed states to measure graduation rates in a variety of ways and to set their own goals for improving those rates. Moreover, there is no requirement that goals be met for subgroups of students, defined by race and poverty. As a result, high school graduation rates, one of the most important indicators of school districts' success in serving students, play almost no role in the NCLB accountability system. One indication of the need to improve graduation rates is that among twenty-two industrialized democracies for which on-time high school graduation rates are available, the United States now ranks nineteenth.[12]

In summary, test-based accountability systems introduced by states and the federal government have had an impact on what happens in American schools, especially those that serve high concentrations of poor children. The challenge now is to revise NCLB and state accountability systems so that children living in poverty make greater gains. The federal government can help make standards-based reforms a success by strengthening the foundation on which they rest, namely, accountability, incentives to serve poor children, and the teaching capacity to serve poor children.

Before turning to my specific recommendations, I want to make clear that they are based on the presumption that the United States will retain its basic governance structure for education. Local communities, operating within boundaries set by states, will make most of the decisions that determine the day-to-day school experiences of children. They will hire teachers and administrators, choose curricula, set the length of the school day and year, and invest in improving the quality of instruction. Individual communities are responsible for educating all students living within their geographic boundaries; they have no responsibility to educate students in neighboring communities. States, in their evolving role, will create content standards, choose tests to measure students' mastery of these standards, determine what requirements college graduates must meet to obtain a teaching license, and fund a significant share of local school spending.

The assumption about governance structure is important because the current structure limits the ability of federal policies to improve the education of poor children. If the governance of American public K–12 education were more centralized, the options for federal policy would be quite different and closer to those that some other industrialized countries have adopted. They might include national content standards and national assessments, a single set of training and licensing requirements for all teachers, assignment of teachers to particular schools in geographic areas encompassing many communities, opportunities for students to attend a wide variety of schools located in nearby communities, and a common strategy for identifying students who are not making good academic progress and for consistently applying intensive intervention strategies.

In an important sense, the governance structure of American public education is evolving. States play larger roles in determining curricular and testing requirements than they did thirty years ago. NCLB marks a larger federal role. Nonetheless, local control remains a central tenet of the educational governance structure.

Improve Accountability

Congress could improve educational accountability by amending NCLB to make test score goals attainable and to develop goals for increasing high school graduation rate requirements.

Make Test Score Goals Ambitious, but Attainable

Robert Linn, one of the nation's foremost experts on educational accountability systems, suggests several constructive changes in the adequate yearly progress provisions of NCLB.[13] One, aimed at reducing the variation across states in the proficiency standard, is to define the minimum score for proficiency (often called the cut score) on a state assessment to be equal to the median score of students in the state who took the test in 2002. Although in some ways an arbitrary choice, 2002 is the first year after passage of NCLB. Linn also recommends requiring that the share of students scoring above that cut score increase by something like 3 percentage points a year—so that the target for 2006 would be 62 percent and that for 2014, 86 percent, rather than 100 percent. Judged against the fastest rates of improvement observed on NAEP tests, these targets would be ambitious but, unlike the current targets, not unrealistic.

Linn also makes a suggestion in response to the problem that schools serving a greater number of the subgroups specified in the law (including poor children, black children, Hispanic children, and children with disabilities) are more likely to fall short of adequate yearly progress than schools serving a more homogeneous group of students.[14] He would amend the so-called safe harbor provision of NCLB—an alternative way for a school to satisfy AYP—so that when a subgroup of students in a school falls short of adequate yearly progress, the school as a whole can still meet the target if the share of students in the subgroup who score in the below-proficient category declines by at least 3 percentage points each year. This change could reduce the disincentives for skilled teachers to work in racially and ethnically diverse schools.

Linn also suggests modifying the safe harbor provision to allow schools to make adequate yearly progress if their students make specified gains in achievement over a school year rather than reaching specific achievement levels, as under current law. Allowing schools to

meet targets by demonstrating growth in students' skills could also reduce the disincentive for skilled teachers to work in schools serving high concentrations of poor children.[15] The Department of Education has shown itself open to such a change. In 2006 it approved applications from five states to participate in a pilot program in which schools could make adequate yearly progress by demonstrating gains in the achievement of students scoring below the proficiency cut score.[16]

Add Serious High School Graduation Rate Requirements

Individual states now estimate high school graduation rates in many different, noncomparable ways. Given the importance of high school graduation in determining the economic future of the country's youth, it makes sense to require that states, districts, and schools measure graduation rates in the same way and that they meet common requirements for improving these graduation rates.

In 2005 the nation's governors signed a "Graduation Counts Compact" that committed their states to implementing a common method for calculating their high school graduation rates.[17] By 2010 thirty-nine states plan to report graduation rates based on this formula. The Department of Education is providing competitive grants to state education departments to develop data systems to track students over time and has already awarded grants totaling more than $52 million to fourteen states. It may thus soon be possible to put in place meaningful accountability provisions to increase high school graduation rates.

Create Incentives for States to Act

Congress could create incentives for states to strengthen high school graduation requirements to reflect the skills that students need for success after graduation and to promote voluntary interdistrict school choice programs.

Strengthen High School Graduation Requirements

Today twenty-two states require high school students to pass exit exams in mathematics and English language arts to earn a high school diploma.[18] But passing these exams does not mean that students are ready either for college or for the demands of jobs with promising futures. Although more than 70 percent of high school graduates enter two- and four-year colleges, more than a quarter must take remedial courses in English and mathematics before registering for courses that provide college credit, and the share is much higher for disadvantaged students. More than 60 percent of employers rate high school graduates' skills in writing and basic math as only "fair" or "poor."[19]

To give educators and students clear signals about the adequacy of the work they do together in high schools, states should align high school standards, assessments, and graduation requirements with the knowledge and skills needed for postsecondary education and work. Public colleges and universities could create incentives for high school students to master the more demanding skills required for high school graduation by committing to base college course placement on students' scores on recalibrated state exams. Knowing that scoring well on high school exit exams would guarantee acceptance into college courses that count toward a degree (as opposed to being funneled into "developmental courses," which do not) would encourage students to do the hard work needed to master important skills.

States that strengthen high school graduation requirements would be likely to strengthen content standards in the earlier grades to prepare students to do more demanding high school work. The variation across states in standards and assessments would likely diminish. Moving toward a common set of national standards and assessments makes sense in a country with a mobile population and an increasingly integrated economy.

Care must be taken in determining precisely which skills are important for success after high school graduation. The tendency is to ratchet up standards in areas such as mathematics, where skills are relatively easy to measure, and to neglect skills such as oral communication, teamwork, and job search and interviewing that are critical to success in postsecondary education and work but are hard to measure.[20]

A ten-year study of career academies illustrates the importance of skills other than reading and math to success after high school. Career academies are small learning communities embedded within a larger high school, whose students take classes together for at least three years from a team of teachers drawn from different disciplines. The academies offer a college preparatory curriculum with a career theme, which enables students to identify relationships among academic subjects and understand how they are applied in a broad field of work. The academies generally include partnerships with local employers, who provide work-based learning opportunities for their students.

In 1993 MDRC, one of the nation's leading contract research firms, undertook an experimental study of the effect of nine career academies serving large shares of students living in poverty. Because there was excess student demand for all nine academies, lotteries determined which interested students were offered places. Both the students who were offered places (the treatment group) and those who lost out in the lottery and enrolled in other school programs (the control group) were followed through high school and for four years after graduation. A variety of indicators of success (reading and math scores, course grades, on-time graduation, college enrollment and completion, labor market earnings) were measured for all participants.

The findings of the evaluation are striking. In both treatment and control groups, academic skills, high school graduation rates, and college enrollment rates were higher, on average, than the national average for students with similar demographic characteristics. (These credentials reflect the greater than average motivation of students who wanted to enroll in career academies.) However, at the end of high school the math and reading skills of students in the treatment group were no higher, on average, than those in the control group. Nonetheless, young men who had been offered places in a career academy earned $10,000 (18 percent) more than men in the control group during the four-year follow-up period after high school. The labor market benefits were especially large for male students who were at risk of dropping out of high school as the experiment began. The explanation for this striking pattern is that enrollment in career academies and the associated opportunities for workplace internships and jobs enabled students to acquire skills that were important to labor market success even though they were not captured by scores on standardized reading and math tests.[21]

Congress could provide funding to help states strengthen high school graduation requirements when it reauthorizes the Higher Education Act or NCLB. Some states have

already begun work. Through the auspices of the American Diploma Project (ADP), a project of the organization Achieve, five states worked together in 2003–04 to develop benchmarks describing the specific English and mathematics skills needed for success in postsecondary education or in jobs with growth potential. Thirty states are now working to align high school standards with the

More than 60 percent of employers rate high school graduates' skills in writing and basic math as only "fair" or "poor."

demands of postsecondary education and work, and a dozen are also upgrading their high school graduation requirements.[22]

In most states realigning high school graduation requirements will entail redesigning exit examinations. As is almost always the case when new exams are introduced, scores will initially be poor but will improve as educators learn to prepare students for them. The question will inevitably arise whether improved exit exam scores reflect better preparation of students for postsecondary education and work or simply score inflation resulting from narrowly focused test preparation. To answer this question, it is necessary also to align the twelfth-grade NAEP English language arts and mathematics examinations with the skills needed for postsecondary education and work and require all states to administer these examinations.

Today the federal government requires states to participate in the NAEP assessment of the

English language arts and mathematical skills of students in grades four and eight. As noted, comparisons of the performance of students on the NAEP tests and on mandatory state tests have revealed how undemanding many state tests are and how low many states have set their thresholds for proficiency. It is important to have similar nationally comparable benchmarks against which to judge states' high school graduation requirements, including their exit examinations. Requiring all states to administer twelfth-grade NAEP tests could provide these benchmarks if two challenges can be overcome. The first is to redesign the NAEP tests to be sure they reflect the skills needed for postsecondary education and work. Progress on this front is under way. In August 2006 the National Assessment Governing Board, the group that sets policy for the NAEP, voted to redesign the NAEP twelfth-grade mathematics examination in accord with skills necessary for postsecondary education and jobs with growth potential.[23] In taking this action the board accepted advice requested from Achieve, sponsor of the American Diploma Project (ADP). The revised NAEP twelfth-grade math examination will thus likely be informed by the work of the ADP.

The second challenge is to convince twelfth-grade students to make their best efforts in answering questions on the NAEP examinations when their scores not only have no consequences for them but are never even known to them. Only if the students give their best effort will the scores serve as a useful audit of the consequences of revising high school graduation requirements. Whether it is possible to elicit the full attention and effort of twelfth-grade students under those circumstances remains to be seen, though several recent experiments show some promise.[24]

Some readers may wonder why states do not simply require that students score above predetermined cut-offs on redesigned twelfth-grade NAEP tests in order to receive a high school diploma. In other words, why not get high school students to take the NAEP tests seriously by making the scores count? There are two complementary answers. First, the NAEP uses a matrix sampling design under which different students are asked to answer different questions. The design permits reliable estimation of the extent to which groups of students have mastered a much broader range of skills than would be the case if all students answered the same questions. But as a consequence, scores are not computed for individual students. Second, critics of test-based accountability often complain that test score gains on high-stakes tests stem from extensive drilling and do not reflect increases in students' mastery of the relevant subject domains.[25] The only way to assess the extent to which this is true is to compare score trends on the high-stakes test with those on a different, broad-based examination. The NAEP tests are designed to serve this audit function.

Promote Interdistrict School Choice
No Child Left Behind requires school districts to give students the option of transferring to a more successful public school if their own school fails to make adequate yearly progress for two years in a row. And the law gives low-achieving children from low-income families priority in requesting transfers. To date, however, this school choice option has been little used, for several reasons. Successful public schools, especially in urban areas, rarely have empty seats and often have long waiting lists.[26] And many school superintendents give parents little or no information about the school choice option. Finally, scores on state tests taken in the

spring of one school year are often not available until after the next school year has begun. (A solution to this problem is to base the NCLB choice option on the most recent accountability data available when families are choosing schools for the next school year.)

Because NCLB as written gives neighboring school districts no real reason to accept students from failing urban schools, the next round of legislation should create strong incentives for states to develop voluntary interdistrict choice programs. Several promising precedents exist. METCO, a grant program funded by the Commonwealth of Massachusetts with the voluntary participation of thirty-four suburban districts near Boston and four near Springfield, has been in operation since 1966 (when it was funded in part by a grant from the U.S. Department of Education). Today it enables 3,300 low-income Boston and Springfield students to attend public schools in other communities. St. Louis also has a voluntary program, under which 12,000 African American children, 75 percent of whom are from low-income families, attend public schools in sixteen suburban districts.[27] Significant state funding provides an incentive for suburban districts to participate in these interdistrict choice programs.

As the METCO and St. Louis programs show, with appropriate incentives, suburban school districts serving primarily middle-class children are willing to educate a nontrivial number of low-income urban students. A recent evaluation found METCO a promising approach to improving the education of some children living in poverty. It increased the reading achievement of participating urban children attending suburban elementary schools and had no lasting negative effects on the achievement of their suburban classmates.[28] Evidence from the St. Louis choice

program is also encouraging.[29] Competitive grants to states for the design and implementation of interdistrict choice programs could make school choice under NCLB a real option for many children from low-income families.

Congress should also amend adequate yearly progress regulations to ensure that suburban districts are not penalized for accepting urban students from low-performing schools. The option of satisfying adequate yearly progress requirements by demonstrating gains in the achievement of initially low-achieving children could be important in this regard.

Although creating interdistrict choice options for low-income children who attend poorly performing schools is important, such programs are likely to serve only a minority of urban children. The reason is that the willingness of suburban communities to voluntarily accept low-income students from urban school districts would diminish as the share of these students in their schools grew. Improving teaching and learning in schools serving high concentrations of poor children must thus be a central part of federal education policy.

Build the Capacity of Schools to Educate Low-Income Students

Setting appropriate goals for student achievement and designing incentives for educators to help all students to meet these goals will improve education for disadvantaged children only if the teachers and administrators doing the work know how to meet the goals. But few schools serving high concentrations of poor children are blessed with many such teachers and administrators. Improving education for children in poverty thus depends on increasing the capacity of educators to deliver consistently high-quality instruction.

The federal role is to catalyze capacity building and to ensure that state and local initiatives are carefully evaluated to learn how they affect student achievement.

Improving Teaching

One consistent finding from three decades of research into what makes schools effective is that some teachers are much better than others in helping children to acquire critical math and reading skills.[30] A second consistent finding is that disadvantaged American children, those who most need the nation's best teachers because their parents lack the resources to compensate for poor schooling, are least likely to get them.

Among the most striking recent evidence is a 2004 study of Teach for America (TFA), a program that recruits academically talented graduates from the nation's best colleges and universities to work for two years in urban and rural schools that face teacher shortages, virtually all of which serve high concentrations of poor children.[31] The study found that a large share of the non-TFA teachers in these schools was remarkably ill prepared to educate children, especially children needing the nation's best teachers. Less than 4 percent had graduated from a college or university classified as at least very competitive, compared with 22 percent of the national teaching force and 70 percent of TFA participants. Almost 30 percent of non-TFA teachers had no student teaching experience. The poor preparation of these teachers helps explain why the average reading score of the students in these schools was in the 13th percentile of the national distribution.

This poor preparation comes as no surprise to anyone who follows American public education. Teaching in schools that serve large shares of disadvantaged children is taxing.

Very few school districts provide extra pay or other inducements to attract talented teachers. As a result, all too often these schools are left with the teachers other schools don't want. Those teachers who can, exercise seniority rights to move on as soon as possible, leaving the schools to search yet again for new teachers.

One response to the poor skills of teachers in high-poverty schools has been professional development aimed at improving these skills and at creating a coherent instructional program. But high teacher turnover rates often thwart such efforts.

Some state departments of education have responded to the consistently poor performance of some schools and school districts by taking them over and appointing new staff to replace incumbent administrators and teachers. Results have varied across settings, but clearly the strategy is no panacea.[32] Creating effective schools is more difficult than changing the leadership. One thing that states have come to understand, however, is that they must increase their capacity to bring about constructive change in troubled schools and school districts.

NCLB acknowledges the importance of teacher quality and mandates a qualified teacher in every one of the nation's classrooms, but it provides no new funding to implement the mandate. Nonetheless, many states and school districts have developed a variety of initiatives to improve instruction in high-poverty schools. For example, fourteen states provide some sort of incentive for teachers to work in a hard-to-staff school.[33] Several, including Florida, California, and Texas, provide bonuses to teachers with National Board certification to move to hard-to-staff schools.[34] And some urban school districts have introduced initiatives aimed at improving education in schools serving high concentrations of poor children. For example, Miami-Dade County has designated its thirty-nine lowest-performing schools as a School Improvement Zone. It is offering teachers a 20 percent pay premium to take a job in one of these schools, working a longer school day and school year.[35]

The federal government must, for two reasons, take a role in building the instructional capacity in high-poverty schools. First, the number of state and district initiatives, while growing, is modest relative to the magnitude of the problem. Second, almost none of these initiatives will be carefully evaluated, so that researchers and policymakers will not be able to take full advantage of them to learn what works. Thus when Congress reauthorizes No Child Left Behind it should include targeted, competitive matching grants to states and school districts to support initiatives in high-poverty schools to attract and retain skilled teachers and administrators and to create leadership academies to train leaders. Each initiative that receives an award should be rigorously evaluated to learn how it affects instructional quality and, ultimately, children's achievement.

Since my recommendation is quite specific—*targeted, competitive matching grants* with a strict *evaluation requirement*—it seems important to defend these design choices. I use the term *targeted grants* to mean grants specifically aimed at improving the quality of teaching in high-poverty schools. I distinguish these from common uses of Title I funds, such as reducing class size and hiring reading specialists to work with students whose reading and math skills are slow to develop. Such uses are common because they do not threaten historic practices in most public school districts, including a common salary scale irrespective of the difficulty of the teaching assignment, seniority in choice of teaching positions, and the right to close the classroom door and teach as one is accustomed to, even if it means that children are exposed to different instructional methods from one year to the next. The targeted

One response to the poor skills of teachers in high-poverty schools has been professional development aimed at improving these skills and at creating a coherent instructional program.

grants would create incentives for districts to challenge these historic practices. The focus would be on attracting skilled teachers and administrators to high-poverty schools and inducing them to work together over an extended time to provide consistently high-quality instruction.

The grants should be competitive rather than formula-based, as provided under Title I, to encourage school districts and states to develop innovative proposals. Innovation is crucial because there is little systematic evidence on the effectiveness of alternative policies to attract and retain skilled teachers and administrators in high-poverty schools. Improving instruction in these schools is thus not simply a matter of having the resources to spend in well-understood, proven ways, but of testing a variety of new strategies to find out what works.

There are two complementary reasons to use matching grants rather than categorical grants that do not require matching contributions from recipients. First, the matching provision increases the total resources devoted to initiatives. Second, requiring a matching contribution is likely to induce recipients to think carefully about the design of their proposals.

The requirement for rigorous evaluations is aimed at maximizing the learning that comes from the grants. Because good evaluations must be planned simultaneously with the initiatives themselves, evaluation plans should be part of all grant applications. Some portion of the federal grant money should be set aside to pay for evaluations. Applicants could be encouraged to leverage their targeted grants by soliciting funding from foundations to pay for part of the evaluation costs—a strategy that states have used successfully to fund evaluations of innovative welfare programs.

Helping Students Who Struggle in High School

The extraordinarily high dropout rate among low-income high school students in urban schools is a pressing national problem.[36] State efforts to strengthen high school graduation requirements are likely to exacerbate this problem unless policymakers do something to improve prospects for students who do not thrive in traditional high schools. If improving high school graduation rates is to become a requirement for making adequate yearly progress, as I have recommended, there is a pressing need for strategies to help students who struggle in high school.

Fifteen years ago, when states began standards-based education reforms, many analysts expected that the problem of struggling high school students would be short-lived.

They thought that the poor reading and math skills of a great many ninth graders stemmed from low-quality elementary school education, and that improving elementary schools would help students succeed in high school. That logic turned out to be faulty. Although many states have improved the reading and math scores of elementary school students, the number of ninth graders who lack the reading and math skills necessary for high school work has not declined. Improving secondary school education itself, both middle school and high school, is perhaps the nation's most pressing education challenge.

Recent research has clarified the challenge of secondary school reform. Among the critical dimensions are creating a personalized and orderly learning environment where students and teachers treat each other respectfully, identifying students with poor academic skills and intervening intensively to improve these skills, improving the quality of instruction and helping students understand the importance of acquiring particular skills and knowledge, and connecting students to the world of work.[37]

Many states are attempting to address this challenge with changes in incentives, in instruction, and in curricular design. But most interventions are not accompanied by high-quality evaluations. Congress could improve the knowledge base on how to improve secondary schools by providing competitive grants to states or groups of states to support innovations, with the requirement that states must submit their innovations to an external evaluation.

Experience in another sector—welfare reform—illustrates the value of the federal role in supporting carefully evaluated state innovations. During the 1980s the U.S. Department of Health and Human Services allowed states wishing to try new strategies for dealing with families in poverty to apply for waivers from federal welfare laws. One condition for being granted a waiver was that the state set aside a share of its federal funds to pay for a rigorous evaluation of the effects of its innovative system. The evaluations of these innovations provided much of the evidence that informed the design of welfare reform in 1996.[38] The same strategy—federal grants coupled with an evaluation requirement—could also increase policymakers' knowledge about the relative effectiveness of alternative statewide solutions to improving the secondary schooling of low-income youth.

In addition to state grants, Washington should provide competitive grants to school districts and community-based partners that are developing alternative educational programs for youth at risk of dropping out of school. Again, the grants should include a requirement for a rigorous external evaluation, with the goal of increasing the supply of successful models from which schools can draw.[39]

Cost
Implementing these recommendations will entail significant costs, though the costs are relatively modest given the importance of the problems that the recommendations address and the social payoff to solving them. Moreover, because the proposals do not involve entitlements, the size of the initiatives could be tailored to federal budget realities. I consider the cost of each proposal briefly, in turn.

It would cost little to revise adequate yearly progress requirements along the lines suggested by Robert Linn as part of the reauthorization of NCLB. The same would be true for making improved high school graduation rates one of the criteria for satisfying those

requirements. But to estimate graduation rates accurately, most states need dramatically improved data systems. It is thus important to continue the Department of Education grant program that helps states develop systems to track individual students over time. Increasing annual funding for those grants from $25 million to $50 million would be a good investment, because high-quality long-term data on students are essential both to good educational policymaking and to evaluating the effects of innovations and new investments. Moreover, because good data systems are low on the education priority list for many state legislatures, substantial grants may be necessary to catalyze progress.

Congress might appropriate another $60 million for grants to states interested in aligning high school graduation requirements with the demands of postsecondary education and work. And it might appropriate another $20 million to push forward research on how to make the twelfth-grade NAEP examinations serve as a benchmark for varying state graduation requirements.

The annual budget of the Massachusetts METCO program, which serves 3,300 students, is roughly $20 million, or $6,000 per student. Using these figures as a base, I estimate that a one-to-one matching grant awarded to states to create interdistrict choice programs might cost the federal government $3,000 per student, on average, including funding for external evaluations. A $120 million annual investment in competitive matching could provide new educational options for approximately 40,000 low-income students attending poorly performing schools. Although this initiative is expensive on a cost-per-student basis, evaluations could provide extremely valuable information about how to design interdistrict choice programs.

The most costly recommendation is the third: targeted competitive matching grants for state and district initiatives to improve teaching in high-poverty schools and to tackle the secondary school problem. To interest districts and states in applying for the matching grants, the federal contributions would have to be large enough to fund the required evaluations and provide significant program money as well. Congress might invite proposals for projects

---

Contrary to the specific provisions of the legislation, federal Title I funding may not have brought about a long-term increase in the resources used to educate disadvantaged children.

---

with a total cost, including evaluations, of up to $20 million a year for up to five years, with a one-to-one matching rate. Thus, the annual federal cost for each project would be a maximum of $10 million. Funding 100 such projects would cost $1 billion.

Competitive matching grants to address the secondary school problem would be somewhat more costly. The annual federal cost for grants to states to reduce dropout rates might be $500 million. Another $800 million a year could usefully go to school districts to develop and test new educational models for increasing high school graduation rates while retaining high standards.[40]

The total annual cost to the federal government of my proposals would be $2.525 billion.[41] That is roughly 20 percent of the $12.7

billion that Congress now allocates under Title I, Part A, of No Child Left Behind for locally designed programs to improve the skills of students at risk of academic failure, especially those attending high-poverty schools.[42] Should the funds for the proposed programs come out of this appropriation? There are arguments on both sides.

The main reason to use existing Title I funds to pay for these programs is that Title I funding has not improved the achievement of the target population of students.[43] Why not reallocate the money to more promising uses? The complication is that, contrary to the specific provisions of the legislation, federal Title I funding may not have brought about a long-term increase in the resources used to educate disadvantaged children. Although an increase in Title I funds allocated to a district does initially raise the district's instructional spending, the increase almost entirely disappears after three years.[44] In other words, the Title I funds end up paying for core expenses, such as teacher salaries and professional development, that otherwise would have been paid for with local or state tax revenue.

How can federal Title I funds end up replacing local and state education funding when the ESEA legislation explicitly prohibits such substitution? Let us consider the example of Central City, an urban district in which all schools are eligible for Title I funds because they serve high concentrations of low-income students. Suppose in 1992 the average spending per student in Central City's schools is $6,000, of which $1,000 is Title I funds. In 1993 Central City receives an increase in Title I funding of $500 per student because the newly available 1990 census shows that the number of low-income students in Central City has grown markedly. In accordance with the law, Central City increases per student funding for the 1993 school year by $500, to a total of $6,500. Over the next several years, however, the purchasing power of the $6,500 is eroded by inflation. To maintain the ability of its schools to purchase the goods and services that they had purchased in 1993, the city council would have had to increase local funding. But facing strong pressures from voters to keep property taxes in check, it does not do so. So by 1995, the real purchasing power of the $6,500 is no greater than that of the $6,000 per student that the district spent in 1992. In effect, the increase in Title I funding has allowed the district over a several-year period to avoid the unpopular tax increase that would have been necessary to keep real per student spending (that is, net of inflation) constant.[45]

If Title I funds used by a district to fund core educational activities were withdrawn, the district would face a fiscal crisis. It would need either to raise taxes to generate more revenue or to reduce spending by eliminating professional development or by laying off teachers and increasing class sizes. Districts under such fiscal pressure would hardly respond favorably to invitations to compete for matching grants for interdistrict choice programs or programs to increase high school graduation rates.

For these reasons, I recommend that federal funds for these programs be new money, added to the federal education budget. Additional funding would address the frequent criticism that NCLB is a laundry list of new unfunded mandates. Districts could use their Title I money to pay for their share of the cost of competitive matching grants.

Limitations and Strengths of the Recommendations

My recommendations for changes in accountability and incentives seem far removed from the classrooms where teaching and learning take place. The proposals to build instructional capacity focus more directly on teaching and learning, but even they do not include a single direct federal program, such as a $5,000 annual salary bonus to skilled teachers who agree to work in high-poverty schools. Why such an indirect federal role? The answer has three parts.

First, the precise design of incentives to attract teachers and principals to high-poverty schools must be negotiated locally. Local circumstances vary far too widely for the federal government to propose a program of fine-grained incentives or resource packages that would consistently improve the quality of education in high-poverty schools. Perhaps when more is known about the effects of locally designed incentive programs, a larger, more focused federal program to improve instruction in high-poverty schools would be appropriate. At this point, however, federal policymakers simply do not have the knowledge base they need to justify a larger direct role.

Second, states and districts are much more likely to embrace initiatives if they are homegrown. More such initiatives are springing up, and the proposed matching grant program would further stimulate growth. The challenge now is to learn which initiatives make a difference to children in high-poverty schools.

Third, NCLB now hampers local efforts to attract and retain talented teachers and administrators in high-poverty schools, especially those serving a racially and ethnically diverse student body. Such schools cannot meet the adequate yearly progress provisions of current law even if they substantially improve students' performances, and the fear of being tarred as working in a failing school discourages talented educators from teaching where they are most needed.

In summary, the federal actions proposed here would strengthen all three legs on which successful standards-based reforms rest: accountability, incentives, and capacity. The proposals would improve the incentives that educators face and provide better benchmarks against which to judge the performances of individual schools and the value of new initiatives. Encouraging states to align high school graduation requirements with the demands of postsecondary education and work should reduce the disjuncture between high schools and the colleges and workplaces where students go after they graduate. Helping states develop interdistrict choice programs could bring to life a critical provision of NCLB, namely, that low-income children attending poorly performing schools should be able to move to better schools.

Finally, providing funds for states and districts to develop initiatives to improve teaching in high-poverty schools and raise the high school graduation rates of low-income youth could, if accompanied by a requirement for rigorous evaluations, increase understanding about how to solve the nation's most pressing educational problem. They would be a wise investment in the nation's future.

Last Words

Beginning with the Elementary and Secondary Education Act of 1965, a major focus of federal education policy has been improving the education of disadvantaged children. No Child Left Behind is the latest federal effort to reach the goal of equal educational opportunity. The new law is not without its strengths—most important, its focus on improving outcomes for children who have historically been poorly served by American schools. As is inevitable in such pathbreaking legislation, the current version of NCLB has many flaws. My proposals would increase the likelihood that a reauthorized NCLB would bring the nation closer to fulfilling the promise of equality of educational opportunity.

Notes

1. Data are from the Current Population Survey and were taken from the Economic Policy Institute Data Zone, www.epinet.org/datazone/05/wagebyed_a.xls.

2. Richard J. Murnane and others, "How Important Are the Cognitive Skills of Teenagers in Predicting Subsequent Earnings?" *Journal of Policy Analysis and Management* 19, no. 4 (Fall 2000): 547–68.

3. Richard J. Murnane, John B. Willett, and Frank Levy, "The Growing Importance of Cognitive Skills," *Review of Economics and Statistics* 77, no. 2 (May 1995): 251–66.

4. National Center for Education Statistics, National Assessment of Educational Progress (NAEP) 2005 Mathematics Assessment (U.S. Department of Education, Institute of Education Sciences).

5. Robert Balfanz and Nettie Legters, "Locating the Dropout Crisis—Which High Schools Produce the Nation's Dropouts? Where Are They Located? Who Attends Them?" (Johns Hopkins University, September 2004), www.csos.jhu.edu/tdhs/rsch/Locating_Dropouts.pdf.

6. For example, 16 percent of public school students in Boston have limited English proficiency, compared with 5 percent of students statewide (http://profiles.doe.mass.edu/home.asp?mode=o&so=-&ot=5&o=164&view=enr).

7. This description of standards-based educational reforms is taken from Frank Levy and Richard J. Murnane, *The New Division of Labor: How Computers Are Creating the Next Job Market* (Princeton University Press, 2004), pp. 134–35.

8. See Center on Education Policy, *Title I Funds: Who's Gaining, Who's Losing and Why* (Washington, 2004), www.cep-dc.org/pubs/TitleIfunds15June2004/TitleIfunds15June2004.pdf.

9. Robert L. Linn, "Accountability: Responsibility and Reasonable Expectations," *Educational Researcher* 32, no. 7 (October 2003): 7.

10. For a discussion of the difficulties in getting the incentives right in accountability systems and the consequences of not doing so, see Helen F. Ladd and Randall P. Walsh, "Implementing Value-Added Measures of School Effectiveness: Getting the Incentives Right," *Economics of Education Review* 21, no. 1 (February 2002): 1–17.

11. Robert L. Linn, "Fixing the NCLB Accountability System," Policy Brief 8 (Los Angeles, Calif.: Center for Research on Evaluation, Standards, and Student Testing, Summer 2005).

12. Organization for Economic Cooperation and Development, "Education at a Glance: Highlights" (Paris, 2006), p. 10, www.oecd.org/dataoecd/44/35/37376068.pdf, p. 10.

13. Robert Linn is distinguished professor emeritus of education at the University of Colorado at Boulder. In this section, the ideas for revising the adequate yearly progress formula are taken from Robert L. Linn, "Toward a More Effective Definition of Adequate Yearly Progress," paper prepared for the Measurement and Accountability Roundtable sponsored by the Chief Justice Earl Warren Institute on Race, Ethnicity and Diversity, Washington, November 16–17, 2006.

14. Thomas J. Kane and Douglas O. Staiger, "Unintended Consequences of Racial Subgroup Rules," in *No Child Left Behind? The Politics and Practice of Accountability*, edited by Paul E. Peterson and Martin R.

West (Brookings, 2003), pp. 152–76. As these authors explain, the greater difficulties that schools with heterogeneous student populations face in meeting adequate yearly progress stem from the instability of statistics based on small numbers of scores.

15. For a discussion of methods of using growth in student achievement to measure adequate yearly progress, see Martin R. West, "No Child Left Behind: How to Give It a Passing Grade," Policy Brief 149 (Brookings, December 2005).

16. Christina A. Samuels and Michelle R. Davis, "2 States Selected for 'Growth Model' Pilot," *Education Week* 25, no. 38 (May 24, 2006): 27–28.

17. The National Governors' Association (NGA) provides a brief description of the Graduation Counts Compact at www.nga.org/Files/pdf/0507GRADCOMPACT.pdf (accessed December 19, 2006). According to the document on this website, states have agreed to "take steps to implement a standard, four-year adjusted cohort graduation rate. States agree to calculate the graduation rate by dividing the number of on-time graduates in a given year by the number of first-time entering ninth graders four years earlier. Graduates are those receiving a high school diploma. The denominator can be adjusted for transfers in and out of the system and data systems will ideally track individual students with a longitudinal student unit record data system. Special education students and recent immigrants with limited English proficiency can be assigned to different cohorts to allow them more time to graduate."

18. Lynn Olson, "Number of Graduation Exams Required by States Levels Off," *Education Week* 26, no. 1 (August 30, 2006): 28, 32.

19. The American Diploma Project, *Ready or Not: Creating a High School Diploma That Counts*, executive summary, p. 2, www.achieve.org/node/552.

20. For a discussion of the reason why these skills are increasingly important in workplaces full of computers, see Levy and Murnane, *The New Division of Labor* (see note 7).

21. James J. Kemple, *Career Academies: Impacts on Labor Market Outcomes and Educational Attainment* (New York: MDRC, March 2004).

22. For a discussion of the standard-setting collaborations among states taking place under the auspices of Achieve, see *Closing the Expectations Gap 2006* (February 2006). In its September 2006 electronic newsletter, *Perspectives*, Achieve reported that the number of states participating in the American Diploma Project had grown to twenty-five.

23. Sean Cavanagh, "NAEP Governing Board Gives Nod to More Complex 12th Grade Math," *Education Week* 26, no. 1 (August 30, 2006): 9.

24. This section draws heavily from *12th Grade Student Achievement in America: A New Vision for NAEP*, a Report to the National Assessment Governing Board, National Commission on NAEP 12th Grade Assessment and Reporting (March 5, 2004).

25. Daniel M. Koretz, "Limitations in the Use of Achievement Tests as Measures of Educators' Productivity," *Journal of Human Resources* 37, no. 4 (Autumn 2002): 752–77.

26. While the law specifies that school districts must create transfer options for students in schools that do not make adequate yearly progress for two years in a row, to date this provision has rarely been enforced.

27. Goodwin Liu and William L. Taylor, "School Choice to Achieve Desegregation," *Fordham Law Review* 74, no. 2 (November 2005): 791–823.

28. Joshua D. Angrist and Kevin Lang, "How Important Are Classroom Peer Effects? Evidence from Boston's Metco Program," *American Economic Review* 94, no. 5 (December 2004): 1613–34.

29. See Liu and Taylor, "School Choice to Achieve Desegregation" (see note 27) for a description of this evidence.

30. See, for example, Steven G. Rivkin, Eric A. Hanushek, and John F. Kain, "Teachers, Schools, and Academic Achievement," *Econometrica* 73, no. 2 (2005): 417–58.

31. Paul T. Decker, Daniel P. Mayer, and Steven Glazerman, *The Effects of Teach for America on Students: Findings from a National Evaluation* (Mathematica Policy Research, June 2004).

32. Kenneth K. Wong and Francis X. Shen, "Do School District Takeovers Work?" *State Education Standard* (National Association of State Boards of Education) (Spring 2002): 19–23.

33. Lynn Olson, "Financial Evolution," *Education Week* 24, no. 17 (January 6, 2005): 8–12, 14.

34. Cynthia Prince, "Higher Pay in Hard-to-Staff Schools: The Case for Financial Incentives" (Arlington, Va.: American Association of School Administrators, June 2002), www.aasa.org/files/PDFs/Publications/ higher_pay.pdf.

35. Learning First Alliance, "A Shared Responsibility: Staffing All High-Poverty, Low-Performing Schools with Effective Teachers and Administrators" (May 2005), p. 6, www.okea.org/NBCTSummit/LFAFinalPDF.pdf. In addition to initiatives that focus specifically on improving the quality of instruction in high-poverty schools, there is a growing interest in basing teachers' pay, at least in part, on evidence of students' test score gains. See, for example, Jennifer Azordegan and others, "Diversifying Teacher Compensation," issue paper (Education Commission of the States, December 2005). A critical question is how particular performance-based pay plans would influence the relative attractiveness of teaching in high-poverty schools.

36. See Gary Orfield, ed., *Dropouts in America: Confronting the Graduation Rate Crisis* (Harvard Education Press, 2004).

37. This list is taken from Janet Quint, *Meeting Five Critical Challenges of High School Reform* (New York: MDRC, May 2006).

38. The Department of Health and Human Services' policy was a response to Section 1115 of the Social Security Act, which allowed the federal government to grant waivers from provisions of the Aid to Families with Dependent Children law to states that wanted to test new welfare reform provisions. One condition for a waiver was that the state commission a rigorous evaluation of the consequences of the trial provisions. See Judith M. Gueron and Edward Pauly, *From Welfare to Work* (New York: Russell Sage, 1991); and Judith M. Gueron and Gayle Hamilton, "The Role of Education and Training in Welfare Reform," Policy Brief (New York: MDRC, 2002).

39. For an example of a high-quality random assignment evaluation of a program to improve high school education, see James J. Kemple, *Career Academies: Impacts on Labor Market Outcomes and Educational Attainment* (New York: MDRC, March 2004).

40. The estimated cost figures for the proposals to increase high school graduation rates are taken from Adria Steinberg, Cassius Johnson, and Hilary Pennington, *Addressing America's Dropout Challenge* (Center for American Progress and Jobs for the Future, November 2006). I also draw heavily on this document for ideas about the design of programs to increase high school graduation rates.

41. This figure includes only the suggested annual increase of $25 million in grants to states to improve data systems. It does not include the $25 million currently allocated to such grants.

42. The $12.7 billion for Title IA of ESEA is the recommendation of the Senate Committee for 2007, as reported on the Department of Education's website: www.ed.gov/about/overview/budget/budget07/07action.xls.

43. H. Wilbert and M. Van Der Klaauw, "Breaking the Link between Poverty and Low Student Achievement: An Evaluation of Title 1," *Journal of Econometrics* (forthcoming 2007).

44. Nora Gordon, "Do Federal Grants Boost School Spending? Evidence from Title I," *Journal of Public Economics* 88, nos.9-10 (2004): 1771–92.

45. The argument in this paragraph is based on Gordon, "Do Federal Grants Boost School Spending?" (see note 44).

Improving the Safety Net for Single Mothers Who Face Serious Barriers to Work

Rebecca M. Blank

Summary

Rebecca Blank explores a weakness of the welfare reforms of the mid-1990s—the failure of the Temporary Assistance to Needy Families program to address the plight of so-called "hard to employ" single mothers and their children. TANF has moved many women on the welfare caseload into work, but the services it provides are not intensive or flexible enough to meet the needs of women with multiple disadvantages who find it difficult to get and keep full-time employment.

Blank notes that many of these women have lost welfare benefits because of their failure to find work. Increasingly, studies show that the number of single mothers who are neither working nor on welfare has grown significantly over the past ten years. Such "disconnected" women now make up 20 to 25 percent of all low-income single mothers, and reported income in these families is extremely low. Disconnected women are likely to report multiple and serious barriers to work, including low education, learning disabilities, health problems, or a history of domestic violence or substance abuse. Counting both longer-term welfare recipients and women who are neither working nor on welfare, Blank estimates that about 2.2 million women who head families are not able to find jobs or, if they do, cannot keep them. And almost 4 million children are in the care of these severely challenged single mothers.

Blank proposes a Temporary and Partial Work Waiver Program to provide more effective employment assistance and other supports for these women and their children. The program she proposes would recognize that some women might be able to work only part-time or be temporarily unable to work. It would supplement their earnings while also offering referral to services that both address their own work barriers and provide help for their children. The support, however, would be temporary. Women would be regularly reassessed for their readiness to return to work or work more hours. Such a program, Blank notes, would require intensive case management. Estimating the cost of such a program is difficult, she explains, because costs would depend heavily on the number of women who participate. But she offers a rough estimate of $2.8 billion, some of which is already being spent as part of the current TANF program.

www.futureofchildren.org

Rebecca M. Blank is the Henry Carter Adams Professor of Public Policy at the Gerald R. Ford School of Public Policy, University of Michigan. The author is grateful to Brian Kovak and Emily Beam for excellent research assistance.

Rebecca M. Blank

Welfare reform efforts during the mid-1990s led all fifty states to increase the scope of welfare-to-work programs and require more welfare recipients to participate in them. Although most of the adult caseload entered employment during the years following reform, some women continue to receive welfare benefits—through the Temporary Assistance for Needy Families (TANF) program—while remaining jobless. Although recent changes in welfare reform law will intensify the demand that women receiving TANF move toward work, not all the unemployed women now on TANF will be able to make the transition to work. And a fast-growing share of single mothers has already left welfare (either voluntarily or involuntarily) but is not working. By my estimate, 20 to 25 percent of all low-income single mothers (those with household income below 200 percent of the official poverty level) fit in this latter category in 2004.

In this article I examine the issues faced by women who have multiple barriers to work and for whom substantial work, at least in the short run, is difficult. These hard-to-employ women are increasingly being moved off TANF in response to growing demands that welfare recipients begin work. They are largely not eligible for disability assistance through the Supplemental Security Income (SSI) program, because although their ability to work is seriously impaired, they do not meet SSI's strict disability requirements. An increasing number of highly disadvantaged single mothers thus cannot access either welfare support or SSI.

To meet the needs of these women, I propose that states design a Temporary and Partial Work Waiver Program to assess family needs, set realistic and limited work requirements (providing at least partial support), and link these women to other services that can help them address the issues that limit their access to employment.

The new program would be more flexible than either TANF or SSI and would serve highly disadvantaged women both on and off welfare. Recognizing that some women cannot move into full-time employment, it would allow for partial work waivers, while continuing to demand that women work as much as they are able to. Recognizing that barriers to work can change over time, it would make waivers temporary and would regularly reassess the women's ability to work. The program would cost about $5,200 per woman served, though precise costs would depend heavily on the nature and availability of special services (such as job training, mental health programs, or substance abuse programs). Assuming that the program operated in all fifty states and that it were used by one-fourth of the low-income single mothers who appear to have difficulty finding work (a maximal participation assumption), it would cost around $2.8 billion a year. Only a portion of that estimate represents new spending; some of these women would receive funding through TANF, and some of the services that would be provided through the new program are already funded from other sources.

The new program would provide services to women and children in some of the nation's poorest families—families that are increasingly disconnected from public support of any kind. It would enable states that wish to provide some type of safety net for these families to balance ongoing work requirements with the recognition that at least some single mothers face formidable barriers to work.

Figure 1. Total AFDC/TANF Caseloads

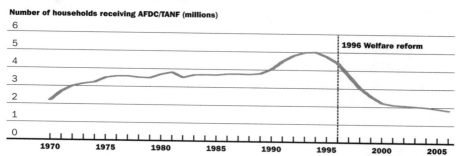

Number of households receiving AFDC/TANF (millions)

Source: Agency for Children and Families, Department of Health and Human Services (www.acf.dhhs.gov).

Note: 2006 data are through March. *AFDC* is the acronym for Aid to Families with Dependent Children. It was the precursor to TANF.

Welfare Reform, Reduced Caseloads, and Increased Work— by Some

As shown in figure 1, welfare caseloads plummeted during the 1990s. Between 1994 and 2004, the number of adults on welfare fell 60 percent, from 5 million to 2 million. Caseloads began falling even before passage of the 1996 welfare reform law. The decline slowed during the early 2000s, when economic growth slowed and unemployment rose, but to many people's surprise it has continued, though many families remain on welfare and only about one-third of these families' adult heads met work requirements in 2003.

The remaining TANF caseload includes at least three groups, only one of which is seriously disconnected from work. One group includes long-term and short-term TANF recipients who are working relatively steadily, especially in states with lower benefit reduction rates (the rate at which benefits are reduced as earnings increase) where women can combine welfare benefits with low-wage work. Another group includes short-term nonworking TANF recipients who use benefits after some economic disruption in their lives, but then leave welfare relatively quickly.

The third group—longer-term recipients who are not working or working only sporadically—is of most concern. Experts estimate that these longer-term (and typically nonworking) welfare recipients make up 40–45 percent of the caseload.[1]

In addition to long-term TANF participants, in some states there are certain families who have been moved off TANF and into special state programs (SSPs). As of 2003, thirty states had created SSPs as a way to avoid counting these families toward their TANF welfare goals. Participants in SSPs are not included in the TANF caseload because they are funded by state dollars rather than the TANF block grant, even though they typically receive benefits on the same formula as those receiving TANF. In 2003, an estimated 320,000 women—14.6 percent of adult welfare recipients—were in an SSP for part or all of the year, although in some states the share is much higher.[2]

The substantial declines in TANF caseloads since the mid-1990s might lead one to expect that the remaining caseload would be more and more heavily populated by the more disadvantaged and longer-term recipients. But though this group represents a large share of the caseload, its share does not seem to have increased.[3] The explanation appears to be that more disadvantaged women have left welfare at about the same rate as more work-ready women. Since the 1996 law was passed, more and more women are being involuntarily terminated from welfare, either through sanctions or through time limits. All states have imposed sanctions on women who do not follow program rules (for example, if they do not show up for welfare-to-work programs). And since states implemented their TANF plans, a federal sixty-month time limit has applied to the majority of the caseload, with about one-fourth of the states imposing even stricter limits. Many studies have noted that more disadvantaged women (those with the characteristics of long-term welfare recipients) are more likely than others to be sanctioned or time limited.[4]

How Many Women Are neither Working nor on Welfare?

Because of the time limits and sanctions that cause women to leave welfare, and because not all women who leave welfare for employment are able to keep their jobs, the share of women who neither work nor receive welfare has been rising. One recent study concludes that six years after welfare reform, as many as 18 percent of former welfare recipients were disconnected from both work and welfare.[5] The well-being of this group of "disconnected" welfare leavers is of increasing concern.[6]

Table 1 shows that these disconnected mothers are becoming a greater and greater share of all low-income single mothers. In the first column, disconnected mothers are defined as those who report no work and no welfare income over the entire past year and do not report "schooling" as a primary activity. In the second column, disconnected mothers are defined more expansively: they are not in

Table 1. Share of Disconnected Low-Income Single Mothers among All Low-Income Single Mothers, 1990–2004

Percent

Year	Definition 1[a]	Definition 2[b]
1990	10	14.8
1995	11.6	16.2
2000	13.7	18.8
2001	16.4	21.7
2002	17.3	22.9
2003	16.5	21
2004	19.6	25.3

Source: Data tabulated by the author from the March Supplement of the Current Population Survey. Includes all single mothers, ages eighteen to fifty-four, living with children aged eighteen or younger, in households where total income is less than 200 percent of the official poverty line.

a. Definition 1: Mother has no welfare or work income reported in the previous year. In 2004, this group numbered 1.35 million.

b. Definition 2: Mother reports no more than $2,000 in earnings and no more than $1,000 in public assistance income over the previous year. In 2004, this group numbered 1.73 million.

school, and they report less than $2,000 in earnings and less than $1,000 in public assistance over the past year.

Under both definitions, the share of disconnected mothers has risen sharply since the early 1990s. The share reporting no work and no welfare income rose 69 percent, from 11.6 percent to 19.6 percent, between 1995 and 2004. The share reporting only limited work or welfare income rose 56 percent, from 16.2 percent to 25.3 percent. As of 2004, between 1.4 million (by the first definition) and 1.7 million (by the second) low-income single mothers qualified as disconnected. Similar increases in the number of women not at work and not on welfare have also been reported in the national Survey of Income and Program Participation and in state-specific surveys.

Who are these disconnected mothers? Table 2 describes their characteristics as reported in 2004, using the same two definitions. Again,

Table 2. Characteristics of Disconnected Low-Income Single Mothers in 2004

Percent, except as indicated

Characteristic	Definition 1	Definition 2
Domestic arrangement		
Living with other adults	50.1	49.9
With a parent	23.5	23.6
With unrelated male	18.2	18.2
Average number of children	1.8	1.8
Income (2003)		
Average self (in 2000 dollars)	4,435	4,287
Average household (in 2000 dollars)	19,607	19,437
Median household (in 2000 dollars)	12,934	12,379
Share with household income below poverty	72.6	73.2
Work		
Labor force participation last year[a]	13.0	28.9
Current labor force participation[b]	20.5	30.0
Race/ethnicity		
White or other non-Hispanic	42.6	44.2
African American, non-Hispanic	28.0	28.6
Hispanic	25.4	23.3
Education		
Less than high school degree	35.2	35.5
High school degree only	37.4	36.7
Disability		
Receiving disability income	3.7	3.1
Disability as reason for not working last year	31.9	31.9

Source: See table 1 for source and definitions.

a. Employed or searching for employment at some point in 2003.
b. Employed or searching for employment last week.

whether they report occasional or very low rates of work and welfare use or report being completely disconnected, the two groups look very similar. About half live in households with other adults: 23 percent with their parents, 18 percent with unrelated men. It is perhaps surprising that the share living with other adults, who may provide potential sources of income, is so low (though it is high relative to less disadvantaged adults). Fully half of these disconnected women have no other adults in the

household to provide additional income. (However, while some observers argue that only single women living without other adults are truly "disconnected," one should note that some single women may have difficulty holding jobs *because* they live with other adults who need care and attention.)

In 2003 these women's personal income averaged around $4,300 (in 2000 dollars). Even though many resided with other adults, their average total household income was less than $20,000. Median incomes were well below average incomes, and for at least half of these women total household income was less than $13,000. Nearly 75 percent had household income below the poverty level. By contrast, 43 percent of "connected" low-income single mothers (that is, those who are working or on welfare) are below the poverty line, while their average household income is more than $27,000. In short, disconnected women live in very poor households, even taking into account their high likelihood of living with another adult. Even if they are receiving additional (unreported) economic help from family and friends outside their household, their resources are so low that they are still likely to be quite poor.

Fewer than half of these disconnected women are white, non-Hispanic; more than one-quarter are African American; another quarter, Hispanic. More than 70 percent have only a high school degree or less. Although only 3 to 4 percent report some sort of disability-related income, around 30 percent report disability or illness as the reason for not working, which suggests that a significant minority have some serious health problems.

By my estimate, there are approximately 1.7 million disconnected single mothers, based on the more expansive definition above. The estimated 40 percent of the single-mother TANF caseload that are long-term cases (I exclude child-only cases in this calculation) and the single mothers in SSP programs together add about another 500,000 disconnected mothers. These rough calculations suggest that some 2.2 million women who head families do not support themselves either with welfare or with their own earnings. That is not a trivial number. If these women have, on average, 1.8 children, almost 4 million children live in these severely economically challenged families.

Why Aren't These Women Working?

A growing research literature has been trying to determine why some women can successfully enter work and why others either do not move into work or do begin to work but cannot hold a stable job. The findings suggest unambiguously that women who do not move into stable employment are disadvantaged along a number of dimensions. Researchers have identified six primary barriers to work.[7]

First, women who stay on welfare or cannot find stable employment have less education—and more learning disabilities—than those who find and keep work. Second, these women are more likely to have past or current problems with substance abuse.[8] Third, they have higher rates of depression and other forms of mental illness, as well as more physical health problems.[9] Fourth, they tend to have younger children or larger families, or both, and they are more likely to be caring for someone with health issues, either a child or another relative. Fifth, they are more likely to report a history of domestic violence or a current relationship that involves domestic violence.[10] Finally, many live in central cities, where welfare caseloads have fallen less than in other parts of the country.[11]

Most welfare leavers who have trouble finding or keeping employment face one or more of these problems. One study finds that more than half—57 percent—had multiple barriers to work, compared with only 17 percent of those who had found work.[12] A series of in-depth assessments of a small group of single mothers who were about to exceed time limits in one county in Minnesota found that all had some combination of serious cognitive limits, mental and physical health issues, a lack of community and social networks, and limited management and decisionmaking skills.[13] Such evidence explains why these long-term TANF recipients have not moved into employment and suggests why they are likely to be jobless after their TANF benefits end.

The success of welfare reform, together with the growth in the number of disconnected women, may be compared to deinstitutionalization and the growth of homelessness during the early 1980s. As Christopher Jencks has suggested, efforts during the 1970s to stop the warehousing of mentally disabled adults in substandard state hospitals appeared at first to be "successful" because the disabled were initially taken in or helped by families.[14] But over time such help became harder to maintain, and homelessness rose within this population. Likewise, the initial success of efforts to move low-skilled single women out of welfare and into employment may not have been sustainable for the more disadvantaged welfare leavers. Over time, families may grow less willing to provide help to single mothers who cannot keep jobs, and disadvantaged women who initially find jobs (for example, in a very strong economy in the late 1990s) are not able to keep them. The result could be an erosion of employment gains among disadvantaged welfare leavers and a rise in the share of women disconnected from both work and welfare. This particular story remains to be proven, but it provides one interpretation for the rising numbers of disconnected women in recent years.

A Growing Policy Concern

Recent changes in federal legislation will increase states' attention to women on welfare who have not successfully transitioned into employment. In January 2006 Congress passed revisions to the TANF legislation that require states to have 50 percent of their current welfare caseloads at work or in work-related programs. Although the original 1996 law also had a 50 percent work requirement, it reduced the share of the caseload required to work in states whose caseloads fell over time. For example, if the caseload fell 25 percent in a given state, that state's work requirement would be 25 percent (50 percent minus 25 percent). Because all states experienced caseload declines, their work requirements declined and, over time, the required share was much lower than the 50 percent standard. The reauthorizing legislation sets the 50 percent work requirement on current caseloads, thereby eliminating previous caseload declines from the work requirement calculation. It also requires states to include women who are in SSPs in their welfare caseloads. States that do not meet this new work requirement will lose part of their federal block grant.[15]

Virtually no state now meets the 50 percent work requirement; some are far from meeting it. Using the counting rules in the new legislation, the average state participation rate—the share of the caseload meeting the work requirement—in 2003 would have been 30 percent.[16] States that do not want to face financial sanctions must find a way to move more of their nonworking caseload, both in TANF and in SSPs, into work.

These new requirements create a strong incentive for states to remove disadvantaged women from the caseload through time limits and sanctions, so that more women on welfare can hold at least part-time work. An increasing share of hard-to-employ women may thus lose TANF benefits and join the already growing group of women who are not on welfare and not working.

A Proposed Policy Response

Public attention over the past fifteen years has focused on moving women into work. It has not yet adequately addressed the reality that some women are not making this transition. It is time to rethink policy for women who face such serious disadvantages, and often so many of them, that full-time and steady employment is not possible. As noted, increasingly these women are losing access to welfare. Many have already left TANF, in part because of sanctions and time limits, and recent changes in the law will only accelerate this process.

Most women in this group also lack access to SSI, the primary federal low-income disability program (the poor elderly do qualify for SSI). During the 1990s, states made a concerted effort to move as many women (or their children) as possible onto SSI, in part because the program is funded primarily by federal dollars, whereas nearly half of welfare dollars are paid by states. To receive SSI, one must meet low-income eligibility standards, have a medical disability that will last at least twelve months, and be unable to engage in "substantial gainful activity" (as defined by a monthly earnings amount). Essentially, an SSI applicant has to prove that she is largely unable to work. Although SSI participants are encouraged to work if they can, not surprisingly a very small share of the SSI caseload does work.[17]

Policy analysts have increasingly been recognizing the need for some sort of temporary or partial disability system that allows people to receive partial support (for problems that limit work but do not create complete disability) or temporary support (for problems that may not be permanent but that limit work in the short term).[18] Such an approach is widely used in European social welfare systems and in private disability systems in the

---

States must address the needs of the growing population of disconnected mothers and their children who are receiving support neither from TANF nor from SSI.

United States. The current public U.S. disability system for low-income people does not recognize that "disability is a dynamic process rather than a static classification."[19] I propose that states create a Temporary and Partial Work Waiver Program to assist hard-to-employ low-income mothers.

States must address the needs of the growing population of disconnected mothers and their children who are receiving support neither from TANF nor from SSI. Women who are not receiving TANF benefits are less likely to receive other services for their children or themselves, including food stamps and Medicaid.[20] States must also address the needs of long-term TANF recipients who need more help in moving to employment than most short-term job search programs can provide. Helping these women deal effectively with their barriers to employment

can move them toward greater economic self-sufficiency and reduce the need for states to impose time limits or sanctions. In short, my proposed program could serve both disadvantaged women in the TANF caseload and women outside TANF who have not found stable employment. (Some other low-income family heads who are not single mothers might need and be eligible for the services provided by this program. For convenience, I discuss the program as if it were available solely to single mothers; in reality, it is likely to be used primarily by them.)

A state Temporary and Partial Work Waiver Program would, like TANF, demand that its clients work as much as possible, but it would provide economic stability and support to highly disadvantaged families. It would have more flexibility than TANF. For example, it would recognize that many of these women may be able to work part time or irregularly even if they cannot work full time; that the circumstances that create work barriers may change, necessitating changes in levels of support; and that these families must be linked with medical and economic supports both to prevent extreme poverty and to ease the severity and duration of the barriers that keep the mothers from work.

What would such a state program look like? It would begin by assessing (and later, as appropriate, reassessing) the family's health problems, the mother's personal and skill limitations, and the family's overall economic situation. Then, if TANF or SSI support was not feasible, it would determine eligibility. Two key questions would be how much work could realistically be expected and how long support should be provided before a reassessment is in order. The program would determine whether barriers to work should be considered full time or partial and would provide support for the family (at the level of TANF monthly benefits) accordingly. For example, a woman whose work barrier is judged to require a 50 percent work waiver would be eligible for 50 percent of the TANF benefit, based on the assumption that she is able to work part time. The program would then refer the mother to other available services, such as mental health services, substance abuse services, counseling on domestic violence, job training, and subsidized child care. Caseworkers would also assist families in applying for programs such as food stamps, the federal nutrition program for infants and children, or Medicaid. Finally the program would involve case management. A caseworker would regularly assess how the family is doing with regard to employment, child well-being, and the use of services.

A client could enter the program in many ways. The TANF system could refer its more disadvantaged clients who have not found jobs. It could also refer people who have lost TANF eligibility either through time limits or through sanctions. Some states may want to refer some new TANF applicants to this program, rather than enrolling them in TANF. The SSI program could refer people turned down for SSI assistance who are not on TANF. People not connected to any public assistance programs could also request help. Some of these clients might receive support in the program through TANF block grant funds and some could be funded out of other dollars.

I would propose setting up the program as a separate funding and program stream that states would administer as part of their TANF-related programs. On the one hand, program participants would be outside the standard TANF caseload counts; they would

not be subject to TANF rules on time limits once they had a waiver, and they would not be counted as part of the state's caseload that is subject to forty-hour work requirements. On the other hand, participants would continue to face work requirements (either current and part-time or forthcoming at the end of their waiver) and could be sanctioned if they do not participate in mental health or counseling services to which they are assigned or if they do not fulfill their (part-time) job search or employment expectations.

Three examples will show how various clients might interact with this system. In the first, a mother who is caring for a partly disabled preschooler is initially given a full work waiver. Once the child reaches school age, the mother is given a partial work waiver and expected to find work that allows her to be home outside school hours.

In the second, a mother who was sanctioned off TANF a year ago but has not been steadily employed is initially assessed and found to have a history of substance abuse. States with substance abuse programs may want to refer her to such a program and to reassess when she has completed it. Some states may be willing to provide a partial waiver but require part-time work. Other states may link her with food stamps and Medicaid and make sure the children are adequately cared for, but refuse additional help given her earlier TANF sanctions.

In the third, a mother who left TANF with a job but has since worked only sporadically is initially assessed and found to have depression and low cognitive functioning. A caseworker might want to make sure she receives medical services for her depression. She may receive a temporary partial work waiver, providing at least part-time support, but face reassessment of her employability after receiving treatment for depression.

Clearly, different state responses are possible in each of these situations, depending on funding capability and the availability of other services. Not all low-income single mothers will be employable in the short run or even in the long run. Some may best be served by being placed in the 20 percent of the TANF caseload that can be waived from time limits. But even highly disadvantaged women can be encouraged to work at least part-time and as regularly as possible. Some women may receive partial benefits over an extended period, with a partial work waiver under this program.

The primary advantage of this system is that it would provide states with flexibility to respond to families for whom current welfare-to-work efforts are not adequate. The system recognizes that not all family heads are able to move into full-time employment and supports them even in some circumstances where TANF funds cannot be used. It recognizes that family circumstances change over time and that women who have trouble holding a full-time job this month might be able to do so in the future. It also allows states to assist and recognize disabilities that are less permanent and severe than those covered by SSI.

A disadvantage of the program is that it would establish a new TANF category with somewhat complex case management. The diversity of needs within this population, however, necessitates extensive case management with multiple service linkages. After all, the greatest value of the program is the flexibility that allows different responses to families with different needs. Still, the primary new part of this program is the assessment and determination system at the front end.

The services it would provide are already available within all states, although there may be limits on how many clients can be served. Services such as payment of benefits and monitoring of work and income levels are standard in TANF programs, and many states already do extensive front-end assessment of new TANF applicants. Women who were referred to additional services would be using existing services for mental and physical health care, substance abuse treatment, or job and child care assistance.

I have described this as a state-specific program responding to the needs of a growing population that is not being served by TANF or SSI. (The details of how the program would interact with TANF requirements would need to be worked out for women who receive some funding from TANF sources.) However, the program could also be more nationally focused. Changing the SSI program over time to allow for more partial or temporary disability determinations would reduce the need for the program.

In states that have 50 percent of their TANF caseload in full-time work activities, as required, the remaining 50 percent of the caseload could be assisted with the assessment and services described in this program. In fact, a woman on TANF might be referred to this program as her work "assignment" by her TANF caseworker. In this sense, the line between TANF cases and cases under the Temporary and Partial Work Waiver Program might be quite blurred; the two groups should overlap.

Finally, this program could also cover people who are not in families with minor children (and not part of the TANF or ex-TANF population). One could imagine using a partial and temporary work waiver system to help adults in such households who have become disconnected from employment, particularly single men who may be struggling to escape from homelessness or drug abuse problems. The American public has traditionally been reluctant to provide much support to adults who are not caring for children or who are not seriously disabled, however, so expanding the program in this way would take some change in public attitudes.

Cost Estimates

The costs of this program are difficult to estimate, because they depend on many different factors. Let me make a few simple assumptions to provide a ballpark cost estimate. Initial assessments will cost about $500. This estimate is on the high end of such costs in demonstration projects, but these disadvantaged families will need extensive assessments. Caseload and tracking services will cost $50 a month, or $600 a year, as a very rough estimate. If a caseworker handles 100 cases (quite a low caseload relative to many programs, but this population will require more intensive help), the monthly cost would be $60,000 a year—to pay the caseworker and provide the computer and support services necessary to deal with the caseload.

The cost of referral services (job search assistance, mental health services, substance abuse treatment) depends heavily on the services provided. Costs can range from $250 for minimal job search assistance to $5,000 for extended treatment programs. I assume that approximately 50 percent of program participants receive some additional services over a year. The nature of these services varies widely, most states have limited slots for more extended treatments, and even families that receive services will not do so continuously. Hence I estimate the annual cost of additional services at an average of $1,000

for each family receiving them (whether minimal or quite expensive services), or $500 per family among all families in the program.

I assume that virtually all women in the program will receive some cash assistance. Some might receive full benefits (if they are fully waived from work); others will receive partial benefits. And I assume that the average fam-

The cost of referral services can range from $250 for minimal job search assistance to $5,000 for extended treatment programs.

ily receives two-thirds of the average state monthly benefit, or $300 a month.

Given these assumptions, the overall cost estimate for the average new entrant into this program in her first year is $5,200, which includes $500 in assessment costs, $600 in case management costs, $500 in other services received, and $3,600 in cash benefits. The cost would be lower if states provided fewer treatment and counseling services and if more women received partial rather than full waivers from work. Costs would be higher if states provided more extensive and more expensive health and counseling services. States could make their own cost estimates for this program, based on their estimated client populations and the types of services they are able to provide.

As noted earlier, as many as 2.2 million women are either disconnected from both welfare and work or are long-term nonworkers on welfare. If the new program served one-quarter of these women, or 550,000 families—a high take-up rate and one likely to result in a maximal cost estimate—the annual cost would be $2.8 billion.

Not all of these costs would require additional spending. Funds are available from other sources to help provide mental and physical health services, substance abuse treatment, child care, employment services, and other treatment services. For at least some of these women, the cash support dollars can come out of TANF. As noted, the primary new cost to states, in both dollars and management expertise, lies in setting up referrals, providing assessment and case management that allows the states to track clients, and staying in touch to encourage them to increase their work efforts and skills.

Additional Policy Issues

Although the program I have outlined highlights some of the needs of these disconnected families, it is not the only possible way to address their needs. Six additional outreach and policy efforts would reinforce existing welfare-to-work efforts and help low-income working women escape poverty.

First, states should make greater efforts to ensure that low-income families who no longer receive TANF support will have access to the programs for which they are eligible, including food stamps, Medicaid, and the earned income tax credit.

Second, states should make sure that subsidized mental health services are available to low-income persons. Increasing evidence suggests that assistance with depression is particularly important for many women struggling to be effective single parents in difficult economic circumstances.[21]

Third, the federal government and the states should expand health insurance programs to ensure that both adults and children in low-income families have access to medical services. Most of the children in these families are covered by Medicaid, although many low-income children receive no regular medical services. If they are not on TANF or SSI, many of the parents in these families are not covered by Medicaid. Programs that expand the reach of Medicaid (or other low-income health insurance programs) can provide treatment for physical and mental health problems in this population and reduce barriers to work.

Fourth, states should make sure that subsidized programs are available to deal with substance abuse problems and domestic violence.

Fifth, the federal statutes should be amended to ensure that TANF does not count individual months in which a woman on welfare meets work requirements against the overall time limit for benefits. Allowing women to work when they can, without fear that they will lose benefits because of their work, will encourage them to take jobs.

Finally, for families that are not participating in any major public assistance programs, the school system may be the best point of contact with the children. Schools can help monitor children's health problems and work with parents to help find assistance for them. Schools can help ensure that eligible children have school breakfast and lunch services. And in worst-case situations, where parents are in serious difficulty, schools are legally required to identify children who are subject to abuse or neglect.

The Administration for Children and Families within the U.S. Department of Health and Human Services has launched several demonstration projects to test programs that go beyond current welfare-to-work efforts in helping these mothers move into work. One program now being evaluated in New York City resembles the program I have proposed. The Personal Roads to Individual Development and Employment (PRIDE) program is designed as a special welfare-to-work program for people judged to be "employable with limitations." It includes extensive assessment and a variety of medical services, as well as assistance finding part-time jobs. The preliminary findings of the evaluation are that a significant share of TANF recipients does not qualify for SSI but also does not seem appropriate for traditional welfare-to-work services. PRIDE clients do increase their work levels, although the levels are still quite low and numerous clients are not able to meet their obligations and are therefore sanctioned.[22] Such demonstration projects, as well as efforts within many states to serve more disadvantaged TANF populations, provide insight about the most effective ways to support and to encourage work among single mothers who have trouble maintaining stable employment.

Conclusion

A public conversation about women for whom welfare-to-work efforts have failed is long overdue. These women do not always evoke public sympathy. They are likely to live in poor neighborhoods, to have a history of drug abuse or sexual abuse, and to face ongoing mental or physical health problems. Public willingness to help them would be low if they lived on their own—just as there is little public interest in helping low-income men with these same problems. But these women are also mothers whose economic instability, poverty, and joblessness affect their children's life opportunities. Policymakers' concerns about this population are evident in the growing interest in research and demonstration projects aimed at the hard-to-employ. As findings from evaluations of the demonstration projects become available, they should be used to inform the design and implementation of new programs such as the one proposed here.

The relative lack of information about this population creates policy challenges. High on the policy agenda must be a database that provides better national information on the extent of long-term welfare use and the problems faced by the more disadvantaged women who leave welfare. The growing number of women who report no work and no welfare support is particularly troublesome. To develop effective policy prescriptions, it is essential to know more about who these women are and how they and their children are coping and surviving.

The success of welfare reform over the past ten years demonstrates that low-income women want to work and provide better futures for their children. A surprisingly large share of women has left welfare and entered the labor force, far greater than even the strongest supporters of welfare reform predicted in 1996. Yet some parents require more assistance than others. Although short-term job search assistance has been effective for many former welfare recipients, it is not effective for all. Greater attention must be given to the needs of mothers who face serious barriers in entering the workforce and whose need for ongoing support may continue even if they are successful in finding low-wage work.

Notes

1. The share of long-term recipients in 2003 is estimated at 40 percent in Michael Wiseman, "Three Views of Welfare Turnover" (George Washington University, 2003). The share of the caseload in long-term spells is 45 percent (based on data from the mid- to late 1990s) in Lashawn Richburg-Hayes and Stephen Freeman, "A Profile of Families Cycling On and Off Welfare," report from MDRC to the Office of the Assistant Secretary for Planning and Evaluation, U.S. Department of Health and Human Services (April 2004).

2. Michael Wiseman, "Another Look at Turnover," Research Memorandum, Human Services Policy Division, Office of the Assistant Secretary for Planning and Evaluation, U.S. Department of Health and Human Services (December 2005).

3. Sheila R. Zedlewski, "Work and Barriers to Work among Welfare Recipients in 2002," *Snapshots of America's Families* 3, no. 3 (Washington: Urban Institute, 2003).

4. A review of this evidence is in Richard Fording, Sanford F. Schram, and Joe Soss, "Devolution, Discretion, and Local Variation in TANF Sanctioning," Discussion Paper Series 2006-04 (University of Kentucky Center for Poverty Research, February 2006); see also LaDonna Pavetti, Michelle K. Derr, and Heather Hesketh, "Review of Sanction Policies and Research Studies," report from Mathematica Policy Research, Inc., to the Office of the Assistant Secretary for Planning and Evaluation, U.S. Department of Health and Human Services (March 2003).

5. Lesley J. Turner, Sheldon Danziger, and Kristin Seefeldt, "Failing the Transition from Welfare to Work: Women Chronically Disconnected from Employment and Cash Welfare," *Social Science Quarterly* 87, no. 2 (June 2006): 227–49.

6. See Gregory Acs and Pamela Loprest, *Leaving Welfare: Employment and Well-Being of Families That Left Welfare in the Post-Entitlement Era* (Kalamazoo, Mich.: W. E. Upjohn Institute, 2004); and Sheila R. Zedlewski and Sandi Nelson, "Families Coping without Earnings or Government Cash Assistance," Assessing the New Federalism, Occasional Paper 64 (Washington: Urban Institute, 2003).

7. Papers that discuss these multiple barriers include Sandra K. Danziger and others, "Barriers to the Employment of Welfare Recipients," in *Prosperity for All? The Economic Boom and African Americans*, edited by Robert Cherry and William Rogers (New York: Russell Sage, 2000); Robert Moffitt and others, "The Characteristics of Families Remaining on Welfare," Welfare, Children, and Families Study, Policy Brief 02-2 (Johns Hopkins University, 2002); Matthew Stagner, Katherine Kortenkamp, and Jane Reardon-Anderson, "Work, Income, and Well-Being among Long-Term Welfare Recipients: Findings from a Survey of California's 'Precarious Families,'" Assessing the New Federalism, Discussion Paper 02-10 (Washington: Urban Institute, 2002); Kristin S. Seefeldt and Sean M. Orzol, "Watching the Clock Tick: Factors Associated with TANF Accumulation," National Poverty Center Working Paper Series 04-9, revised (Ann Arbor: University of Michigan, May 2005); and Ellen Meara and Richard G. Frank, "Welfare Reform, Work Requirements, and Employment Barriers," Working Paper 12480 (Cambridge, Mass.: National Bureau of Economic Research, 2006).

8. A particularly good discussion of this issue is in Lisa R. Metsch and Harold Pollack, "Welfare Reform and Substance Abuse," *Milbank Quarterly* 83, no. 1 (2005): 65–99.

9. A good summary of the research literature on health limitations among disadvantaged single mothers is in Mark Nadel, Steve Wamhoff, and Michael Wiseman, "Disability, Welfare Reform, and Supplemental Security Income," *Social Security Bulletin* 65, no. 3 (2003–04): 14–30.

10. A summary of the recent research is in Stephanie Riger, Susan L. Staggs, and Paul Schewe, "Intimate Partner Violence as an Obstacle to Employment among Mothers Affected by Welfare Reform," *Journal of Social Issues* 60, no.4 (2004): 801–18.

11. See the discussion in Margy Waller and Alan Berube, "Timing Out: Long-Term Welfare Caseloads in Large Cities and Counties" (Center on Urban and Metropolitan Policy, Brookings, September 2002).

12. Pamela Loprest, "Disconnected Welfare Leavers Face Serious Risks," *Snapshots of America's Families* 3, no. 7 (Washington: Urban Institute, 2003).

13. LaDonna A. Pavetti and Jacqueline Kauff, "When Five Years Is Not Enough: Identifying and Addressing the Needs of Families Nearing the TANF Time Limit in Ramsey County, Minnesota," Lessons from the Field (Princeton, N.J.: Mathematica Policy Research, March 2006).

14. Christopher Jencks, *The Homeless* (Harvard University Press, 1994).

15. For more information on these legislative changes, see Center for Best Practices, "The Wait Is Over, the Work Begins: Implementing the New TANF Legislation," issue brief (National Governors' Association, June 14, 2006).

16. Mark Greenberg, "Conference TANF Agreement Requires States to Increase Work Participation by 69 Percent, but New Funding Meets Only a Fraction of New Costs" (Washington: Center for Law and Social Policy, January 11, 2006).

17. For an excellent discussion of the SSI program, see Mary C. Daly and Richard V. Burkhauser, "The Supplemental Security Income Program," in *Means-Tested Transfer Programs in the United States*, edited by Robert A. Moffitt (University of Chicago Press, 2003).

18. For instance, see David Wittenburg and Pamela J. Loprest, "A More Work-Focused Disability Program? Challenges and Options" (Washington: Urban Institute, November 2003); and U.S. General Accounting Office, "SSA Disability: Other Programs May Provide Lessons for Improving Return-to-Work Efforts," testimony before the Subcommittee on Social Security, Committee on Ways and Means, U.S. House of Representatives, GAO/T-HEHS-00-151 (January 2001).

19. Richard V. Burkhauser and Mary C. Daly, "U.S. Disability Policy in a Changing Environment," *Journal of Economic Literature* 15, no.1 (Winter 2002): 219.

20. Sheila Zedlewski and others, "Is There a System Supporting Low-Income Working Families?" Low-Income Working Families Paper 4 (Washington: Urban Institute, February 2006).

21. Mary Clare Lennon, Juliana Blome, and Kevin English, "Depression and Low-Income Women: Challenges for TANF and Welfare-to-Work Policies and Programs," report from the National Center for Children in Poverty to the Center for Mental Health Services of the Substance Abuse and Mental Health Services Administration, U.S. Department of Health and Human Services (March 2001).

22. Dan Bloom, Cynthia Miller, and Gilda Azurdia, "Early Results from the New York City PRIDE Evaluation," presentation prepared for the APPAM Fall Research Conference, Madison, Wis., November 2-4, 2006. The PRIDE evaluation is being carried out by a random-assessment methodology.